# How Hollywood Works

# How Hollywood Works

Janet Wasko

**SAGE Publications**
London • Thousand Oaks • New Delhi

© Janet Wasko 2003

First Published 2003

Apart from any fair dealing for the purposes of research or
private study, or criticism or review, as permitted under the
Copyright, Designs and Patents Act, 1988, this publication
may be reproduced, stored or transmitted in any form, or by
any means, only with the prior permission in writing of the
publishers, or in the case of reprographic reproduction, in
accordance with the terms of licences issued by the
Copyright Licensing Agency. Inquiries concerning
reproduction outside those terms should be sent to the
publishers.

 SAGE Publications Ltd
6 Bonhill Street
London EC2A 4PU

SAGE Publications Inc
2455 Teller Road
Thousand Oaks, California 91320

SAGE Publications India Pvt Ltd
B-42, Panchsheel Enclave
Post Box 4109
New Delhi – 100 017

**British Library Cataloguing in Publication data**

A catalogue record for this book is available from the British
Library

ISBN 0 7619 6813 X
ISBN 0 7619 6814 8 (pbk)

**Library of Congress Control Number: 2003102339**

Typeset by Mayhew Typesetting, Rhayader, Powys
Printed and bound in Great Britain by TJ International, Padstow, Cornwall

# Contents

# List of Tables

# Introduction

This book is about the US motion picture industry – its structure and policies, its operations and practices. It focuses on the commodity nature of Hollywood film, or the process that is involved in turning raw materials and labor into feature films that are distributed as commodities to different retail outlets. It describes the process of film production, distribution and exhibition or retail – a process that involves different markets where materials, labor, and products are bought and sold. In other words, it details how Hollywood works as an industry that manufactures commodities.

While media industries may be converging, there are still distinct differences in the ways that specific media, such as films, are produced and distributed, at least for the present. The aim of the book is to survey and critique the current policies and structure of the US film industry, as well as its relationships to other media industries.

The focus of the discussion is on theatrical motion pictures produced by the mainstream film industry, also known as Hollywood. A good deal of attention is paid to the major players or the studios that dominate Hollywood. Importantly, these few companies are part of transnational, diversified entertainment conglomerates, involved in a wide range of media activities.

## Why this book?

Many books describe the film production and marketing process, but usually from an industrial perspective and mostly aimed at people who want to get into the industry (also known as "wannabes"). Nearly all these discussions are celebratory and rarely does an analyst step back to look at the industry critically within a more general economic, political, and social context. This attitude is perpetuated in the massive amount of press coverage that Hollywood receives (and encourages), as well as the popular myths and lore that circulate about the industry.

Because of the role that Hollywood films play in the creation and recreation of societal values and ideas, an understanding of the way that this industry works is seriously needed. More in-depth study of film also demands attention to the mechanics of the industry, in addition to the study of film texts, genres and audiences. (Further discussion of the theoretical approach used in this study is presented at the end of this chapter as some readers may be less interested in these issues and may want to skip this section.)


## Industry Characteristics

This discussion of how Hollywood works focuses on the typical processes for the manufacture and marketing of Hollywood films. It describes Hollywood as an industry that produces and distributes commodities, and thus is similar to other industries that manufacture and produce products for profit. However, many Hollywood analysts stress that the film industry is different, with a set of unique characteristics that defies typical economic analysis. Some of these analysts even argue that the conventional measures of concentration and competition are not applicable to the film industry (for instance, De Vany and Eckert, 1991).

But how are the film industry and the film commodity different? An important and fundamental point is that each film is a unique product – a different set of circumstances, deals, and players are involved for every film. While it is possible to point to general tendencies in the film industry, there are always exceptions due to the unique quality of each film commodity.

Another characteristic often identified by film economists relates to the cyclical nature of the industry, and thus the constantly changing policies and practices. It should also be pointed out, however, that the industry's development is necessarily linked to general economic cycles. For instance, even though new technological developments (such as VCRs or multiplex theaters) are regularly introduced, the economic climate will influence their reception in the marketplace.

Most often, Hollywood analysts argue that the film business is not only unique, but risky, uncertain, and even chaotic. The industry's key trade association, the Motion Picture Association of America (MPAA) purposely explains this point on their website:

> Moviemaking is an inherently risky business. Contrary to popular belief that moviemaking is always profitable, in actuality, only one in ten films ever retrieves its investment from domestic exhibition. In fact, four out of ten movies *never* recoup the original investment. In 2000, the average major studio film cost $55 million to produce with an extra $27 million to advertise and market, a total cost of over $80 million per film. No other nation in the world risks such immense capital to make, finance, produce and market their films. (Emphasis in the original) (http://www.mpaa.org/anti-piracy/)

Nevertheless, the industry overall does survive and companies continue to thrive, having adopted various organizational and policy responses to such risks. Despite the cyclical nature of the industry and the variety of unique deals, there are general, ongoing tendencies and characteristics that do not change. In other words, there may be change, but there is also continuity. A few of these general tendencies need to be examined before looking more closely at the industry and its practices.

## General Tendencies: Profit/Power/Paucity

### Profit

Motion pictures developed in the USA as an industry and have continued to operate in this mode for over a century. Above all, profit is the primary driving force and guiding principle for the industry. Capital is used in different ways to achieve that goal. Inevitably, individuals and corporations come and go as companies move from one project to another, to other businesses, to new or more profitable technologies. Nothing is sacred – not even film. As Thomas Guback (1978) pointed out many years ago: "the ultimate product of the motion picture business is profit; motion pictures are but a means to that end". A Hollywood executive explained it this way:

> Studios exist to make money. If they don't make a lot of money producing movies, there's no reason for them to exist, because they

don't offer anything else. They offer entertainment, but you don't need studios to make entertainment. You don't need studios to make movies. The reason they exist is to make money. (Taylor, 1999, p. 59)

The profit motive and the commodity nature of film have implications for the kind of films that are produced (and not produced), who makes them, how they are distributed, and where/when they are viewed. While it is common to call film an art form, at least Hollywood film cannot be understood without the context in which it is actually produced and distributed, that is, within an industrial, capitalist structure.

## Power

A common understanding is that every relationship in Hollywood is defined by power. Although power influences relationships throughout society, it seems that in Hollywood, these relations are far more blatant and conspicuous. As exemplified in the discussions that follow in this book, power is often a determining factor in deals and decision-making, as well as the overall context in which Hollywood works.

*Premiere* magazine's yearly "Power List" and *Variety*'s annual book of "Power Players" are indications of this phenomenon (for example, Petrikin et al., 1999). In these assessments, one's clout is often determined by one's track record or most recent success. Daniels et al. (1998, p. 280) provide another example: "it isn't unusual for a studio lawyer to call a competitor to verify the producer's 'quotes.' Antitrust implications aside, the lesson is, what you have accomplished in the past plays a direct role in what you can negotiate for the future."

## Paucity

It is a challenge to generalize about the economic aspects of the motion picture industry or the commodity nature of Hollywood films. Practically every film industry researcher has acknowledged the problems of securing basic industry data and reliable information on deals and relationships. Outside people dealing with Hollywood, as well as even some within the industry, often express frustration at the difficulties of understanding the complexities of the industry, as well as finding reliable information. As media analyst Harold Vogel observes: "The lack of access to real numbers in this industry is astounding and it's getting worse all the time. We have no way to judge Hollywood's actual return on equity, nor can we accurately assess the year-to-year health of the film business."[1]

## Limitations and Features

This overview of the film business also is intentionally limited in certain ways. The focus is on feature films produced and/or distributed by the current US film industry. The emphasis is on the major Hollywood production/distribution companies, also called the studios, because of their clear domination of the entire industry. Much less attention will be given to independent production and distribution, as many other industry-oriented books focus on these areas. There also is less depth about the historical evolution of the US film industry, which is the focus of a number of books and edited volumes. And, finally, even though this volume is about how Hollywood works, it should not be considered a "how-to" book. The aim is to provide a critical overview of the production, distribution, and exhibition or retail sectors of the US film industry, plus how the industry expands, promotes, and protects its business.

This overview of Hollywood draws on a variety of sources. While specific references may not always be cited, the primary trade publication, *Variety*, has been a fundamental reference for the bulk of material on industry practices and players. But industry representatives also have been consulted, both in interviews as well as via the multitude of books and articles written by current and former Hollywood insiders. While most of these publications are written for industry wannabes, they also provide significant and revealing material on film production and distribution by experienced and (sometimes) insightful industry professionals. Other materials have been provided by various academic studies, discussed briefly in the next section.

In addition to describing how Hollywood works, key issues will be referred to throughout the book. These points refer to a variety of questions and problems that have been raised in connection to the development of film and the film industry, as well as its role in society.

## Approaches to Film Studies

In the late 1970s, Thomas Guback wrote an essay entitled "Are We Looking at the Right Things in Film?", in which he argued that the study of cinema focussed overwhelmingly on criticism and theory, with a dash of atheoretical history (Guback 1978). Guback's main point was that film studies typically neglected the analysis of cinema as an economic institution and as a medium of communication. And, though more attention is given these days to the economics of film by cinema scholars, legal scholars, and economists, it might be argued that some of Guback's concerns are still quite germane.

More specific attention to economics also has been evident in the field of communication and media studies during the past decade, with scholars identifying media economics as a distinct focus of research activity. Examples include texts by Picard (1989), Albarron (1996), and Alexander et al. (1993), as well as *The Journal of Media Economics*, which was introduced in 1988. The goal of the journal, as stated in its Contributor Information section, is "to broaden understanding and discussion of the impact of economic and financial activities on media operations and managerial decisions." Generally, these media economics texts and the journal echo the concerns of mainsteam (neo-classical) economics. As the journal's first editor explains: "Media economics is concerned with how media operators meet the informational and entertainment wants and needs of audiences, advertisers and society with available resources. It deals with the factors influencing production of media goods and services and the allocation of those products for consumption" (Picard, 1989, p. 7).

For the most part, the emphasis of media economics is on microeconomic issues rather than macro-analysis, and focusses primarily on producers and consumers in media markets. Typically, the concern is how media industries and companies can succeed, prosper, or move forward. While competition may be assessed, little emphasis is placed on questions of ownership or the implications of concentrated ownership and control. These approaches avoid any kind of moral grounding, as most studies emphasize description (or "what is") rather than critique (or "what ought to be"). This distinction is highlighted in a description of the industrial organization model by Douglas Gomery:

> The industrial organization model of structure, conduct, and performance provides a powerful and useful analytical framework for

economic analysis. Using it, the analyst seeks to define the size and scope of the structure of an industry and then go on to examine its economic behavior. Both of these steps require analyzing the status and operations of the industry, not as the analyst wishes it were. Evaluation of its performance is the final step, a careful weighing of 'what is' versus 'what ought to be.' (Gomery, 1989, p. 58)

Generally, economic approaches to film can be characterized as Allen and Gomery did in their discussion of economic film history in 1985. They describe, and obviously favor, an *institutional* or *industrial organizational model*, following Gomery's description above. Examples of an industrial analysis include Gomery's early work on the introduction of sound, followed by studies of exhibition, etc. More recently, Justin Wyatt's analysis of "high concept" as a dominant force in contemporary Hollywood draws directly on industrial organization economics (1994, pp. 65–66).

In addition, economic analysis has been directed at the film industry by an increasing number of economists and financial analysts. These studies primarily use neo-classical economic analysis and econometrics in an attempt to understand the film industry's activities. Meanwhile, legal scholars are increasingly looking at the film industry, sometimes applying economic analysis as part of their work.

The approach used in this book might be referred to as the *political economy of film*. While a political economic approach has been distinctly identified in communication scholarship, it is much less common within film studies. The political economy of film incorporates those characteristics that define political economy generally, as well as its application to the study of media and communications.

In *The Political Economy of Communication*, Vincent Mosco defined this version of political economy as "the study of the social relations, particularly power relations, that mutually constitute the production, distribution and consumption of resources" (1996, p. 25). He explains that political economy is about survival and control, or how societies are organized to produce what is necessary to survive, and how order is maintained to meet societal goals. Mosco further delineates four central characteristics of critical political economy, which are helpful in understanding this approach:

1   *Social change and history*. Political economy continues the tradition of classic economic theorists, uncovering the dynamics of capitalism – its cyclical nature, the growth of monopoly capital, the state apparatus, etc.

2   *Social totality*. Political economy is a holistic approach, or, in concrete terms, explores the relationship among commodities, institutions, social relations, and hegemony, exploring the determination among these elements, although some elements are stressed more than others.

3   *Moral philosophy*. Critical political economy also follows the classical theorists' emphasis on moral philosophy, including not only analysis of the economic system, but discussion of the policy problems and moral issues which arise from it. For some contemparary scholars, this is the distinguishing characteristic of political economy.

4   *Praxis*. Finally, political economists attempt to transcend the distinction between research and policy, orienting their work towards actual social change and practice. As Karl Marx explained: "Philosophers have sought to understand the system, the point is to change it."

Mosco's model draws strongly on the work of British political economists Graham Murdock and Peter Golding, who distinguished critical political economy from mainstream economics: it is holistic, historical, centrally concerned with the balance between capitalist enterprise and public intervention, and "goes beyond technical issues of efficiency to engage with basic moral questions of justice, equity and the public good" (Golding and Murdock, 1991).

These explanations set the stage or provide the grounding for applying political economy to the study of communication. The academic study of communication has not always embraced economic analysis, much less a political economic approach. During the 1940s and 1950s, communication scholars focussed primarily on individual effects and psychologically-oriented research, with little concern for the economic context in which media is produced, distributed and consumed.

In the 1950s and early 1960s, former FCC economist and University of Illinois professor, Dallas Smythe, urged scholars to consider communication as an important component of the economy and to understand it as an economic entity. In 1960, he presented one of the first applications of political economy to communication, defining the approach as the study of political policies and economic processes, their interrelations and their mutual influence on social institutions. He argued that the central purpose of applying political economy to communication was to evaluate the effects of communication agencies in terms of the policies by which they are organized and operated, or to study the structure and policies of communication institutions in their social settings. Smythe further delineated research questions emanating from policies of production, allocation or distribution, and capital, organization and control, concluding that the studies that might evolve from these areas were practically endless.

In the 1970s, Murdock and Golding defined political economy of communication as fundamentally interested in studying communication and media as commodities produced by capitalist industries (Murdock and Golding, 1974). The article represented "a ground-breaking exercise . . . a conceptual map for a political economic analysis of the media where none existed in British literature" (Mosco, 1996, p. 102). A later work placed political economy within the broader framework of critical and Marxian theory, with links to the Frankfurt School, as well as to other critical theorists (Murdock and Golding, 1979). Nicholas Garnham (1979) further outlined the approach, noting that the political economy of communication involves analyzing "the modes of cultural production and consumption developed within capitalist societies."

Political economy draws upon several disciplines – specifically history, economics, sociology, and political science. And, while some may question whether or not a specific methodology is involved, the study of political economy draws on a wide range of techniques and methods, including not only Marxist economics, but methods used in history and sociology, especially power structure research and institutional analysis.

Because historical analysis is mandatory, the approach is able to provide important insight into social change and movement. Political economy becomes crucial in order to document communication in its total social context. Understanding interrelationships between media and communication industries and sites of power in society is necessary for the complete analysis of communications. This approach also challenges common myths about our economic and political system, especially the notions of pluralism, free enterprise, competition, etc. Through study of ownership and control, political economists analyze relations of power and confirm a class system and structural inequalities. In that the position includes economic *and* political analysis, it is therefore necessary grounding for ideological readings and cultural analysis. And through identification of contradictions, political economic analysis provides strategies for intervention, resistance and change.

Fundamentally, the political economy of film analyzes motion pictures as commodities produced and distributed within a capitalist industrial structure. As Pendakur notes, film as a commodity must be seen as a "tangible product and intangible service" (1990, pp. 39–40). Similar to industrial analysts, the approach is most definitely interested in questions pertaining to market structure and performance, but a political economist analyzing these issues more often would challenge the myths of competition, independence, globalization, etc., and view the film industry as part of the larger communication and media industry and society as a whole.

For instance, the US film industry is not only important because its films are popular worldwide. Indeed, that is only the tip of the iceberg. Rather than celebrate Hollywood's success, political economists are interested in how US films came to dominate international film markets, what mechanisms are in place to sustain such market dominance, how the State becomes involved, how the export of film is related to marketing of other media products, what the implications are for indigenous film industries in other countries, and what political/cultural implications may stem from the situation. Most importantly, the political and ideological implications of these economic arrangements are relevant, as film must also be placed within an entire social, economic, and political context and critiqued in terms of the contribution to maintaining and reproducing structures of power.

Indeed, the focus on one medium or industry, such as film, may be seen as antithetical to political economy's attempt to go beyond merely describing the economic organization of the media industries. The political economic study of film must incorporate not only a description of the state of the industry, but, as Mosco explains, "a theoretical understanding of these developments, situating them within a wider capitalist totality encompassing class and other social relations [offering a] sustained critique from a moral evaluative position" (1996, p. 115).

Some key distinctions between political economy and other models are the recognition and critique of the uneven distribution of power and wealth represented by the industry, the attention paid to labor issues and alternatives to commercial film, and the attempts to challenge the industry rather than accepting the status quo.

While perhaps not as recognized as other approaches, the political economy of film is represented in a wide range of research. Some classic economic studies fit much of the above description, but were not explicitly identified as political economy. For instance, Klingender and Legg's *Money Behind the Screen* (1937) examined finance capital in the film industry in 1937, tracing studio owners and their capitalist backers, while Mae Huettig's (1944) study of the film industry in the 1930s documented the power inherent in the various sectors of the industry.

More recently, Guback's work, especially those studies focussing on international film markets, represent ideal examples of political economy of film. *The International Film Industry* presented primary documentation about how the US domination of European film industries intensified after 1945, with the direct assistance of the US government (Guback, 1969). He followed this classic study with several articles documenting the international extension of US film companies in the 1970s and 1980s, especially emphasizing the role of the State in these activities (Balio, 1976). In another article, Guback defended a nation's right to resist Hollywood's domination and develop its own film industry based on economic and cultural factors (Guback, 1989). And finally, in an in-depth outline of the US film industry in *Who Owns the Media?*, Guback presented a strong critique of Hollywood's structure and practices, as opposed to the other industrially-oriented articles in the same volume (Compaine, 1982).

Pendakur's (1990) study of the Canadian film industry employs a radical political economy of film, but also incorporates industrial organization theory to examine the market structure of Canadian film. "Marxian political economy's concern with power in class ·societies and its emphasis on a dialectical view of history help explain how the battle to create an indigenous film industry has been fought in Canada, in whose interests, and with what outcome" (ibid., p. 39). Pendakur (1998) also examined labor issues in film, adding to the growing literature documenting the history of labor organizations and workers in the US film industry.

Meanwhile, many other scholars have taken a political economic approach in looking at various aspects of film. Garnham incorporated an analysis of the "Economics of the US Motion Picture Industry" to exemplify the production of culture in his (1990) collection, *Capitalism and Communication*. Aksoy and Robins' (1992) recent study of the motion picture industry also is a good example of a study that focusses on issues of concentration and globalization, and draws fundamentally on political economy. Another example is Prindle's (1993) *Risky Business: The Political Economy of Hollywood*, which especially emphasizes the social and political implications of Hollywood's unique industrial structure.

In my own work, I have presented critiques of capital, technology, and labor as they pertain to Hollywood. *Movies and Money* (1982) presents the historical development of relationships between

Hollywood and financial institutions, while *Hollywood in the Information Age* (1994) examined continuity and change in the US film industry related to the introduction of new technologies during the 1980s and early 1990s. In addition, "Hollywood meets Madison Avenue" considered the ongoing commercialization of film by focussing on the growth of product placement, tie-ins, and merchandising activities in film marketing (Wasko et al., 1993), while an overview of Hollywood labor unions was presented in a collection on global media production (Wasko, 1998).

Despite these various studies (and many more that will be referred to in this text), it still might be argued that political economy is much less common in film studies than in communication research. If so, then why? It is possible that Guback's explanations in the essay mentioned previously are still relevant. He argued that one of the reasons that there is so much textual film analysis is the relatively easy access to film texts to study. In other words, scholars depend on the material that is available for study, whether film texts or industry-supplied information. Even though more popular media attention now centers on the film or entertainment industry through stories and programs (such as *Entertainment Tonight*), including stories that explore film production and box office numbers, it is mostly coverage generated by the industry itself and hardly critical.

As noted previously, it is still a challenge to find reliable and relevant data about the film industry on which to base a critical analysis. For instance, where can one find accurate and consistent production figures beyond the rumor mill, as reported in *Variety* or other trade publications? Rare glimpses into studio accounting are provided by court cases, as in Art Buchwald's *Coming to America* suit (see O'Donnell and McDougal, 1992). But these cases still are limited and infrequent.

The type of information that is available lends itself especially well to congratulatory coverage of the industry's triumphs. However, it also might be argued that much scholarly writing on the industry is not critical, anyway, resisting any criticism of the status quo, and basically supportive of the way things are. Even when information is available, the commerical and profit-motivated goals of the industry are assumed, and rarely questioned.

On the other hand, one might also wonder why film is less often included in much of the work in political economy of communication. While film appears in general overviews of communication or media industries, it seems to receive less careful analysis than other forms of media (Jowett and Linton, 1980). One obvious reason may be the academic fragmentation that still sometimes separates film studies from media and communication studies, in university organizational charts, professional organizations, and scholarly journals. Of course, one explanation is that film studies typically has been based in the humanities, while communication and media studies tend to draw more on the social sciences. Beyond this fragmentation, though, there also may be different perceptions of film's importance for communication scholars. For some film simply represents "entertainment," thus not as worthy of scholarly attention as news and information programming, or computer and information technologies.

These oversights need to be addressed if we are to understand film in its actual social context. These days, film must be considered as part of the larger communications and media industry. More than ever before, distribution outlets such as cable and satellite services link news, information and entertainment programs; and sometime in the future, it seems likely that there will be further links via new digital and multimedia forms. It is no longer novel to observe that news is looking more like entertainment, with new forms evolving, such as infotainment, docudramas, etc.

Importantly, these activities usually are under the same corporate ownership. Films are produced by the same companies that are involved with other media and communications activities, and it is no secret that fewer and fewer giant corporations control these activities. These transnational corporations have diversified into all areas of the media, sometimes attempting to maximize profitability by building synergy between their corporate divisions. For some of these companies, film plays a key role in these synergistic efforts, as corporations such as the Walt Disney Company build product lines which begin with a film, but continue through television, cable, publishing, theme parks, merchandising, etc. These days, companies like Disney not only distribute products to these outlets, but also own the outlets.

In addition, it may be useful for communication scholars to look more closely at the international expansion of the US film industry to better understand the historical evolution of current globalization trends. While the expansion of global markets may be relatively new for some media, the US film industry developed global marketing techniques as early as the 1920s and continues its dominant position in international media markets today.

As the film industry and its wealth become ever more concentrated, it is increasingly difficult to avoid the issues and analysis that a political economy of film offers. This volume is an attempt to present this kind of analysis and confront these important issues.

## Note

1  M. Amdur, "H'w'd Burns as Feds Fiddle," *Variety*, 29 July 2002, pp. 1, 51.

# Production

1

The entire production process for a Hollywood motion picture – from development to theatrical release – typically takes from one to two years. During this time, raw materials and labor are combined to create a film commodity that is then bought and sold in various markets. Film production has been called a "project enterprise," in that no two films are created in the same way. Nevertheless, the overall process is similar enough to permit a description of the production process for a "typical film."

Contrary to popular belief, Hollywood films do not begin when the camera starts rolling, but involve a somewhat lengthy and complex development and pre-production phase during which an idea is turned into a script and preparations are made for actual production followed by post-production (Figure 1.1).

> concept (writer) >> manager/agent >> producer >>
> studio executive >> development deal >>
> studio president/chairman >> green light >>
> pre-production >> production >> post-production

FIGURE 1.1  *From conception to development to production*

## Acquisition/development

> I have an idea for a film, and if I had just a little more money, I could develop it into a concept. (Quoted in Cones, 1992, p. 97)

Ideas for Hollywood films come from many sources. Some screenplays are from original ideas or fiction; some are based on actual events or individual's lives. However, a good number of Hollywood films are adaptations from other sources, such as books, television programs, comic books, and plays, or represent sequels or remakes of other films.

The prevailing wisdom is that around 50 percent of Hollywood films are adaptations. An informal survey of *Variety*'s top 100 films by gross earning for the years 2001 and 2002 and for all time revealed that Hollywood films often draw on previous works for inspiration. Books, biopics, and sequels to previous blockbusters represent primary sources used by the industry, while both comic book and video games represent emerging frontiers. Perhaps more importantly, films based on previous works consistently rated among the highest grossing films.[1]

## Issue: Hollywood and creativity

These points draw attention to the issue of creativity, a topic that attracts a good deal of attention, both inside and outside of the industry. As we shall see, there are economic factors that contribute to this ongoing reliance on recycled ideas, already-proven stories and movie remakes and sequels. Repetition of stories and characters may also have cultural significance. Nevertheless, it is relevant at this point to at least question some of the extreme claims about the originality and genius of Hollywood fare.

## Properties and Copyright

In Hollywood, film material rather quickly becomes known as property, defined by the industry as "an idea, concept, outline, synopsis, treatment, short story, magazine article, novel, screenplay or other literary form that someone has a legal right to develop to the exclusion of others and which may form the basis of a motion picture." An underlying property is "the literary or other work upon which right to produce and distribute a motion picture are based" (Cones, 1992, p. 413).

The idea of a property implies some kind of value and ownership, and thus involves copyright law. In fact, copyright is a fundamental base for the film industry as commodities are built and exploited from the rights to specific properties. A copyright can be described simply as a form of protection provided by law to authors of "original works of authorship," including literary, dramatic, musical, artistic, and certain other intellectual works. This protection is available to both published and unpublished works.

In the USA, the 1976 Copyright Act (Section 106) generally gives the owner of copyright the exclusive right to do (or authorize others to do) the following:

> To reproduce the work in copies; To prepare derivative works based upon the work; To distribute copies . . . to the public by sale or other transfer of ownership, or by rental, lease, or lending; To perform the work publicly; To display the copyrighted work publicly, including the individual images of a motion picture or other audiovisual work. (http://www.copyright.gov/circs/circ1.html)

It is important to realize, also, that copyright protection applies only to the expression of an idea, not the idea itself. In other words, works must be "fixed in a tangible medium of expression" (Cones, 1992, p. 110).

A film idea that develops from another source usually already involves a set of rights. For instance, book contracts usually specify film rights.[2] Thus, even before a screenplay is produced, ownership rights (and usually some kind of payment or royalties) may be involved. That is, unless a source is in the public domain, which means either that the work was not copyrighted or the term of copyright protection has expired. The material therefore is available for anyone to use and not subject to copyright protection. The rights to film ideas are often contested, with infamous lawsuits emanating from squabbles over copyright infringement, plagiarism, etc.

Overall, the Hollywood script market is relatively complex, as there are many ways that a script may emerge. An idea, concept or a complete film script may originate with a writer, an agency or manager, a producer or production company, a director, or a studio executive. In each case, a slightly different process is involved.

### The players

Before describing the script market, it will be helpful to introduce some of the players involved in the process: writers, agents and managers, lawyers, producers, and production companies. In Hollywood, powerful people are often referred to as "players." However, in this discussion, all participants in the process will be referred to as players, with the important distinction that some players are more powerful than others.

*Writers.* Everyone in Hollywood seems to have a screenplay or an idea for a film.[3] It is not uncommon that directors or producers also are writers. However, only a relatively small number of writers actually make a living from screenwriting and typically writers have little clout in the industry.

In the past, writers typically had studio contracts or deals to develop ideas or options, from which scripts were written. More recently, a major writer works with an agent or manager to sell an idea or script (which sometimes is packaged to include talent) to a producer, who then tries to interest a studio executive in a development deal.

*WGA.* The Writers Guild of America is the collective bargaining representative for writers in the motion picture, broadcast, cable, interactive, and new media industries. The guild's history can be traced back to 1912 when the Authors Guild was first organized as a protective association for writers of books, short stories, articles, etc. Subsequently, drama writers formed the Dramatists Guild and joined forces with the Authors Guild, which then became the Authors League. In 1921, the Screen Writers Guild was formed as a branch of the Authors League, however, the organization operated more as a club than a guild.

Finally, in 1937, the Screen Writers Guild became the collective bargaining agent of all writers in the motion picture industry. Collective bargaining actually started in 1939, with the first contract negotiated with film producers in 1942. A revised organizational structure was initiated in 1954, separating the Writers Guild of America, west (WGAw), with offices in Los Angeles, from the Writers Guild of America, East (WGAE), in New York.

*Salaries/Payments.* While it may be difficult to determine how many people claim to be Hollywood screenwriters, it is even more difficult to assess how many writers in the industry actually make a living from their writing efforts. According to the WGAw, 4,525 members reported earnings in 2001, while 8,841 members filed a dues declaration in at least one quarter of that year. Thus, the guild reported a 51.2 percent employment rate. However, only 1,870 of those employed were designated as "screen" writers, and that group received a total of $387.8 million in 2001. (The highest number of employed writers were employed in television.) But the guild also points out that the general steady state of employment understates the turnover within the ranks of the employed, with as much as 20 percent of the workforce turning over each year.

While the minimum that a writer must be paid for an original screenplay was around $29,500 in 2001, much higher amounts are often negotiated (as discussed below). Writers also receive fees for story treatments, first drafts, rewrites, polishing existing scripts, etc. Other important earnings come from residuals and royalties. During 2001, the earnings of writers reporting to the WGAw totaled $782.1 million. The lowest-paid 25 percent of employed members earned less than $28,091, while the highest-paid 5 percent earned more than $567,626 during 2001.

Screen credits.   Another area of crucial importance to writers (and other players) is the issue of screen credits, or the sequence, position, and size of credits on the screen, at the front and end of a film, and in movie advertisements. The order of front credits is often: distributor, producer or production company, director, principal stars, and then film title. However, there are variations. Credits or billing issues may be significant negotiating points in employment agreements and the guilds have developed detailed and often complex rules.

For instance, the WGA rules generally require a 33 percent contribution from the first writer for credit, while subsequent writers must contribute 50 percent. However, when an executive on a project also becomes a subsequent writer, such executives must contribute "more than 50%" to receive credit; if part of a team, that contribution must be "substantially more than 60%" for credit.

Credits are a vital issue for many Hollywood writers not only because of their impact on their reputations, but because bonuses and residuals are based on which writers receive final credit.

Agents/Agencies.   Writers, as well as other Hollywood players, often use agents, managers or lawyers, to represent them in business negotiations and career planning. Generally, an agent or agency serves as an intermediary and represents a client. Agents typically negotiate employment contracts, sell scripts, help find financing, or act as intermediaries between two or more companies that need to work together on a project. The standard commission for agents is 10 percent, thus *Variety*'s name for agencies, 10-percenters. In addition, the agency gets an interest in possible future versions of the product (for example, a television show that is syndicated), in the form of royalties and residuals.

In California, agencies are licensed and regulated by the state through the California Talent Agency Act. Agencies also are certified by or are signatories of one of the guilds (the WGA or the Screen

Actors Guild (SAG), discussed below). Some agencies are organized into the Association of Talent Agents (ATA), which has negotiated agreements with the talent unions and guilds for over 60 years. Another group representing agents is the National Association of Talent Representatives. In 2002, these two professional associations represented around 150 talent agencies (mostly in LA and New York), however, SAG and/or WGA also approved 350 other agencies.[4]

A few agencies are full-service organizations and handle a wide range of industry workers; others specialize in certain categories, such as actors or writers. Such organizations are either called talent agencies or literary agents, depending on what kind of talent is represented.

Agencies often are assumed to have tremendous clout and power in Hollywood, especially for their ability to put together film packages. The major talent agencies are closely held and many of their intangible assets are hard to value. But some aspects of the business – such as its ability to take a sizeable stake in the profits generated from packaging television shows – can generate substantial revenues.

CAA.   The agency business became especially powerful in the late 1970s. Creative Associates Agency (CAA) was started in 1975 by a group of breakaway talent agents from the William Morris Agency, led by Michael Ovitz, who is given credit for greatly expanding the agency business. Initially an important television packager, CAA under Ovitz's direction expanded into film, investment banking, and advertising, becoming the dominant talent agency in Hollywood. Ovitz also became involved in advising media companies and was credited with helping arrange the sale of several of the Hollywood majors in the 1980s, including MCA to the Matsushita Electric Company and Columbia to the Sony Corporation.

Under his aegis, CAA acquired a client list of some 150 directors, 130 actors and 250 writers, enabling Ovitz and his company to exert a dominant influence on major Hollywood productions through the packaging of talent. For instance, Ovitz was credited with putting together the major elements for successful films such as *Rain Man* and *Jurassic Park*. Even though agency packaging had been typical for TV production, such deals were more or less unheard of for film projects. Prior to the 1960s, the studios arranged projects through their ongoing contractual relationships with producers and talent. As the studio system evaporated, the door was open for others to make such arrangements. CAA stepped into this role when they began to assemble packages from their pool of directors, actors, and screenwriters. Consequently, the agency was able to attract more talent,

TABLE 1.1  *Leading Hollywood talent agencies*

| INTERNATIONAL CREATIVE MANAGEMENT (ICM) | CREATIVE ARTISTS AGENCY (CAA) |
|---|---|
| • represents 2,500 clients in film, theater, music, publishing, and new media<br>• represents stars such as Julia Roberts and Mel Gibson<br>• owns stake in entertainment producer Razorfish Studios<br>• around $125 million in sales (1998)<br>• rumored to be worth between $100 million and $150 million<br>• CEO Jeff Berg owns about 30% of the agency<br>• 500 employees | • founded in 1975 by a group of former William Morris agents<br>• represents clients in film, TV, music, and literature<br>• has a 40% stake in ad firm Shepardson Stern & Kaminsky<br>• offers marketing services to corporate clients such as Coca-Cola<br>• sales around $200 million (1999)<br>• 400 employees |
| WILLIAM MORRIS AGENCY INC. (WMA) | UNITED TALENT AGENCY INC. (UTA) |
| • started in 1898 as William Morris, a vaudeville agent<br>• employee-owned agency<br>• strength in music and TV division<br>• represents authors, athletes, and comedians, as well as various corporations<br>• sales around $170 million (1999)<br>• 450 employees | • represents actors, directors, writers, musicians, and others in entertainment<br>• clients include actor Harrison Ford and writer/director M. Night Shyamalan. |

*Source*: Hoover's Online (hoovers.com), *Variety* (variety.com)

who received increasingly higher salaries negotiated (or demanded) by CAA.

In addition to CAA, a handful of companies dominate the agency business in Hollywood. These include International Creative Management (ICM), the William Morris Agency Inc. (WMA), and United Talent Agency Inc. (UTA), (Table 1.1).

Agencies also can become involved with product placement deals (or the arrangements made for branded products to be featured in films). Not only are agencies often aware of film projects from their conception, they represent writers who can add a product or company name to a script in the first draft and then sell that placement to corporate clients. In addition, directors can be encouraged by their agent to feature the product prominently in the film. (More on product placement in Chapter 4.)

**Management companies.**  Recently, managers and management companies have been developing as power players in Hollywood. Managers are similar to agencies in that they advise talent and perform comparable functions. Managers receive fees of 15 percent or more, and have been aggressively moving into agencies' territories. More importantly, management companies are allowed to develop and produce film and television projects, a function that gives them a considerable advantage over agencies. In other words, managers have been allowed a more extensive role in their clients' careers than agents.

Again, Ovitz was involved with the growing role of managers through the formation of the Artists Management Group (AMG). After achieving some success in a variety of innovative schemes, AMG merged with The Firm in 2002. In addition to its core TV movie and music talent representation businesses, the Firm owned the Pony footwear brand and had joint ventures with toy maker Build-a-Bear Workshops and "Arthur the Aardvark" creator Marc Brown. Late in 2002, The Firm announced an arrangement to share equally in the profits of the Virgin Drinks Group's newly formed North American subsidiary, and to control its marketing and distribution in the USA. The Firm described itself as a brand management company, focussing on "businesses on which young consumers lavish discretionary income," including music, concerts, movies, TV, footwear, apparel and beverages.

Some of the other large management companies are Industry Entertainment, Brillstein-Grey Entertainment, and 3 Arts Entertainment.

**Entertainment lawyers.**    While not everyone in Hollywood may use an agent or manager, many players (especially power players) and virtually every company ultimately enlists legal services to deal with the increasingly complex motion picture business. Thus, the number of entertainment lawyers dealing with Hollywood has grown dramatically over the years. While it is difficult to estimate the size of this sub-industry, a survey in the 2000 volume of the *Martindale-Hubbell Law Directory* reports more than 400 entertainment lawyers in Los Angeles alone.[5]

The legal framework for motion picture production and distribution is built on contract, copyright, labor, and competition law. More specifically lawyers may focus on finance, liability, litigation, intellectual property, contracts, copyrights, production and distribution rights, syndication, taxation, and publication within the entertainment industries.

Obviously, a wide range of agreements and contracts are used during the production and distribution of a motion picture.[6] For instance, option agreements are used to acquire rights to a literary property, and often combined with a literary property acquisition agreement. In addition, the ownership rights of a literary property must be researched, especially if it is not original material.

In fact, the selection of a film title is a key area involving legal resources. Consideration must be given as to whether a title is similar to another film title and if there is any possibility for litigation. Although insurance may cover some of these problems, legal research is usually undertaken to avoid the problem. Title searching in the USA is done in a number of ways. The MPAA (see Chapter 5) maintains a Title Registration Bureau, where the studios regularly register titles even before a film is made. The studios have agreed among themselves not to use motion picture titles which are confusingly similar to those which are registered. Titles have not been able to be registered in the past unless they are titles for a series. It is not common for a motion picture title to be registered as a trademark, except for those that have significant merchandising potential.

Defamation and privacy issues also are legal considerations during the pre-production process. For instance, a screenplay may portray an individual in a questionable or untruthful way, thus risking a claim for invasion of privacy as well as for defamation. Privacy issues may emerge if the film is deemed to be offensive and intrudes on an individual's privacy, or if the film includes private facts previously known but kept out of the public eye. Such claims are limited, however, especially when they involve public figures. Whether or not privacy or defamation issues exist, a producer may use legal counsel to arrange for various releases.

Other legal agreements are involved in the financing of a motion picture, although these vary according to the type of financing. As discussed below, bank financing or pre-sale contracts may be involved and thus require complex and important legal contracts.

Entertainment lawyers also are involved in negotiating agreements that deal with talent, resolving disputes, and drawing up contracts – lots of contracts for lots of deals. The contracts involved in the distribution and licensing of films and film-related products may seem never-ending and all of them involve constant legal expertise.

The studios have their own legal departments that prepare contracts and handle legal issues during all stages of a film's life. Other lawyers specialize in film law work independently, often in the Los Angeles area, but also around New York or other areas where there is significant film business.

In addition, there are a growing number of law firms that either include entertainment law or focus primarily on film law, and those firms are becoming more active across the entertainment field. For example, the law firms of Katten Muchin Zavis of Chicago and Rosenman & Colin of New York merged in 2002. Both companies already had prominent entertainment and media practices, but the combined firm, KMZ Rosenman, was to include more than 600 lawyers, with offices in New York, Chicago, and Los Angeles. The clientele for the new company included a wide range of clients. KMZ's clients alone included Vivendi Universal, Miramax, Showtime and Sony Entertainment. But the new organization promised to serve companies and players in the entertainment, music, and new media industries, and counsel them on various business dealings. Among the activities that the firm lists on its website are licensing and rights management, production issues, corporate transactions (such as acquisitions and joint ventures), litigation, intellectual property, distribution and merchandising, labor and employment issues, and tax and estate planning.

A few other law firms that have become prominent in the film and television industry in the Los Angeles area are Harold A. Friedman, William M. Kaplan and Charles Silverberg. Not surprisingly, there are a few professional organizations that represent entertainment lawyers. The International Association of Entertainment Lawyers was formed in 1977 and consists of over 260 lawyers, in 23 countries. Meanwhile, the Black Entertainment and Sports Lawyers Association was formed in 1980 and represents African-American lawyers in entertainment and sports law.

**Producers.**    A producer typically guides a film through development, pre-production and production, acquires a script, selects talent, secures financing or convinces a studio to fund the film. However, there are many kinds of producers, including executive producer, line producer, associate producer, and co-producer. Sometimes a producer's credit is given to a power player who contributes in some way to getting a project off the ground.

It is possible that a producer may initiate a project, but work under the supervision of one of the major studios, receiving a straight producing fee ($250,000 to $500,000), plus some kind of participation in net profits. Other producers may be involved with production companies that handle the acquisition, development, and packaging of material for production, and have ongoing relationships with major distributors (more in the next section).

**PGA.**    The Producers Guild of America (PGA) is a professional organization that represents, protects, and promotes the interests of producers and (since 2001) all those on the career path to becoming producers (for instance, production managers). The organization includes around 1,350 members and has been concerned with health benefits for its members and the proliferation of unjustifiable producer credits.

The PGA emerged in 1966 from the Screen Producers Guild, which was founded as an elite social club in 1950. Since then, there have been ongoing challenges to the PGA's status as a collective bargaining agent as it is argued that producers are actually supervisors or managers. Much more detail about these issues and the role of producers is presented throughout the following discussions of film production and distribution.

## The Script Market

So, again, an idea or concept for a film or an original screenplay may originate with a writer, producer or director, who may work with an agent/manager to interest a producer in the property. A producer also may purchase an option, or a temporary purchase of rights to a property for a specific period of time for a fee. Others who may become involved in the script market are development executives (who work with a project through development) and trackers (studio people who specifically follow the script market) (see Taylor, 1999, for more background on these players).

The process of selling the idea or script may include a pitch, that is, when a writer (typically) verbally describes a project or story to a development executive or other potential buyer. Since the end of the 1980s, pitches have been somewhat difficult to arrange and probably only possible for established screenwriters. However, pitches have not disappeared and may become more common in the future, as some of these processes are cyclical.

Many scripts are written in hopes of purchase by a producer or studio and referred to as spec scripts.[7] The process often involves readers or script analysts who prepare script coverage for studio executives, producers, and agents who do not have time to read every script. Coverage includes a short synopsis of the screenplay, a rating of the script (from poor to excellent), plus an overall assessment as to whether to consider, recommend, or pass on the project. Most scripts (one estimate is 99 percent) receive a recommendation of pass. Readers are interns, students, recent graduates, or aspiring screenwriters, who may freelance from their homes, receiving $25–$50 per script.

An agent also can circulate a spec script, trying to build a buzz around the property and create a bidding war. The sale of spec scripts boomed throughout the 1990s, as did the prices paid for them.[8] After Shane Black (*Lethal Weapon*) sold *The Last Boy Scout* for $1.75 million in 1990, the "million dollar script" became commonplace. Then, only a few years later, Black received $4 million for *The Long Kiss Goodnight*. Despite attempts by the studios to hold script prices down, at the end of the 1990s, million-dollar scripts were 'almost routine,' and even unknowns succeeded in selling spec scripts. For instance, when M. Night Shyamalan was basically a Hollywood newcomer, he received $2.25 million for *The Sixth Sense* spec script, with a green light (a go-ahead for production) on its purchase (Taylor, 1999).

### Issue: Script quality

For wannabe Hollywood screenwriters, there is a plethora of advice available in various forms, such as books, on-line sources, seminars, etc. For instance, a simple dictum from one such publication, *Hollywood 101*: "Write what sells" (Levy, 2000, p. 53). This is in accord with veteran screenwriter, William Goldman's point: "the business pays attention only to writers who write movies that are commercially viable" (1989, p. 95).

Some think that the spec script process is increasingly problematic, as the bidding process boosts the appeal of mediocre scripts that then attract inflated prices. Taylor (1999) notes that nearly all spec scripts must be rewritten before they are produced, but many are especially weak and the selection process is often irrational.

One of the alleged problems is that everyone is looking for the next big hit, the next blockbuster, or the next franchise (a movie that spawns merchandising and sequels). Since no one knows what will actually work, decisions are not based on quality, but the money-making potential of the material. In other words, a "bottom-line mentality" prevails. As one producer notes: "I would say 90 percent of the screenplays are purchased based on financial concerns and . . . what it's going to bring the studio. It really starts at the financial end" (Taylor, 1999, p. 58).

Other problems have to do with the "scare factor" – executives scared of losing their jobs, as well as scripts that are bought because of their potential as star vehicles or potential packages.

Another trend is the high concept film – an easily expressed, extremely commercial idea, where the story can be told in a few lines. High concept films are usually action or melodrama with recognizable stars. (For a thorough discussion of high concept films, see Wyatt, 1994.)

*Studio films.* Concepts or script ideas sometimes are initiated in-house or within a major studio. After securing the rights to an idea or the movie rights to an existing literary property, a studio may hire a writer to prepare a script or at least, a first draft, often with the guidance of the studio's development staff. Obviously, these films proceed quite differently from independent or out-of-house films. However, the exact role played by various producers, studios and production companies in the evolution of a script and an eventual film is sometimes difficult to assess. As one report has noted: "The often-complex transactions involved in bringing a film to market make analysis of the production industry difficult. Without detailed inside knowledge it can be impossible to determine the actual producer of a film" (Grummitt, 2001, p. 4). But it also must be noted that most of the scripts developed by the studios, no matter where they originate, never actually get produced. Estimating the number of scripts that do not emerge as finished films is nearly impossible, for the same reason noted above.

However, it is possible to determine how many films are released and by whom (see Table 1.2). Of the 185 new films released by MPAA members and their subsidiaries in 2000, one estimate is that the studios themselves released 109 films, while their subsidiaries were responsible for 76. One hundred of these films were actually produced or co-produced by the studios, at a cost of approximately $5.5

TABLE 1.2    *Feature films released in the USA, 1990–2002*

|  | Total | MPAA | Other distributors |
|---|---|---|---|
| 2002 | 467 | 225 | 242 |
| 2001 | 482 | 196 | 286 |
| 2000 | 478 | 197 | 281 |
| 1999 | 461 | 218 | 243 |
| 1998 | 509 | 235 | 235 |
| 1997 | 510 | 253 | 257 |
| 1996 | 471 | 240 | 231 |
| 1995 | 411 | 234 | 177 |
| 1990 | 410 | 169 | 241 |

*Source*: MPAA

billion. These films accounted for 75 percent of the North American box office in 2000 (ibid., 2001, p. 5).

**PACTs.**  Some players have ongoing arrangements or production contracts (pacts) with the studios for development and output. Many pacts involve production companies, but some individual players also have pacts with a specific studio or company. *Variety* categorizes pacts as follows:

- a first-look deal, which may provide a producer with overhead (and which may be supplemented by additional outside financing);
- an equity partnership, under which a studio and a company's backers share in both the shingle's [company's] overhead and profits;
- a distribution deal, under which a company is wholly financed by outside partners and utilizes only the studio's distribution and marketing arms. (Facts on Pacts, 2001, variety.com)

Table 1.3 presents a few examples of pacts that were in place in November 2002. While some of these companies represent important players in the industry and are able to command preferential deals, their "independence" is still relative because of their dependence on the majors for distribution. Daniels et al. (1998, p. 213) call them dependent-independent producers, although others in the industry still refer to them as independent. It also is revealing to find that the top box office films often involve these companies with ongoing pacts with the major studios.

The following section presents brief profiles of a few successful and active Hollywood production companies. None of these companies are "independent" in that they all have relationships with the major distribution companies.

**Imagine Entertainment.**  Formed in 1986 by Brian Grazer and Ron Howard, Imagine Entertainment produces films and television programs. The company's films include numerous Howard-directed pieces such as *Apollo 13* and *A Beautiful Mind* (which won Academy Awards for Best Picture and Best Director), as well as films by others such as Eddie Murphy's *The Nutty Professor*. The firm was publicly traded as Imagine Film Entertainment until becoming privately-held in 1993 under its current name.

**Spyglass Entertainment Inc.**  Spyglass was founded in 1998 by Hollywood producers, Gary Barber and Roger Birnbaum. The privately-held

TABLE 1.3   *Pacts 2002: selected agreements between studios and production companies*

DISNEY
- Boxing Cat (Tim Allen)
- Jerry Bruckheimer Films
- HYDE PARK (Ashok Amritraj) second-look deal
- Live Planet (Ben Affleck, Matt Damon)
- Garry Marshall
- PANDEMONIUM PICTURES (Bill Mechanic)
- Satchel 'N' Jackson co. (Spike Lee)
- SPYGLASS (Roger Birnbaum, Gary Barber) equity partner

DREAMWORKS
- Gravier Productions (Woody Allen) distribution deal
- ImageMovers (Robert Zemeckis)
- Montecito Pictures (Tom Pollock, Ivan Reitman)
- Zanuck Co. (Richard Zanuck, Lili Fini Zanuck)

FOX
- ICON (Mel Gibson, Bruce Davey)
- Lightstorm (James Cameron)
- Scott Free Prod. (Ridley & Tony Scott)
- NEW REGENCY (Arnon Milchan) equity partner w/all Fox divisions
- Ten Thirteen (Chris Carter)

MGM
- Cheyenne Enterprises (Bruce Willis, Arnold Rifkin)
- HYDE PARK (Ashok Amritraj)
- David Ladd Films
- Lion Rock (Terence Chang, John Woo)

MIRAMAX
- Cohen Pictures (Bobby Cohen)
- Craven/Maddalena Films (Wes Craven, Marianne Maddalena)
- Los Hooligans (Robert Rodriguez, Elizabeth Avellan)

NEW LINE
- Benderspink (JC Spink, Chris Bender)
- Cube Vision (Ice Cube)
- Indelible Pictures (David Fincher, Art Linson)

PARAMOUNT
- Alphaville Productions (Sean Daniel, Jim Jacks)
- C/W Productions (Tom Cruise, Paula Wagner)

- KOPELSON/INTERTAINMENT (Arnold Kopelson, Anne Kopelson) distribution deal
- LAKESHORE (Tom Rosenberg) equity partner
- Manhattan Project (David Brown)
- MTV Films
- MUTUAL FILM COMPANY (Gary Levinsohn, Don Granger) equity partner
- Nickelodeon Movies

SONY
- ESCAPE ARTISTS (Jason Blumenthal, et al.) equity partner
- Gracie Films (James Brooks)
- Heartburn (Nora Ephron)
- Overbrook Ent. (Will Smith, James Lassiter)
- PARIAH (Gavin Paolone)
- REVOLUTION (Joe Roth) equity partner

UNITED ARTISTS
- AMERICAN ZOETROPE (Francis Ford Coppola) distribution deal
- Revolution (Michael Winterbottom, Andrew Eaton)

UNIVERSAL
- Imagine (Brian Grazer, Ron Howard)
- Jersey Films (Danny DeVito, Michael Shamberg, Stacey Sher)
- Kennedy/Marshall (Frank Marshall, Kathleen Kennedy)
- Mandalay (Peter Guber)
- Playtone (Tom Hanks, Gary Goetzman)
- Tribeca (Robert De Niro, Jane Rosenthal)
- WORKING TITLE (Tim Bevan, Eric Fellner) equity partner

WARNER BROS.
- ALCON (Andrew Kosove, Broderick Johnson) distribution deal
- BEL-AIR (Steve Reuther) financial partner
- CASTLE ROCK (Martin Shafer) equity partner
- FRANCHISE (Elie Samaha) distribution deal
- GAYLORD/PANDORA (Hunt Lowry) distribution deal
- Malpaso (Clint Eastwood)
- MORGAN CREEK (James Robinson) distribution deal
- Section 8 (George Clooney, Steven Soderbergh)
- SHANGRI-LA (Steve Bing) distribution deal
- VILLAGE ROADSHOW (Bruce Berman)

*Source*: *Variety* (variety.com), Facts on Pacts – Winter 2002

NOTE: Production company names in all caps indicate that the company had co-financing capabilities. "Equity partner" indicates that the studio had an investment in the production company. "Distribution deals" indicates that the company may have wholly financed some or all of its films.

company is responsible for such films as *The Sixth Sense*, *The Insider*, and *Shanghai Noon*. Spyglass funds three to four films a year through its partnership with J.P. Morgan Chase Bank and distributes movies through an exclusive deal with The Walt Disney Company, which owns a 10 percent stake in the company. Spyglass also has pay-TV deals in Europe with CANAL+ Group, Sogecable and Kirch Media. In 2002, Spyglass Entertainment Television was formed to handle TV projects.

**Mandalay Entertainment.** Mandalay was founded in 1995 by former Columbia Pictures head, Peter Guber, and former entertainment lawyer, Paul Schaeffer. The company has produced such films as *Sleepy Hollow* and *Enemy at the Gates*, but also produces movies and series for television (*Cupid*, *Sole Survivor*) and non-fiction movies (*Galapagos – IMAX 3D*). Lions Gate Distribution is a partial owner of the company. (More on Lions Gate in the next chapter.)

**Lucasfilm, Ltd.** Created in 1971, Lucasfilm, Ltd. is the privately held company that handles the business affairs of the companies in filmmaker George Lucas' empire: THX, Ltd., Skywalker Sound, Industrial Light & Magic, and Lucas Productions. Lucasfilm is one of the most successful Hollywood production companies with five of the 20 highest grossing films of all time. Lucasfilm's productions also have received 17 Academy Awards. The 1999 release, *Star Wars Episode I – The Phantom Menace*, grossed about $920 million worldwide and is ranked third on *Variety*'s all-time box-office list. The company is estimated to have received $1.5 billion in sales in 2001 and employs around 2,000 people.

**Hyde Park Entertainment.** Hyde Park has a first-look deal, co-financing and co-production deal with MGM, with a similar five-year arrangement at Disney, which released *Moonlight Mile*. The company's leaders are Ashok Amritraj and Jon Jashni. Hyde Park typically produces around four titles a year with budgets between $20 and $80 million. The company provides the bulk of its overhead, with MGM providing office space at its Santa Monica headquarters. Hyde Park's production financing is underwritten by Natexis Banques Populaires, which provided financing for *Moonlight Mile*. Hyde Park also has output deals with companies in Switzerland, South Africa, Turkey, and Israel.

## Issue: Access to the script market

Although it has been argued that the spec system provides opportunities for new writers, the market is still quite selective. Taylor (1999) has described it as a "closed auction," while another producer poses an interesting question:

> Are agencies inhibiting free trade as a result of only giving it to such and such an individual? The agencies say, "We're gonna give this spec to you, you, and you to look at first, and we are going to decide who we want to give it to." That, to me, is a closed market, and they are basically monopolizing their talent and distributing it to certain individuals. (Quoted in Taylor, 1999, p. 57)

For instance, 20th Century Fox purchased film rights to Michael Crichton's novel *Prey* for close to $5 million in 2002. Fox executives were approached about the rights several weeks before they received the manuscript and concluded the deal over one weekend. The book was sent only to Fox – a rare event in Hollywood, where literary rights are typically shopped to the highest bidder and ultimately spread across several companies.[9]

The most successful writers and producers do not always go through the spec script process, *per se*. As illustrated by the Crichton example above, some players with an established track record have the clout to "short-circuit the standard development process and have a film approved on the strength of their interest alone" (Daniels et al., 1998).

Often when a script moves forward in Hollywood, some major players are involved, as illustrated in another example of a script deal reported in *Variety*:

> In a deal worth $400,000 against $1 million, Universal and Imagine Entertainment topper Brian Grazer bought "Inside Man," a spec script by neophyte scribe Russell Gewirtz that will be developed as a possible directing vehicle for Grazer's Imagine partner Ron Howard. Gewirtz, a lawyer-turned-scribe, crafted a crime thriller that revolves around a hostage situation at a bank, with a tough cop matching wits with a clever robber. CAA brokered the deal and Daniel Rosenberg, who developed the script with the scribe, will be exec producer. The script had several suitors, but execs Scott Stuber and Donna Langley were able to persuade the scribe to take a U turn.[10]

Again, it is impossible to estimate how many ideas or concepts for films and scripts based on those ideas do not make it to the development stage. Many elements must come together for a film to actually become a commodity. One might argue that some films that actually do make it to the screen actually should not have been developed or produced. But it seems clear that some ideas and some scripts have a better chance than others.

## Development deals

Development generally refers to the initial stage in the preparation of a film, or in other words, those activities related to turning an idea or concept into a finished screenplay.[11] More specifically, the development stage may include activities related to organizing a concept, acquiring rights, preparing an outline, synopsis, and treatment, as well as writing, polishing and revising script drafts.

Again, film properties develop differently, depending on who is involved and when. While it may be risky to generalize, a "typical" or "model" process will be described here. Development deals are agreements with a studio or production company to provide funding for a writer, producer, or director to develop a project. Not all projects receive the same amount of funding and many do not make it through the full series of development steps. Development financing may come from different sources – the major studios draw on corporate funds, while independents may draw on a wider variety of sources, as discussed below. Development deals also may include contingencies that must be met before the movie can move into actual production. The process, which can take as little as eight months or as long as two years, may involve approving the writer, script, budget, director, and lead actors.

Often the first step is for the writer to prepare a treatment, which outlines the scenes, major characters, action, and locations in about 20–50 pages. A first draft, second draft, rewrite, and polish usually follow a treatment. At every step, various participants or players offer suggestions in the form of development notes.

If they haven't been arranged already through a package deal, for instance, directors and main stars may be hired at this point. These players may receive frontend payments, which would include their salaries and other perks which are negotiated, and backend payments, such as profit participation, or some kind of share in the receipts from the film (to be discussed in the next chapter).

Deferred payments involve cast or crew members who receive some or all of their compensation after the film is released in order to reduce production costs. A deferred fee is generally paid from revenues generated from a completed motion picture, and if a movie is not finished, or it does not generate significant revenue, then the deferred payment holder may not be paid for his/her contribution.

## Film costs/budgets

During development, a line producer is hired to oversee physical production of the film, which includes preparing the budget and other preliminary material. The budget is organized with above-the-line and below-the-line costs, which also is the way that labor is referred to. Above-the-line costs include major creative costs or participants (writer, director, actors, and producer) as well as script and story development costs. Below-the-line items are technical expenses (equipment, film stock, printing, etc.) and technical labor.

Generally, motion picture production is labor-intensive, meaning the largest part of the budget is spent on labor. The cost of key talent (especially actors/actresses) is a significant part of the budget for a typical Hollywood film. Above-the-line talent can often represent 50 percent of a production budget, and has been identified as one of the key reasons why the costs of Hollywood films have skyrocketed.

Table 1.4 reveals that the average cost to produce a Hollywood feature film has increased dramatically over the last few decades. One measure of a film's expense is its negative cost or the amount spent on actual production costs. However, there also are additional costs involving studio overhead and interest expenses. Thus, the actual cost

TABLE 1.4    *Average negative and marketing costs for feature films*

| Year | Average Negative Cost[1] (in millions) | Average Marketing Costs[2] (in millions) |
|------|----------------------------------------|------------------------------------------|
| 2002 | $58.8 | $30.6 |
| 2001 | 47.7 | 31.1 |
| 2000 | 54.8 | 27.3 |
| 1999 | 51.5 | 24.5 |
| 1998 | 52.7 | 25.3 |
| 1995 | 36.4 | 17.7 |
| 1990 | 26.8 | 11.9 |
| 1985 | 16.8 | 5.2 |

*Source*: MPAA

[1] Negative cost includes production costs, studio overhead and capitalized interest.

[2] Marketing costs include prints and advertising.

of manufacturing a completed negative may be inflated beyond what was actually spent to produce the film. As reported by the MPAA, in 1975 the average negative cost was around $5 million; by 1987 that amount was over $20 million. In 2002, the average had risen to $58.8 million.[12] (Marketing costs will be discussed in the next chapter and Chapter 5.)

## Financing

Financing usually is arranged during development and becomes a significant factor in determining whether a film will be made and who will be involved. Again, financing strategies and funding sources are different for major films and independent productions. A funding source's influence or involvement in the production/distribution of a film also may vary, depending on the clout of the major participants or players.

*Funding sources.*   While financing is a major challenge for most independent filmmakers, it is less problematic for a film project that involves the major studios. The cost of development and production may be paid by the studio, which will then own the film outright. (Various charges and fees are associated with this support, which will be discussed in the next chapter.)

It is important to note at this point that the major Hollywood companies do not fund film production solely through profits. At least the potential for extensive resources are available through the studios' well-heeled parent corporations, as well as from ongoing financial relationships with banks and other financial institutions. These sources may provide capital for various activities, including film production. While these financial sources (especially banks) may not become involved in decisions about which films to produce, they are always involved in the financial health and overall management of the company and become more involved and restrictive when a company is doing poorly. (See Wasko, 1982, for more discussion of Hollywood's historical relationship with banking institutions.)

Production loans for individual films also are possible from banks, however, collateral is always required to secure the loan and a distribution agreement with a major studio is often required. Independent filmmakers may find it especially difficult to find bank financing, however, some financial institutions specialize in this type of business. A few large banks have many years of experience in dealing with Hollywood companies (City National, Chase National, Chemical, and Bank of America). Meanwhile, other financial institutions have developed this expertise, but may also find that this type of financing is quite challenging. For instance, Comerica Entertainment Group, a division of Comerica Bank-California, was especially active in financing independently produced feature films between 2000–2002.

Independent producers are often forced to rely heavily on pre-sales to other distribution outlets, such as TV networks, pay cable channels, and home video companies. In other words, a producer may arrange for production financing from a pay-TV channel, in exchange for the right to run the film first in the pay-TV market. Similar rights in foreign territories also are sources of funding, especially for independent films. The availability of such funding fluctuates, sometimes providing ample funds for film production, other times drying up completely.

Meanwhile, other sources of funding for some films include merchandising and product placement arrangements. While not all films may be able to tap these sources of production funding, it is not uncommon for Hollywood films to feature numerous products that are not accidental, but purposely placed in exchange for fees that may offset production costs.

Another source of production funding is investment capital in the form of limited partnerships, which may be organized for a specific film or group of films. Several general partners (often, the producers) may initiate and control the partnership, with limited partners serving as investors with no control and no financial liabilities beyond the amount they have invested.

Independent filmmakers also may seek grants from various sources. For example, the film *Stand and Deliver*'s budget of $1.37 million came from the Corporation for Public Broadcasting, American Playhouse, ARCO Corporation, National Science Foundation, and Ford Foundation, in addition to a few product placement deals.

*Co-productions.* Actually, cooperative production ventures have been prevalent in the past and US film production in Europe has a long history, albeit, with numerous ups and downs. Co-productions grew dramatically in the late 1980s as companies were not just picking up films for distribution or simply financing projects, but becoming active in "creative partnerships."

Sometimes complete funding is provided, through a combination of pre-sales and a domestic US distribution agreement. Financing is available from distribution companies, pay-TV (such as HBO) and cable companies (such as Turner and the USA Network). Such financing may be available for independents, especially if the film has overseas potential. However, when such co-production funds are slim, projects associated with the US majors (again) have the advantage.

*Completion guarantees.*   It is possible that a financier or bank may require a completion guarantee to assure that the film is actually finished. A completion bond is a form of insurance that guarantees financing to complete a film in the event that the producer exceeds the budget. If a bond is used, the completion guarantor sometimes assumes control over the production, as well as receiving a preferential position over other investors in recouping funds.

### Green lights/development hell/turnaround

When all of these various elements are in place (which may take many years), a film project may receive a green light from a studio executive and move into (pre-)production. If a script is in development but never receives production funds, it is said to be in development hell. A former screenwriter has estimated that 85 percent of studio-purchased spec scripts end up in development hell (Taylor, 1999). However, even if a film is not produced, the studios are able to recoup development costs from other films' budgets as part of studio overhead charges (more on this in the next chapter).

Development itself is a controversial process, especially because of the constant rewriting of scripts. The major studios tend to have different philosophies about development, including the number of projects in development, who becomes involved in the rewriting process, etc. In addition, decisions about which films are given a green light are made based on many factors, not just the quality of the idea or concept. For instance, a film may provide a vehicle for a star or director or it may be a high-powered studio executive's special project. However, favored film projects may also never receive a green light because of management changes.

Even though one studio may abandon a project, it is possible for another one to pick up the project and make it into a successful film. Again, if a studio project is abandoned, the costs are written off to the studio's overhead or perhaps charged to a producer's multi-picture deal. A classic example was *E.T.: The Extra-Terrestrial*, which was developed and dropped by Columbia Pictures, but picked up by Universal. As they say, the rest is history.

## Pre-production

Pre-production begins when a developed property is approved for production and may take from two to six months, of course, with the usual proviso that every film is different. While 400–500 films are released in the USA each year by Hollywood companies, obviously, many, many film ideas or scripts never reach the production stage (see Table 1.2). However, if a major film does begin production, it will usually be completed, as too much money has already been invested in the project for it to be abandoned.

### Organizing production

After a film is given the green light, various elements are assembled that are necessary to manufacture the film. Locations are scouted and selected, final casting is done, and key production personnel are hired. Each of these areas will be discussed further below.

Meanwhile, the final budget, shooting script, and shooting schedule also are prepared. A line producer or unit production manager handles some of these details and the logistics of the entire company and production process. Although these positions are similar, a line producer often has greater creative involvement.

Decisions are made as well about the equipment needed during production. Often, production companies hire or lease machinery, tools or gear needed for production as rentals eliminate the need to purchase and maintain equipment.

In addition, an account is established for the film, with all costs, time, and materials charged against a job or charge number. Importantly, producers or studio representatives review charges on a regular basis, watching for costs that may be inappropriately charged to the film. Motion picture accountants explain that this "job-order cost procedure" is similar to the process used in specialty manufacturing or accounting systems used by service businesses (Daniels et al., 1998, p. 183). This process becomes especially important when the revenues and costs for a film are eventually distributed (as will be explained in the next chapter).

A number of firms offer services to assist companies during production, including payroll and production accounting. Accounting firms such as Arthur Anderson & Co., Coopers & Lybrand, Deloitte & Touche, Ernst & Young, KPMG Peat Marwick, and Price Waterhouse, have been involved in the motion picture accounting business.

## Locations

Decisions are often made about locations during development and firmed up during pre-production. Decisions about whether to shoot on a studio lot or another location involve creative judgments, but are also very much influenced by economic factors. A script may call for a specific location; however, recreating the site in a studio or on a backlot may be less costly in the end.

While a good deal of production for Hollywood films takes place at studios and on location in and around Hollywood and the San Fernando Valley, film companies are often drawn to other locations for economic reasons. For instance, during 2001, around 170 features were shot in New York City, with film and TV companies spending $5 billion on production in the city, which generated $500 million in tax revenues. These days, film production is being deliberately lured away from Southern California by film commissions offering various incentives, as well as the attraction of lower labor costs.

*Film commissions.*   Film commissions at the local, state, and national level attempt to attract productions to their locations. The first commission was formed in the USA in the late 1940s. More commissions developed in response to the need for local government liaisons who could coordinate services such as police, state troopers and highway patrols, road and highway departments, fire departments, park rangers, and all of the other essential municipal and government services for location shooting. The Association of Film Commissioners (AFCI), formed in 1975, represents a worldwide network of more than 300 commissions from 30 countries.

As more production companies began to look for realistic and varied locations, more cities and states began to see the need for production coordination. But most importantly, they were also keenly aware of the economic benefits brought by film and video production companies to their areas. Indeed, a multiplier effect is often experienced as the local economy can take in as much as three times the amount that a production company actually spends on location.

The services provided by film commissions have expanded in response to the growth of location shooting. Film commissions provide a number of services for film producers, from scouting locations within their area to trouble-shooting with local officials and helping cut through paperwork and bureaucratic red tape. Some provide economic incentives, such as tax rebates and hotel discounts for location scouts. Others offer a variety of other free services like research for screenwriters or liaison work with local government agencies.

Film commissions have been set up by cities, counties, states, provinces and federal governments, and are generally operated and funded by various agencies of government, such as governors' offices, mayors' offices, county boards of supervisors, chambers of commerce, convention and visitors bureaus, travel commissions, and business and economic development departments. Their primary responsibility is to attract film and video production to their areas so that film companies will hire local crews and talent, rent local equipment, use hotel rooms, rental cars, catering services, and other goods and services supplied on location. While supporting businesses in their area, filmmaking attracts visitors. Film scenes at a particular location are "soft-sell" vehicles that also promote that location as a desirable site for future tourism and industry.

Various incentives are offered to attract film production to locations. For example, the State of Louisiana launched a major production-incentives program featuring film production tax credits in 2002. Under the new legislation, qualifying productions could earn tax credits of up to 15 percent of the total production expenditures in the state. In addition, a financing fund was organized to attract producers to the state.

## Issue: Fragmentation and runaway production

Because of the proliferation of film production in many locations, some attention has been given to the issue of whether the US motion picture industry is still centralized in Southern California. Some scholars argue that the film industry is characterized by flexible specialization, with activities at different locations. From their base in urban planning, Storper, Christopherson and others argue that the film industry has been restructured from the integrated, mass-production studio system of the 1930s and 1940s (a Fordist model) to a disintegrated and flexible system based on independent and specialized production (a post-Fordist model). Thus, the film industry provides an example of flexible specialization's viability for other industrial sectors to emulate (Storper and Christopherson, 1987).

While these interpretations describe some important changes in the US film industry of the late twentieth century, the analysis is severely handicapped by the emphasis on production and the neglect of the key roles played by distribution, exhibition, and financing. Aksoy and Robins (1992) have provided an excellent critique of the flexible specialization thesis:

> For them [Storper and Christopherson] the major transformation in the American film industry is centered around the reorganization of produc-tion, and, more particularly, around the changing relationship between technical and social divisions of labor in production. It is as if the Hollywood industrial story begins and ends with the production of films.

The flexible specialization argument also overlooks the considerable concentration of post-production in California. Even with growing post-production activities in Florida, Vancouver, and Toronto, an argument can be made that Hollywood is still a focal point for production planning, post-production and distribution. A Hollywood insider explains it this way:

> There is still some truth to the notion of Hollywood as a place located in Southern California. The district of Hollywood is still more or less the geographic center of a cluster of production facilities, soundstages, office buildings, and studio ranches, stretching from Culver City, Venice, and Santa Monica in the south, to Glendale, Burbank, North Hollywood, and even the Simi Valley in the north. The dozen or so companies that control more than half of the world's entertainment have headquarters in Los Angeles, within a thirty-mile radius of Holly-wood. The executives, agents, producers, actors, and directors are there. The meetings to decide what movies will be made are held there. At some point, every major figure in world entertainment has to come to Hollywood, if only to accept an Academy Award.[13]

Nevertheless, shooting on location is common for various reasons. In some discussions of this issue, economic runaway has been defined as "US-developed feature films, movies for television, TV shows or series that are filmed in another country for economic reasons" (SAG/DGA, 1999). The SAG/DGA study of runaway production in 1999 reported that the total economic impact as a result of US economic runaway film and television production was $10.3 billion in 1998, up more than fivefold since the beginning of the decade.

The report noted that Canada had captured the vast majority of economic runaways, with 81 percent of the total. Although US domestic feature film production grew 8.2 percent annually from 1990 to 1998, US features produced in Canada grew 17.4 percent annually during the same time period. In addition to the substantial impact on DGA and SAG members (directors, unit production managers, assistant directors, principal and supporting actors, stunt and background performers), the guilds' study noted that the greatest impact in terms of lost employment opportunities was felt by below-the-line workers.

Further, the total employment impact of US runaway production on entertainment industry workers rose 241 percent from 1990 to 1998, with the number of full-time equivalent positions lost rising from 6,900 in 1990 to 23,500 in 1998 – a cumulative total of 125,100 positions. Meanwhile, a Dept. of Commerce study released in 2001 mirrored the SAG/DGA findings, concluding that film and TV work continues to leave the USA at an accelerating rate (US Dept. of Commerce, 2001).

Some small anti-runaway advances have emerged in recent years, such as streamlined local permitting and California's $45 million three-year incentive program, which reimburses filmmakers for permits, public equipment, and safety costs. (More discussion of this issue, and how the industry is calling on the government for assistance, will be presented in Chapter 6.)

### Labor markets/labor organizations

While actors and directors receive much of the attention and publicity, the Hollywood workforce includes a wide range of laborers, from carpenters and office workers to artists, and lab technicians. According to MPAA data, 582,900 people were employed in the US motion picture industry in 2002. (This figure includes video rental employees.)

Hollywood workers sell their labor to employers in a labor market that is both similar and different to other industries. Generally, the motion picture production is labor-intensive and the industry is highly unionized. Hollywood unions and guilds negotiate basic agreements, which specify minimum salaries (or scale), working conditions, residuals, benefits, etc. However, individual workers also negotiate their own contracts, sometimes with the assistance of an agent or manager, as explained previously.

Since 1982, the Alliance of Motion Picture & Television Producers (AMPTP) has been the primary trade association that negotiates industry-wide collective bargaining agreements that cover actors, craftspersons, directors, musicians, technicians, and writers – virtually all the people who work on theatrical motion pictures and television programs. In these negotiations, the AMPTP represents over 350 production companies and studios.

Some of the unions and guilds involved in these negotiations include the American Federation of Musicians; American Federation of Television and Radio Artists; Directors Guild of America; International Alliance of Theatrical Stage Employees; International Brotherhood of Electrical Workers; Screen Actors Guild; International Brotherhood of Teamsters; and Writers Guild of America. Because of the significance of labor in the process of manufacturing film com-modities, more discussion of some of these labor organizations, their role in Hollywood production, and the status of labor power will be presented in the next few sections.

## Hollywood unions and guilds

Early in the industry's history, film workers were organized by trade unions from related industries, such as the theater and the electrical industry. Eventually unions and guilds were formed specifically to organize Hollywood workers, and most of these labor groups are still active in the film and television industries. But similar to other US labor organizations, the Hollywood unions and guilds continue to be challenged by political and economic developments in society in general, and the film industry, in particular.

The global expansion of the film industry over the last few decades has proven to be especially problematic for US film workers, as well as presenting problems for cinema workers in other parts of the world. Although the global film market has grown over the last few decades, a political economic analysis focussing on labor issues presents a less cheery picture for trade unions and workers in the entertainment business. Though some top stars, writers and directors are benefiting mightily from these developments, a more careful look at the power relations in Hollywood reveals a rather different picture for many other workers.

TABLE 1.5   *Trade unions active in the US film industry*

|  | Founded | Membership |
|---|---|---|
| Above-the-Line Organizations |  |  |
| Directors Guild of America (DGA) | 1937 | 12,000 |
| Screen Actors Guild (SAG) | 1936 | 98,000 |
| Writers Guild of America (WGA) | 1954 |  |
| WGAw |  | 8,500 |
| WGAE |  | 4,000 |
| Below-the-Line Organizations |  |  |
| International Alliance of Theatrical & Stage Employees & Motion Picture Operators (IATSE) | 1893 | 100,000 |
| National Association of Broadcast Employees and Technicians (NABET)[a] | 1933 | 10,000 |

*Source*: *Encyclopedia of Associations*, 2003

[a] NABET became part of the Communication Workers of America (CWA) in January 1994.

Film workers represent a highly skilled and specialized labor force, but unemployment is high. For instance, it has been estimated that 85 percent of actors are out of work most of the time. There are some unusual or unique characteristics, as well. Some workers, such as writers, directors and actors, share in the profits of films through profit participation deals. Others may become employers themselves through their own independent production companies or in projects where they serve as producer or director. (An example: Mel Gibson worked as director and actor in *Braveheart*, but also was one of the film's producers.) There also are keen differences between above-the-line and below-the-line workers, with consequent differences between the labor organizations that represent these different types of labor (see Nielsen, 1985). Moreover, the organization of entertainment unions along craft lines rather than a vertical, industrial structure, has tended to inhibit labor unity within the industry.

Only a brief introduction to the major trade organizations will be given here, followed by a discussion of current issues (see Table 1.5 for a summary of the main labor organizations and their membership figures[14]).

### Above-the-line guilds

*DGA.*   The Directors Guild of America represents directors, unit production managers, assistant directors and technical coordinators in television and film. The guild was formed in 1960 from the merger of the Screen Directors Guild and the Radio and Television Directors Guild. The organization's membership was more than 12,000 in 2003.

While a producer manages the overall film project, the director is in charge of production and is usually considered the "primary creative force" in a film's manufacture. The director controls the action and dialogue in front of the camera and is therefore responsible for interpreting and expressing the intentions of the screen writer and producer as set out in the screenplay. The director is usually hired by the producer, although some directors also become involved as some kind of producer in some films.

It is interesting to note that most directors make only one movie, while only a handful make ten or more, even though, as one study has argued, "Director pay, the number of movies they make, and the box office grosses of their movies are statistically self-similar" (De Vany, 2002).

The DGA negotiates a Basic Agreement for its members, who then arrange individual contracts with the producer or producing company with terms and conditions applicable to a specific film. Director's agreements include employment details (salary, etc.), but also issues relating to creative control. More specifically, details regarding the director's cut and final cut of a film are delineated.

Prompted especially by the introduction of colorized films, the DGA has lobbied strongly for a moral rights law for creative personnel to prevent changes in their work (Stumer, 1992).

**SAG.**   While actors and actresses have played an important role in the industry's evolution, their involvement in the film business has shifted over the years. On the one hand, actors sell their labor to producers in a market just as other workers do. However, as many film theorists have discussed, the nature of actors as unique "stars" presents some interesting dynamics that differ from other Hollywood laborers.

Indeed, stars long ago became commodities, bought, and sold by Hollywood companies, representing "brands" with identifiable names, faces, and other characteristics. In recent Hollywood history, some successful actors and a few actresses have parlayed this "clout" into sizable salaries and shares in films' profits (see McDonald, 2000). In addition, actors are sometimes film producers, investing their own capital in film projects and serving both as laborer (actor) and management (producer) at the same time.

The Screen Actors Guild (SAG) was organized in 1933, after several other organizations had attempted to organize film performers, including the Academy of Motion Picture Arts and Sciences (Prindle, 1988; Clark, 1995). The early history of SAG was dominated by the attempt to establish a guild shop, but more recently has focused on gaining compensation for actors in the constantly expanding forms of distribution (television, video cassettes, etc.). SAG's concern with compensation is not an insignificant issue considering that its members gained more than $1 billion in 1987 merely from residual payments for TV reruns of old films. Much more revenue has been earned from home video and other new distribution outlets.

Again, SAG negotiates a Basic Agreement for its members, however, individual actors/actresses also contract for individual films, sometimes using agents or managers to represent them, as noted previously.

In 1992 the Screen Extras Guild's (SEG) 3,600 members became a part of SAG's union coverage, primarily because SEG lacked the clout to deal with producers and most extras were working non-union. Serious discussions of a merger continue between SAG and the American Federation of Television and Radio Artists (AFTRA). AFTRA was formed in 1937 to represent radio and then television performers. The organization's primary jurisdiction is in live television, but AFTRA shares jurisdiction with SAG for taped television productions. AFTRA organizes over 80,000 performers in radio, television and sometimes, film.

The American Federation of Musicians (AFM) represents musicians across many industries, including film. The trade group, which was formed in the 1890s, has negotiated contracts with the film industry since 1944, and has been especially concerned with new technological developments in sound recording.

## Below-the-line unions

*The International Association of Theatrical and Stage Employees (IATSE or IA).*   This has been the most powerful union in the US film industry. Formed at the end of the nineteenth century, IATSE organized stage employees in the USA and Canada. As the entertainment industry expanded, IATSE grew to include motion picture projectionists and technical workers at the Hollywood studios and film exchanges throughout North America. When television was introduced, IATSE organized technical workers in the new medium.

IATSE's history includes some dismal chapters from the 1930s when racketeers and criminals extorted funds from union members, as well as assisting in the ugly blacklisting activities that tainted Hollywood in the 1940s (Nielsen, 1985; Horne, 2001).

The IATSE currently represents technicians, artisans and craftspersons in the entertainment industry, including live theater, film and television production, and trade shows. More than 500 local unions in the USA and Canada are affiliated with IA.[15] IATSE has a tradition of local autonomy, with a variety of craft-based locals involved in collective bargaining agreements. However, nationwide agreements for film production personnel are negotiated with the AMPTP, as noted above.

IA covers a wide range of employees in film production, distribution and exhibition. Among the classifications of workers represented are art directors, story analysts, animators, set designers and set decorators, scenic artists, graphic artists, set painters, grips, electricians, property persons, set builders, teachers, costumers, make-up artists, hair stylists, motion picture and still camerapersons, sound technicians, editors, script supervisors, laboratory technicians, projectionists, utility workers, first aid employees, inspection, shipping, booking and other distribution employees. IA's bargaining strength comes from this "complete coverage" of all the crafts involved in the production of theatrical, motion picture or television products, with workers involved in every phase of a production, from its conception through every aspect of its exploitation.

*The National Association for Broadcast Employees and Technicians (NABET).* This labor organization grew first out of radio, and then television broadcasting. The union was organized at the National Broadcasting Corporation (NBC) as a company union (an industrial organization rather than craft oriented) as an alternative to the larger and more powerful IBEW (Koenig, 1970). NABET's relatively militant history is replete with squirmishes with IBEW and IATSE, as well as continuous rumors of a merger with the larger IATSE.

In 1990, NABET's Local 15, which organized 1,500 freelance film and tape technicians in New York, merged with IATSE. Then, in 1992, most of the other NABET locals joined the Communication Workers of America (CWA), effective January 1994. About 9,300 NABET members became a part of the much larger CWA, which represents 600,000 workers in telecommunications, printing, broadcasting, health care, and the public sector.

While most of NABET's members were to be moved to an independent broadcasting arm within CWA, NABET's West Coast Local 531 agreed to merge with IATSE because of its 500 members' closer affiliation with the film industry. Thus, IATSE became the only union in the USA to represent behind-the-camera film workers.

*The International Brotherhood of Teamsters.*  This is the largest and strongest union in the USA and also is active in the motion picture industry, organizing studio transportation workers on the West Coast and various other workers. The Teamsters claim a general membership of around 1.4 million; its Hollywood Local 399 has approximately 4,000 members who work as truck drivers and security personnel in the film industry. (The Teamsters also have organized workers involved with other aspects of corporate Hollywood's activities, as discussed below.)

### Issue: labor and power

The biggest headache facing Hollywood unions and guilds is the proliferation of non-union production in the Los Angeles area as well as at production sites all over the country and the world. As always, employers are trying to lower labor costs and there is a ready supply of non-union workers, both in Hollywood and other locations. In addition, the established entertainment unions are perceived as uncooperative and too demanding.

The abundance of available labor also may be related to the popularity of media in general. The growth of media education at universities and colleges, as well as the increased visibility of film and television production in the popular press, means that there is a glut of eager workers for Hollywood companies to employ, very often, without union affiliation. An example: over 3,000 applications are submitted to the DGA's Assistant Directors Training Program each year – only 12 are chosen. Hollywood also seems to have a fantasy quality, even non-production work in the film industry seems glamorous.

While studios try to blame unreasonable union demands for the increase of non-union production and the flight to non-union locations, labor leaders (especially from below-the-line unions) claim that they are not the problem. They point to the sky-rocketing costs of above-the-line talent, with especially high salaries going to high-profile actors and actresses. As one union official explains, "Until they can control their above-the-line costs and their own studio's executives, they'll never bring costs back in line. They can beat us until we do it for free, but if Julia Roberts still wants 76 million bucks, the picture is still going to cost."[16]

The lack of unity among entertainment unions also has been blamed for the growth of non-union filming. Some of the mergers mentioned previously may help to alleviate this problem, yet the organization of labor along craft lines still exacerbates the situation.

The lure of lower budgets with non-union workers has attracted producers to right-to-work states, such as Florida, as well as other states that have recognized film and television production as a boost to local economies, as noted above. Meanwhile, foreign locations, such as Eastern Europe and parts of the Developing World, offer low-budgets and exotic locations.

Pressure from the availability of a non-union option and runaway production has forced the unions to make concessions during contract negotiations. An example was IATSE's contract negotiation process with the AMPTP, when a strike was barely averted with a new contract accepted in December 1993. During intense contract negotiations, some argued that IA had lost its clout. Even if the union went on strike, the producers and other observers felt that there was enough non-union labor to continue production. They also assumed that IA members themselves would have worked non-union jobs if a strike had been called.

Meanwhile, New York unions also have accepted concessions to lower labor costs and compete with Los Angeles. The East Coast Council – a coalition of seven motion picture and television production unions – has actively tried to lure work away from Hollywood, with substantial changes in contracts and concessions, including wage reductions of up to 50 percent.

While Hollywood companies have become more diversified, union representation also has followed. The different types of businesses incorporated by Hollywood companies have involved further differentiation of labor, making it difficult for workers to form a united front against one corporation. For instance, workers employed by Disney include animators at the Disney Studio, hockey players on Disney's hockey team, the Mighty Ducks, and Jungle Cruise operators at Disney's various theme parks.

The differentiation of labor is especially apparent at the theme parks owned by many Hollywood companies, in particular, Disney, Universal, Paramount, and Warners. Workers at these sites are represented by a wide array of labor organizations, many of which are unrelated to those unions active in the film industry.

Generally, then, the trend towards diversification has contributed to a weakening of trade unions' power as well as a further lack of unity among workers. As *Los Angeles Times* labor reporter, Harry Bernstein, once observed:

> These days, corporate tycoons own conglomerates that include busi-nesses other than studios and networks. They may enjoy movie-making, but money seems to be their primary goal. So if production is stopped by a film industry strike, their income may be slowed, but money can still roll in from other sources.[17]

A CWA official explained their merger with NABET in straightfor-ward terms, highlighting labor's current concerns with unity and globalization:

> In this day and age, with all the concentration of corporate power, it's become an advantage for unions to band together and join their resources and strength. It certainly helps when unions have to take on these multinational corporate structures, as especially evidenced in the communications and broadcasting fields.[18]

So the pressures are mounting on labor organizations in the enter-tainment field. Hollywood unions and guilds have faced difficult struggles in the past, combating a range of problems from union recognition in the 1930s to ideological assaults such as the black-listing period of the 1940s and 1950s. They continue to face further challenges from anti-union sentiments as well as power struggles with diversified corporations actively involved in international markets, as will be described in the chapters that follow.

*Professional organizations.*    While Hollywood workers often are represented by labor organizations, many professional groups also have been organized. For example, the American Cinema Editors (ACE), an honorary society of motion picture editors, was founded in 1950. Film editors are voted into membership on the basis of their professional achievements, their dedication to the education of others and their commitment to the craft of editing. Another example is the American Society of Cinematographers, which was formed 76 years ago as an educational, cultural and professional organization. Membership is by invitation, extended only to directors of photography with distin-guished credits in the industry. Meanwhile, the Society of Camera Operators, formed in 1978, is an honorary organization composed of several hundred men and women internationally, who make their living operating film and/or video cameras in the cinematic media.

Another professional organization is the Society of Motion Picture and Television Engineers (SMPTE), the leading technical society for the motion picture industry. SMPTE was founded in 1916 to advance theory and development in the motion imaging field. More than 10,000 SMPTE members are spread throughout 85 countries and include engineers, technical directors, cameramen, editors, technicians, manufacturers, educators, and consultants. SMPTE publishes ANSI-approved Standards, Recommended Practices, and Engineering Guidelines, *SMPTE Journal* and its peer-reviewed technical papers. SMPTE goals include developing industry standards, education through seminars, and communicating the latest developments in technology.

## Principal photography/production

Principal photography is usually the most costly part of manufacturing a film and typically takes from 6–12 weeks. Again, there are always exceptions. While the structure of production is relatively flexible, it is similar to the construction industry. In other words, film productions are organized as short-term combinations of directors, actors, and crews, plus various subcontractors who come together to construct a motion picture.

A good deal of attention has been given to this part of the production process, which may be seen as the most glamorous and/or creative part of the manufacture of the film commodity. While some economic issues may emerge during principal photography, only a few will be mentioned briefly here. Obviously, there is always the issue of adhering to the budget, and the problems that may lead to over-budget productions. Creative decisions inevitably will be influenced by the availability of funds.

In addition, the clout or power of various players has enormous influence on decision-making on the set. Perhaps not surprisingly, the involvement of producers, investors or studio representatives (collectively called The Suits) is often claimed to have a chilling effect on the creative process.

## Post-production

Although editing usually begins during principal photography, it continues after shooting concludes, as other elements of the film are added: scoring, mixing, dialogue, music, sound effects, and special effects. Post-production may take 4–8 months. As noted above, some of these activities may take place in other locations, however, post-production is still mostly centralized in Hollywood.


## Hollywood services industry

An infrastructure for film production and post-production has developed in the Los Angeles area, which includes a wide range of motion picture-related businesses. Many companies are involved in servicing the motion picture industry, including those that deal with film stock, laboratories, camera equipment, sound recording and equipment, properties, costumes, set design and construction, lighting equipment, etc. There is even an association for the businesses that manufacture, supply and produce entertainment equipment, called the Entertainment Services and Technology Association.

Though some of these services may be offered in other locations, Los Angeles is still a centralized location for most of these activities. For instance, Los Angeles is home to roughly 400 sound stages with more than 4.4 million square feet of space.

While it is impossible to describe these businesses in any detail here, a few of the major companies involved in these markets are profiled below.

*Eastman Kodak Company.*    One of the largest companies servicing the film industry is Eastman Kodak, which has a long history in Hollywood. With sales of over $13 billion in 2001, and over 75,000 employees, Kodak continues to be the world's number one manufacturer of photographic film, ahead of Fuji Photo Film. However, the company also has developed digital imaging media and other products for both amateur and professional photographers. Kodak is an important source of film, paper, and processing equipment for the entertainment industries.

*Technicolor.*    The Camarillo, California-based company first brought color to movies more than 80 years ago and still claims to be the world's number one processor and distributor of motion picture film as well as the largest independent manufacturer and distributor of DVDs, CDs, and videocassettes. The company also offers content services (post-production, release print service labs), exhibition services (film print distribution, digital distribution, on-screen advertising space, in-theater distribution of promotional materials), and home entertainment services (video duplication, and DVD and CD replication, plus packaging, distribution, warehousing and fulfillment services). Technicolor is owned by Thomson Multimedia, with sales of 10.5 billion Euros (US $9.3 billion) in 2001 and 73,000 employees in more than 30 countries. Thomson is involved with a wide range of video technologies, systems, finished products and services to consumers and professionals in the entertainment and media industries.

*Panavision Inc.* Panavision claims to be the number one maker of cameras for the motion picture and TV industries. Although the company's equipment was used in the production of about three-quarters of the movies produced by the major film studios in 2001, it is not available for sale – its equipment can only be rented from Panavision or its agents. Its camera systems are made up of cameras, lenses, and accessories. A Panasonic subsidiary, Lee Filters, makes and sells lighting, color-correction, and diffusion filters; subsidiary Lee Lighting rents lighting equipment in the UK.

*Dolby Laboratories, Inc.* Dolby produces and sells a wide range of film technologies, mostly involving sound systems. Dolby audio systems are used in the motion picture, broadcasting and music industries, as well as being licensed for use in the consumer electronics industry. The privately-held company is based in San Francisco.

*Avid Technology Inc.* Avid produces digital editing systems used by the film, music, and television industries. Its products, including Film Composer, Symphony, and Avid Xpress, are used by film studios, postproduction facilities, and television stations. Its Digidesign unit markets the ProTools line of sound editing systems. Avid also makes animation design software, newsroom automation systems, and digital storage systems. Nearly 50 percent of sales (which were over $434 million in 2001) come from outside North America. Software giant Microsoft has a 12 percent stake in the company.

*Laser-Pacific Media Corp.* This company provides a variety of post-production services, primarily for TV shows. Its two facilities in Hollywood, California, offer film processing, film-to-videotape transfer, sound mixing, and digital editing. The company also offers mastering for home video and digital versatile disc (DVD) projects and post-production services for high-definition television. In addition to television, Laser-Pacific also serves motion picture studios like

New Line Cinema and Paramount. The company has received five Emmy Awards for outstanding achievement in engineering development.

**THX, Ltd.**    The company that is named after George Lucas's first feature film *THX 1138* was spun off from Lucasfilm in 2002 and is comprised of five divisions: THX Studio, THX Cinema, THX Home, THX Mobile, and THX Games. The company is devoted to improving the sound and image quality of motion pictures, home and automotive entertainment systems, computer games, and gaming consoles. Skywalker Sound is another Lucas subsidiary which offers a wide range of sound services.

**Special effects (f/x).**    The area of special effects has grown dramatically over the last decades, as new computer and digital technologies continue to produce a wide range of filmic magic. Because of the significance of this area, a bit more detail is provided here. Obviously, special effects have implications for the type of films that are made, as well as influencing production costs.

The primary aim of special effects is to create things that don't actually exist. Some of the techniques used by the earliest filmmakers, such as double exposures and miniaturized models, are still employed. *King Kong* (originally released in 1933) represented a landmark in special effects and incorporated many of the same techniques used by today's special effects teams: models, matte paintings for foreground and backgrounds, rear projections, miniature or enlarged props and miniaturized sets, combined with live action.

However, the use of computers, robotics and digital technologies over the past 20 years has added to the sophistication of the effects process, and enhanced the filmmaker's ability to create nearly anything imaginable on film. There is a wide variety of optical or special effects, which are constantly changing as every film has its own set of unique requirements which inspire effects masters to create new techniques. Only a few of these techniques can be discussed here.

First, the use of computerized cameras has made stop-motion techniques smoother and more believable, while image compositing has become more complex. Meanwhile, computers have been used not only to assist in manipulating images, but to create new ones. Computer Generated Imaging (CGI) has reached a new level of sophistication, as characters, objects, and settings can be created and then composited with real images (or live action).

Other types of effects can be achieved through digital image processing, including manipulation of color, contrast, saturation, sharpness, and shape of images. Certain elements of images can be removed, making it possible to repair damaged film, or eliminate unwanted parts of scenes. Examples are the flying sequences in many films, which used heavy cable guides that could be electronically "painted" out of each shot.

Another possibility is to create situations that seem real, but are actually computer enhanced. Rearranging scenes from famous films, as well as inserting current actors in historical footage is not only a possibility, but a reality as seen in some of the scenes in *Forrest Gump*.

For some films, the number of effects can be staggering. Yet, some of these techniques and technologies actually save time, as effects can be done quicker and involve fewer people. For instance, computerized human images have been integrated into films and the possibility of synthetic actors is certainly possible.

The special effects boom has led to the creation of a few new companies. An example is Apogee Productions, which was formed in 1977 by a group led by John Dykstra, who had worked on the special effects for *Star Wars*. Their first project was the television series, *Battlestar Galactica*, but they went on to produce spectacular images, models, mechanized props, and/or optical composites for over 50 feature films and television programs. Apogee also serves the varied interests of the entertainment business, designing and manufacturing a wide array of special effects devices and theme park attractions, as well as producing commercials, feature films, and television movies.

However, one company seems to dominate the special effects market. Industrial Light and Magic, formed by George Lucas while producing *Star Wars*, claims to do more business in the special effects field than its five major competitors combined. The company has worked on six of the top ten box office hits in history and has created some of the most spectacular effects work in the industry.

## Production issues

It is fairly uncontroversial to state that decisions made about which scripts are sold, how they are developed, and which ones are green lighted and actually produced are guided by a bottom-line or box-office mentality, at least for major Hollywood films. Obviously, such decisions also affect the creativity of the players involved. For instance, as a script goes through the development process, it's often changed and reworked to the point that some writers don't even recognize their original work. As Kawin explains:

> A script may pass through the hands of many writers before it is ready to be produced, and even the revised final is likely to be modified by the director and the actors while the picture is being shot. The editor, too, may affect the "script" by deleting a line or a speech that turned out not to play well, and the decisions that follow previews may entirely change the outcome of a story. (1992, p. 310)

Important decisions about what is shot (or not shot) during principal photography and the final cut also are made by those in positions of power. While the last stage of the editing process involves a director's cut, the final version of the picture is almost always in the hands of the distributor or the financier of the film, unless a director has a good deal of clout. For instance, as another industry insider reports: "I have seen bad test screenings, where the director of the film has final cut and the head of the studio wants the director to change the movie, fix the ending" (PBS, 2001). Generally, creativity is tempered by clout and power, and decisions are made within the parameters of the box office.

However, even with the prevailing financial mentality, those with power or clout often do not know any better than anyone else what will be popular with an audience. As screenwriter William Goldman wrote in *Adventures in the Screen Trade*: "nobody knows anything in the movie business because no one can predict popular taste" (1989, p. 39) Goldman explains further: "nobody really knows which films will be big. There are no sure-fire commercial ideas anymore. And there are no unbreakable rules."

While these remarks echo the theme of riskiness mentioned previously, the industry also tries to eliminate this uncertainty in various ways – by focussing on blockbusters featuring well-known stars and/or by basing films on already-recognizable stories and characters.

While success in Hollywood may be unpredictable, explanations abound. For instance, some claim that the movies that get made reflect the executive mentality but the movies that are successful reflect the audience (Squire, 1992, p. 95). This explanation, however, underestimates the amount of effort and expense that is devoted to convincing audiences to see or buy a film or the products associated with the film. Marketing and promotion begin during production, continue during shooting, and become especially significant upon a film's release. (More discussion of these activities will be included in Chapter 5.)

As noted previously, the production of Hollywood films attracts a good deal of attention from the press, academics, and the public. It also attracts a good deal of capital. The total investment in producing or acquiring films for release in the USA in 2000 was $7.75 billion (not including advertising or marketing expenses) (Grummitt, 2001, p. 5). As such, it is important to understand how the film commodity is produced. However, it is vital to understand how films are distributed, for as we will find in the next chapter, distribution holds the key to power in Hollywood.

## Notes

1  For 2001, approximately 31% of the top 100 films and approximately 44% of the top 25 films drew on previous works. For 2002, derivative films represented approximately 39% of the top 100 and approximately 56% of the top 25 films. For all time, approximately 53% of the top 100 films, and approximately 64% of the top 25 films were derivative. The numbers are approximate because some films' original sources could not be identified and a few films (most evidently, *The Lion King*) have contested origin. Thanks to Randy Nichols, University of Oregon, for this analysis.

2  For instance, for this book, the publishers have "the sole and exclusive right . . . to license the Work or any abridgement of the Work or any substantial part of the Work in all media in all languages for the legal term of copyright throughout the world." This would include, if one could imagine, the rights to a feature film based on this book.

3  This is nicely portrayed in Robert Altman's film, *The Player*, a brilliant representation of the film industry. In fact, Hollywood is rather fond of making films about itself, exemplified by the classic *Sunset Boulevard*, as well as more recent examples such as *The Big Picture*, *Get Shorty*, *Bowfinger*, *A Star is Born*, *Cecil B. Demented*, *Ed Wood*, *Celebrity*, *Chaplin*, *Full Frontal*, *Bugsy*, *Swimming with Sharks*, *Wag the Dog*, *America's Sweethearts*, *Jay and Silent Bob Strike Back*, *Last Action Hero*, *The Majestic*, *ED-TV*, *The Purple Rose of Cairo*, *Shadow of the Vampire*, *State and Main*, *Simone*, *The Muse* . . . and the list goes on.

4  Significant changes in these relationships were being considered at the end of 2002, with the agencies calling for more flexibility from the guilds.

5  This does not include other important sections of the Los Angeles area, such as the San Fernando Valley.

6  Some of this discussion is drawn from Paul D. Supnik's "Motion Picture Production and Distribution – An Overview of the United States Perspective" http://www.supnik.com.

7  Scripts that are sent directly to a production company or one of the studios are usually not even opened, as complications (and lawsuits) arise

if a script later develops as a film that follows (or is claimed to follow) the unsolicited script too closely.

8 Taylor (1999, p. 11) explains that the first big spec script sale was *Butch Cassidy and the Sundance Kid*, which was "auctioned" and sold for $400,000 in the late 1960s. However, the industry's preoccupation with spec scripts began after the Writers Guild strike of 1988, when agents deluged the studios with scripts for sale (ibid., pp. 7–9).

9 *Variety* noted that the deal was

> an unusual feat of big-money, bicoastal synergy for News Corp., corporate parent of Fox and Crichton's publisher, HarperCollins. Opting not to shop the manuscript on the open market, HarperCollins, which keeps an office on the Fox lot, has long nurtured its ties to the studio. The publisher, which bought "Prey" last year in a two-book deal worth $40 million, will launch the tome in English-speaking territories around the world in November. The cross-promotional possibilities at News Corp. are considerable. Company can time paperback publication to the release of the feature and the rollout of licensing and merchandise deals, which are part of the franchise rights contained in the film deal." (Dave McNary, "Crichton Nabs a Foxy $5 mil," *Variety*, 25 July 2002)

10 M. Fleming, "U, Imagine: 'Inside' job," *Variety*, September 2002. Such announcements are a regular feature of the trade press, as players and companies continuously communicate deals and other information, in order to make further deals.

11 Some of the discussion in this section draws on information from Cones (1992), Benedetti (2002), and others.

12 This amount is tricky to estimate, as there may be fluctuations due to high/low budgeted films in any one year. In addition, financial reporting changed in 2000, when abandoned project costs were no longer included in studio overhead, and thus not a part of negative costs.

13 Christopher Vogler, *Opening the Doors to Hollywood*, excerpt from http://screenwriters.com/hn/writing/cda.html.

14 The history of Hollywood labor organizations, while neglected for many years by scholars, has received increased attention during the past few decades (Clark, 1995; Hartsough, 1995; Nielsen, 1985; Prindle, 1988; Horne, 2001; Nielsen and Nailes, 1995). However, most of these excellent studies have focused on the historical background of Hollywood labor, with less attention given to more recent developments, such as corporate diversification and globalization. Background for the unions and guilds discussed has been based on a variety of sources, but especially descriptions in Gary M. Fink, *Labor Unions*, Westport, CT: Greenwood Press, 1977.

15 Some idea of the diversity of IATSE's membership is possible by considering the union's Hollywood locals: Local 44 – Affiliated Property Craftspersons; Local 767 – First Aid; Local 80 – Motion Picture Studio Grips; Local 790 – Illustrators & Matte Artists; Local 600 – Int'l Photographers Guild / West Coast; Local 816 – Scenic Artists Local 695 – International Sound Technicians; Local 818 – Publicists; Local 700 – Editors Guild / West Coast; Local 839 – Screen Cartoonists; Local 705 – Motion Picture Costumers;

Local 847 – Set Designers & Model Makers; Local 706 – Make-Up Artists & Hair Stylists; Local 854 – Screen Story Analysts; Local 717 – Production Office Coordinators & Accountants; Local 871 – Script Supervisors; Local 727 – Motion Picture Craft Service; Local 876 – Art Directors; Local 728 – Studio Electrical Lighting Technicians; Local 884 – Studio Teachers & Welfare Workers; Local 729 – Set Painters & Sign Writers; Local 892 – Costume Designers.

16 D. Cox, "IA Hits 'Hidden' Pix," *Daily Variety*, 18 May 1994, p. 1.

17 H. Bernstein, "Hollywood May Take the Drama Out of Settling Disputes," *Los Angeles Times*, 11 April 1989, p. 1.

18 K. O'Steen, "NABET Council Approves Merger with CWA," *Daily Variety*, 17 June 1992, p. 1.

# Distribution   2

## Distribution Companies: The Majors

Film production often attracts the greatest attention to Hollywood, as the popular press, encouraged by the Hollywood promotional machine itself, focuses on new stars, hot directors, and exciting scripts. But the glamour of movie production is closely wound up with the business of film distribution. Production teams often work directly for major production/distribution companies and independent production companies often need to deal with them if their film is ultimately to appear in theaters and video stores around the country and the world. The major distributors dominate the film business. So, to understand how Hollywood works, one must ultimately confront distribution and thus ultimately encounter the Hollywood majors. This chapter will present profiles of the major distributors and their parent conglomerates, as well as outlining the distribution process.

From the 1950s onward, the majors became part of diversified conglomerates, no longer depending on movies as their only source of income, but involved in a wide range of cultural production, from audio-visual products to theme park operations. Interest in Hollywood firms became especially intense at the end of the 1980s with a fury of mergers and consolidation. Deregulation, privatization, technological developments, and the opening of new international markets contributed to this concentrated growth. Interestingly, foreign interests were attracted to these conglomerates for many of the same reasons that Hollywood increasingly was looking to international markets. At the end of the twentieth century, several of the Hollywood majors were owned by foreign companies – Columbia/Tri-Star by Sony, Universal by Vivendi, and Fox by News Corp.

Hollywood is dominated by a handful of companies that draw much of their power from film distribution, which is central to the film business. Despite the presumed risk involved in film distribution, the major distribution companies manage to survive and (usually) profit.

As we shall see in the latter section of this chapter, the distribution process is designed to benefit the distributors, but not necessarily production companies. In addition to their positions within diversified conglomerates, the majors have distinct advantages that include distribution profits, enormous film libraries, and access to capital. As industry insiders Daniels et al. (1998, p. 5) observe: "The studios have Oz-like power over the motion picture industry and cash in abundance. Or perhaps more properly, access to abundant capital."

The majors claim to encounter intense competition in the film industry, as well as in other activities. Yet, many companies have attempted to enter the distribution business over the years and have failed. Examples included the so-called "instant majors" of the 1970s/ 1980s (National General, Cinerama) and more recently Orion, DEG, Lorimar, Embassy, and Allied Artists. In other words, the major distributors still dominate, as indicated by the fact that eight companies received 95 percent of the box office revenues in the USA and Canada in 2000.

At one time, one could depict Hollywood as a "three-tier society." At the top were the big studios or the majors – Paramount, Twentieth Century Fox, Warner, Universal, Disney, and Columbia. The second tier included a handful of smaller or less influential production and/ or distribution companies, or minor majors, including MGM/UA, Orion, Carolco, and New Line Cinema. And at the bottom were the much smaller and often struggling "independent" distributors and production companies.

The majors still dominate the top tier, however, there are far fewer second tier companies and some have been taken over by the majors (Miramax, New Line, etc.). Others have faded into oblivion (Orion). The only new company on the scene that has significant clout is Dreamworks (which will be described more fully below).

The majors' trade organization is the MPAA, which will receive more attention in Chapter 5. The organization is concerned with legislation affecting the motion picture industry, piracy and copyright issues, and administering the rating system. Meanwhile, the American Film Market Association (AFMA) represents and works with independent distributors.

## Profiles of the Major Studios and Parent Companies

One of the problems in outlining the activities of these corporations is the ongoing restructuring and realignment. The major corporations and their subsidiaries are constantly merged and unmerged, while boards of directors and managers continuously make decisions to move into different markets, trying best to predict what products will be the most lucrative and profitable. Nevertheless, it is still possible to talk about ongoing tendencies and/or trends that characterize the major distribution companies and their parent corporations. The discussion below and the accompanying tables present overviews of the parent companies for each of the major Hollywood distributors, as they were organized at the end of 2002.

## AOL Time Warner/Warner Brothers

Warner Brothers Pictures operated under the roof of the diversified conglomerate Warner Communications Inc. from the late 1960s through the end of the 1980s. In January 1990, Time Inc. and Warner Communications Inc. merged to form one of the largest communications companies in the world. Despite a huge debt, the merger was defended as necessary to compete globally, as well as to take advantage of technological, political and social changes. In 2001, Time Warner then merged with America OnLine (AOL), to create what is claimed to be the largest entertainment conglomerate in the world.

As indicated in Table 2.1, AOLTW is divided into several divisions: AOL, Cable, Filmed Entertainment, Networks, Music, and Publishing. Approximately 22 percent of its revenue comes from its AOL division, which represents the largest source of revenue for the company. AOLTW has a 15-person board of directors, with companies such as XO Communications, Hilton Hotels, Fannie Mae, and Colgate-Palmolive represented.

*Warner Brothers Pictures* had sales of nearly $7 billion in 2001, thanks to top-grossing *Harry Potter and the Sorcerer's Stone*, as well as other notable hits. Video and DVD products are distributed through Warner Home Video. But AOLTW also owns other film companies, as well.

*New Line Cinema* was founded in 1967 by Robert Shaye, but is now a wholly owned subsidiary of AOL Time Warner's Turner Broadcasting. The company produces and distributes movies such as *Austin Powers in Goldmember*, *Blow*, and *Rush Hour 2*. New Line also is responsible for the *Lord of the Rings* trilogy. The company distributes its films on video and DVD through New Line Home Video, and licenses and develops television and merchandising through New Line Television.

TABLE 2.1   *AOL Time Warner*
Total Revenue (2001): $38,234 million
Filmed Entertainment Revenue (2001): $8,759 million
Employees: 89,300

### AMERICA ONLINE
AOL Services, AOL Anywhere, AOL International, CompuServe, ICQ, MapQuest, Moviefone, Netscape, AOL Music, AOL Local, AOL Instant Messenger, AOL Broadband

### NETWORKS
**Turner Broadcasting System**
TBS Superstation, Turner Network Television, Cartoon Network, Boomerang, TCM Europe, Cartoon Network Europe, TNT Latin America, Cartoon Network Latin America, Turner South, TCM & Cartoon Network/Asia Pacific, Atlanta Braves, Atlanta Hawks, Atlanta Thrashers, Phillip Arena, the WB Television Network, Kids' WB!, CNN/U.S., CNN Headline News, CNN International, CNNfn, CNN en Espanol, CNN Airport Network, CNNRadio, CNNRadio Noticias, CNN Newsource, CNN.com, CNNMoney.com, CNNfyi.com, CNNSI.com, CNN.com.br, CNN.com.Europe, CNN.de, CNN.dk, CNNenEspanol.com, CNNItalia.it, CNN.com Asia, CNNArabic.com
**Joint ventures**
Cartoon Network Japan, Court TV, CETV, NBC/Turner NASCAR Races, Viva +, CNN+, CNN Turk, n-tv
**Home Box Office**
HBO, HBO2, HBO2 Signature, HBO Comedy, HBO Zone, HBO Latino, Cinemax, MoreMAX, ActionMAX, ThrillerMAX, WMAX, @MAX, 5StarMAX, OuterMAX, HBO Independent Productions, HBO Downtown Productions
**Joint ventures**
Comedy Central, HBO Asia, HBO Brasil, HBO Czech, HBO Hungary, HBO India, HBO Korea, HBO Ole, HBO Poland, HBO Romania, A&E Mundo, E! Latin America, SET Latin America, WBTV Latin America, Latin America History Channel

### FILMED ENTERTAINMENT
**Warner Bros.**
Warner Bros. Pictures, Warner Bros. Television, Warner Bros. Animation (including Looney Tunes, Hanna-Barbera), Castle Rock Entertainment, Telepictures Productions, Warner Home Video, Warner Bros. Consumer Products, Warner Bros. International Theaters, Warner Bros. Online, DC Comics (includes MAD Magazine)
**New Line Cinema**
New Line Cinema, Fine Line Features, New Line Home Entertainment, New Line International Releasing, New Line New Media, New Line Television, New Line Distribution, New Line Merchandising/Licensing, New Line Music

### MUSIC
**Warner Music Group**
The Atlantic Recording Corporation; Elektra Entertainment Group, Inc.; Warner Bros. Records, Inc.; Warner Music International (includes Warner Music Latina, Inc); Warner Strategic Marketing, Inc. (includes Rhino Entertainment Company, Warner Commercial Marketing, Warner Special Products, Inc.; WMG Soundtracks); Word Entertainment; Warner/Cheppel Music, Inc. (includes Warner Bros. Publications U.S., Inc.); WEA Inc. (includes Ivy Hill Corporation, Warner-Elektra-Atlantic Corporation, and WEA Manufacturing, Inc.); Alternative Distribution Alliance; Giant Merchandising
**Joint ventures**
The Columbia House Company, Maveric Recording Company, Music Choice

### PUBLISHING
**Time, Inc.**
Time, Sports Illustrated, People,

TABLE 2.1 (*cont.*)

Entertainment Weekly, Fortune, Money, In Style, Real Simple, Time for Kids, Sports Illustrated for Kids, Sports Illustrated Women, Teen People, People en Espanol, FSB: Fortune Small Business, Business 2.0, Mutual Funds, Southern Living, Progressive Farmer, Southern Accents, Sunset, Cooking Light, Coastal Living, For the Love of Cross Stitch, For the Love of Quilting, Parenting, Baby Talk, Health, In Style U.K., In Style Australia, In Style Germany, Time Asia, Time Canada, Time Atlantic, Time Latin America, Time South Pacific, Popular Science, Who Weekly, Outdoor Life, Field & Stream, Golf Magazine, Yachting, Motor Boating, Salt Water Sportsman, Ski, Skiing, Freeze, This Old House, TransWorld Stance, TransWorld Surf, TransWorld Skate-boarding, TransWorld Snowboarding, TransWorld Motorcross, TransWorld BMX, Ride BMX, Skiing Trade News, TransWorld Skateboarding Business, TransWorld Snowboarding Business, TransWorld Surf Business, BMX Business News, Amateur Gardening, Motor Boats Monthly, Muzik, 19, Now Style Series, 4x4, Amateur Photographer Angler's Mail, Cage & Aviary Birds, Park Home & Holiday Caravan, Chat, Country Life, Cycling Weekly, Horse & Hound, NME, Now, Shooting Times & Country Magazine, Practical Boat Owner, Practical parenting, Prediction, Racecar Engineering, Woman, Woman's Own, Woman's Weekly, Woman Feelgood, Woman's Own Life, Woman's Weekly, TV & Satellite Weekly, TVTimes, The Railway Magazine, Rugby World, Ships Monthly, Soaplife, Sporting Gun, What's On TV, Mizz, Mizz Specials, Webuser, Caravan Magazine, The Guitar Magazine, VolksWorld, World Soccer, Beautiful Homes, Bird Keeper, Stamp Magazine, The Field, The Golf, Uncut, What Digital Camera, Cars & Car

Conversions, Chat Passion Series, Classic Boat, Country Homes & Interiors, Creating Beautiful Homes, Woman & Home, Yachting Monthly Aeroplane Monthly, Superbike, Cycle Sport, Decanter, Essentials, Evening, Family Circle, Women & Golf, Shoot Monthly, Hair, Wedding & Home, Woman's Weekly Fiction Special, International Boat Industry, Farm Holiday Guides, Jets, Golf Monthly, Hi-Fi News, Homes & Gardens, Horse, Ideal Home Land Rover World, Living etc., Loaded, Marie Claire, MBR–Mountain Bike Rider, MiniWorld, Model Collector, Motor Caravan, Motor Boat & Yachting

Time Life, Inc.; Oxmoor House, Leisure Arts; Sunset Books; Media Networks, Inc.; First Moments, Targeted Media Inc.; Time Inc. Custom Publishing; Synapse; Time Distribution Services; Time Inc. Home Entertainment; Time Customer Service; Warner Publisher Services, This Old House Ventures, Inc.
***Joint ventures***
BOOKSPAN, Essence Communications Partners, European Magazines Unlimited, Avantages S.A.
***AOL Time Warner Book Group***
Little, Brown and Company Adult Trade Books; Warner Books; Little, Brown and Company Children's Publishing; Bulfinch Press Warner Faith, Time Warner AudioBooks; Time Warner Books UK

### CABLE
***Local News Channels***
Bay News 9, Tampa FL; Central Florida News 13, Orlando FL (joint venture); NY1 news, NY; News 8, Austin TX; $/ News, Rochester NY; Raleigh NC
***Joint ventures***
Road Runner, Time Warner Telecom, Inc., inDemand, Kansas City Cable Partners, Texas Cable Partners

*Sources*: 2001 Annual Report and Hoover's OnLine (www.hoovers.com)

Meanwhile, *Fine Line Features* is the subsidiary of New Line that produces, acquires, and distributes art house films such as *Storytelling, Human Nature, Cherish, Before Night Falls, Shine,* and *Dancer in the Dark.*

Turner Broadcasting also owns *Castle Rock Entertainment,* a production company responsible for *When Harry Met Sally, A Few Good Men,* and *The Shawshank Redemption.* The company also produces television programming, including *Seinfeld* and the short-lived *Michael Richards Show.* It was formed in 1987 by five media moguls including director Rob Reiner, Glenn Padnick, Andrew Scheinman, Alan Horn, and Martin Shafer. Castle Rock has produced seven movies based on Stephen King novels and takes its corporate name from the fictional Maine town that serves as the setting for many King stories.

### The Walt Disney Company/Buena Vista

The Walt Disney Company claims to be the No. 2 media conglomerate in the world and probably the most synergistic of the Hollywood majors. The company that began as an independent studio producing cartoons distributed by other companies has moved into the ranks of the majors. Since the reshuffling of owners and managers in 1984, the Disney empire has extended its tentacles more widely and more tenaciously. And, as with most of the Hollywood majors, the company's expansion did not depend solely on motion pictures, but on a wide array of business activities which aggressively exploit the Disney name and its characters.

As illustrated in Table 2.2, the Walt Disney Company is organized into divisions representing Studio Entertainment, Parks and Resorts, Consumer Products, and Media Networks. These divisions accounted for 24 percent, 28 percent, 10 percent, and 38 percent of the company's 2001 revenues, respectively.

The company's film production and distribution division is *Walt Disney Studio Entertainment,* which attracted nearly $7 billion in sales in 2002. The distribution arm is called *Buena Vista Distribution,* while live-action and animated titles, such as *Atlantis* and *Pearl Harbor,* are produced through Walt Disney Pictures, Touchstone, and Hollywood Pictures.

Disney also owns *Miramax Film,* the "independent" distribution company that was formed in 1979 by brothers and co-chairmen Harvey and Bob Weinstein. Miramax Film produces and distributes

TABLE 2.2 *The Walt Disney Company*
Total Revenue (2001): $25.3 billion
Studio Entertainment (2001): $6.1 billion
Employees: 114,000

### MEDIA NETWORKS

ABC Television Network
TV Stations:
WABC (NY), KABC (LA), WLS (Chicago), WPWI (Philadelphia), KGO (San Francisco), KTRK (Houston), WTVD (Raleigh-Durham), KFSN (Fresno), WJRT (Flint, Mich.), WTVG (Toledo)

ABC Radio Network
Radio Stations:
WABC, KPLI (NY), KABC, KSPN, KDIS, KLOS (LA), WLS, WMVP, WRDZ, WPJX, WZZN (Chicago), KGO, KSFO, KMKY (San Francisco), WWJZ (Philadelphia), KMKI, WBAP, KSCS, KMEO, KESN (Dallas), WJR, WDRQ, WDVD (Detroit), WMAL, WJZW, WRQX (Washington), KMIC (Houston), WMYM (Miami), WDWD, WKHX, WYAY (Atlanta), KKDZ (Seattle), KDIZ, KQRS, KXXR, WGVX, WGVY, WGVZ (Minneapolis), KMIK (Phoenix), WSDZ (St. Louis), WEAE (Pittsburgh), WMMI (Tampa), KADZ , KDDZ (Denver), WMMK (Cleveland), WKMI (Boston), KIID (Sacramento), WDDZ (Providence), WGFY (Charlotte), WDYZ (Orlando), WMNE (W. Palm Beach), WDZY (Richmond), WDZK (Hartford)

ABC Internet Operations, Disney and family-branded Internet Operations: ESPN, Inc., ABC Family, Disney Channel, Disney Channel International, Toon Disney, SoapNet

### *Joint ventures*

A&E (37.5% stake) includes A&E International and Biography
Lifetime (50% stake) includes Lifetime Movie Network
E! Entertainment Television (39.6% stake) includes Style
The History Channel ((37.5%) includes the History Channel International

### STUDIO ENTERTAINMENT

Walt Disney Pictures, Touchstone Pictures, Hollywood Pictures, Miramax Films, Dimension Films

Walt Disney Television, Buena Vista Television

Buena Vista Home Entertainment
Buena Vista Music Group:
Walt Disney Records, Walt Disney Music Publishing, Hollywood Records, Mammoth Records, Lyric Sheet Records

Buena Vista Theatrical Group

### PARKS AND RESORTS

Disneyland Resort, Disney California Adventure
Walt Disney World Resort (Magic Kingdom, Epcot Center, Disney-MGM Studios, Animal Kingdom)
Tokyo Disney Resort, Tokyo DisneySea, Disneyland Resort Paris
Disney Vacation Club
Disney Cruise Line

Disney Regional Entertainment:
ESPN Zones (in Anaheim, Las Vegas, Denver, Chicago, Atlanta, Washington D.C., Baltimore, and NY)

Walt Disney Imagineering

Anaheim Sports, Inc. (Mighty Ducks, Anaheim Angels)

### CONSUMER PRODUCTS

Disney Licensing, Disney Hardlines, Disney Toys, Disney Apparel, Disney Publishing, Hyperion Books, Disney Interactive

The Disney Store, Disney Store.com, Disney Catalog

TABLE 2.2    *(cont.)*

|  | Direct-to-Retail Agreements<br>North America: JC Penny, K-Mart, Wal-Mart, Zellars (Canada)<br>Europe: C&A (Belgium), H&M (Belgium), Lindex (Norway), Oviesse (Italy), Tesco (U.K.)<br>Latin America: C&A (Brazil) |
| --- | --- |

SOURCES: 2001 Annual Report, 2001 Fact Sheet, and Hoover's OnLine (www.hoovers.com)

independent and foreign films, such as *Pulp Fiction*, *Clerks*, and *Amélie*. Although known for distributing and producing quirky art house films, Miramax also has distributed more mainstream movies such as *Serendipity* and *All the Pretty Horses*. Disney acquired the firm in 1993.

Miramax owns *Dimension Films*, a production company that reinvigorated the teen horror genre with the *Scream* and *Scary Movie* series. More recently, the company has expanded its scope with films such as *Spy Kids*.

### News Corporation Limited/Twentieth Century Fox

Twentieth Century Fox, the company started by William Fox, and one of the Hollywood majors since the 1920s, was purchased by Rupert Murdoch's News Corporation in 1985. News Corp. is truly a global media and entertainment empire, as the company's 2001 Annual Report boasts: "Producing and distributing the most compelling content to the farthest reaches of the globe." The company's revenues for 2002 were over $16 billion.

Murdoch's family owns about 30 percent of the company, which is claimed to be valued at around $11 billion. Furthermore, the company claims to be the largest English-language newspaper publisher in the world, with paid weekly circulation of over 15.5 million. However, News Corp.'s activities go far beyond newspapers, with extensive ownership of magazines, books, and newsprint manufacturing, as well as television, film, video and satellite distribution of entertainment and information, in addition to a variety of other companies (see Table 2.3).

News Corporation divides its business into Filmed Entertainment, Television, Cable Network Programming, Magazines/Inserts, Newspapers, Book Publishing, and Other. By group, revenues break down

TABLE 2.3  *The News Corporation*

Total Revenue (2001): $25,578 million (Australian)
Filmed Entertainment Revenue (2001): $6,625 million (Australian)
Employees: 30,000

**FILMED ENTERTAINMENT**
### *Fox Filmed Entertainment*
Twentieth Century Fox Film Corp
Fox 2000 Pictures
Fox Searchlight Pictures
Fox Music
Twentieth Century Fox Home Entertainment
Twentieth Century Fox Licensing and Merchandising
Fox Interactive
Twentieth Century Fox Television
Fox Television Studios
Blue Sky Studios
Fox Studios Baja (Mexico)
### *Joint ventures*
Regency Televsion (50% stake)
Fox Studios Australia (50% stake)

**TELEVISION**
### *United States*
FOX Broadcasting Company
Fox Television Stations
  WNYW (NY)
  KTTV (LA)
  WFLD (Chicago)
  WTXF (Philadelphia)
  WFXT (Boston)
  KDFW (Dallas)
  KDFI (Dallas)
  WTTG (Washington, DC)
  WJBK (Detroit)
  WAGA (Atlanta)
  KRIV (Houston)
  WTVT (Tampa)
  WJW (Cleveland)
  KSAZ (Phoenix)
  KDVR (Denver)
  KTVI (St. Louis)
  WDAF (Kansas City)
  WITI (Milwaukee)
  KSTU (Salt Lake City)
  WBRC (Birmingham, AL)
  WHBQ (Memphis)
  WGHP (Greensboro, NC)
  KTBC (Austin)
  Chris-Craft (10 Stations)
Twentieth Television
Echostar Commuications Corporation (5% stake)

TABLE 2.3   *(cont.)*

---

**UK & Europe**
British Sky Broadcasting (36.3% stake)
Stream (50%)
Balkan News Corporation
**Asia (except Japan)**
STAR
Channel [V] Music Networks Limited Partnership
  Phoenix Satellite Television Holdings Limited (37.6%)
ESPN STAR Sports (50%)
VIVA Cinema (50%)
Asia Sports Group Limited (20%)
**Japan**
SKY PerfecTV! (8.1%)
News Broadcasting Japan (80%)
JSky Sports (14.3%)
Sky Movies Corporation (50%)
Nihon Eiga Satellite Broadcasting (15%)
**Latin America**
Canal Fox
Sky Latin America DTH Platforms
Mexico – Innova (30%)
Brazil – NetSat (36%)
Sky Multi-Country Partners (30%)
Telecine (b) (12.5%)
Cine Canal (b) (22.5%)
**Australia and New Zealand**
FOXTEL (25%)
Fox Sports Australia (50%)
Sky Network Television (29.5%)

**CABLE NETWORK PROGRAMMING**
**United States**
Fox News Channel (a)
Fox Cable Networks Group (a)
FX
Fox Movie Channel
Fox Sports Networks
Fox Regional Sports Networks
  (13 owned and operated) (d)
Regional Programming Partners (b) (40%)
  (interests in 8 regional sports networks,
  Metro Channels, New York Knicks,
  New York Rangers, Madison Square Garden and Radio City Music Hall)
Sunshine Network (b) (63%)
Speedvision Network (b) (32%)
Outdoor Life Network (b) (33%)
Fox Sports International (b) (50%)
CTV SportsNet (b) (20%)
National Sports Partners (b) (50%)
National Advertising Partners (b) (50%)
National Geographic Channel – Domestic (b) (66.7%)
National Geographic Channel – International (b) (50%)

TABLE 2.3   *(cont.)*

---

Fox Family Worldwide (b) (49.5%)
Los Angeles Dodgers
STAPLES Center (b) (40%)
LA Sports and Entertainment District (b) (40%)
HealthSouth Training Center (b) (40%)
Fox Sports Skybox (b) (70%)
**Asia**
Hathway Cable & Datacom Private Ltd. (26%)
KOOs Group (15 Affiliated Cable Systems) (20%)

## NEWSPAPERS
### United States
New York Post
### United Kingdom
The Times
The Sunday Times
The Sun
News of the World
TSL Education
### Australia
More than 100 national, metropolitan, suburban, regional and Sunday titles,
including the following:
The Australian
The Weekend Australian
The Daily Telegraph
The Sunday Telegraph
Herald Sun
Sunday Herald Sun
The Courier-Mail (41.7%)
Sunday Mail (Qld) (41.7%)
Northern Territory News
Sunday Territorian
The Advertiser
Sunday Mail (SA)
The Mercury
Sunday Tasmanian
The Sunday Times
### New Zealand
Independent Newspapers (44.3%)
Pacific Islands Monthly
### Fiji
The Fiji Times
Sunday Times
### Papua New Guinea
Post-Courier (63%)

## MAGAZINES AND INSERTS
### United States and Canada
Gemstar-TV Guide International Inc (38.5%)
News America Marketing
In-Store

TABLE 2.3   *(cont.)*

---

FSI (SmartSource Magazine)
SmartSource iGroup
News Marketing Canada
The Weekly Standard
**Australia**
InsideOut
**New Zealand**
Independent Newspapers (44.3%)
(14 national magazines)

**BOOK PUBLISHING**
**United States, Canada, United Kingdom & Europe and Australasia**
HarperCollins Publishers

**OTHER**
**United States**
Healtheon/WebMD (0.6%)
Rawkus Entertainment (80%)
OmniSky Corporation (17.4%)
**United Kingdom and Europe**
NDS (79%)
epartners
Broadsystem
Broadsystem Ventures
The Wireless Group (19%)
Convoys Group
Sky Radio (71.5%)
Radio 538 (42%)
News Outdoor Group (75%)
**Australia and Asia**
News Interactive
News Connect
Festival Records
National Rugby League (50%)
Netease.com (8.5%)
Indya.com (37.5%)
Explocity.com (25%)
ndiaproperties.com (19.9%)
Egurucool.com (15%)
Baazee.com (15%)

---

*Source*: 2001 Annual Report and *Hoover's*.

into the following percentages: Filmed Entertainment (26 percent), Television (27 percent), Cable Network Programming (11 percent), Magazines/Inserts (7 percent), Newspapers (18 percent), Book Publishing (7 percent), and Other (4 percent).

*Twentieth Century Fox* reported sales of over $4 billion in 2001 and has released record-breaking hits such as *Titanic* and *Star Wars*. In addition, the company owns *Fox 2000*, which also produces big budget Hollywood films, while *Fox Searchlight Pictures* produces smaller art house films (*Waking Ned Divine*, *The Full Monty*, *The Ice Storm*, and *Boys Don't Cry*).

## Viacom, Inc./Paramount

Paramount Pictures represents an interesting example of corporate trends for the major Hollywood studios during the post-WWII period. One of the original major motion picture studios, Paramount was engulfed by Gulf + Western (G+W) in 1967, and currently is owned by another diversified entertainment conglomerate, Viacom, Inc. Chairman and CEO Sumner Redstone controls 68 percent of Viacom, which is divided into six segments: Cable Networks, Television, Infinity, Entertainment, Video, and Publishing (see Table 2.4). The company's various holdings include CBS, MTV, Nickelodeon, VH1, BET, Viacom Outdoor, Infinity, UPN, TV Land, The New TNN, CMT: Country Music Television, Showtime, Blockbuster, and Simon & Schuster.

*Paramount Pictures* owns a library with more than 2,500 titles, including Oscar winners such as *Forrest Gump*, *Braveheart*, and *Titanic* (the highest-grossing motion picture of all time) and more recent releases *The Sum of All Fears*, *We Were Soldiers*, *Orange County*, and *Changing Lanes*. *Paramount Home Entertainment* handles the videocassette and DVD business, while Paramount's international distribution is part of *United International Pictures* (*UIP*), in which Viacom has a 33 percent interest.

*Paramount Classics* is Viacom's specialty film division that produces and distributes art house films such as *Focus*, *The Virgin Suicides*, and *You Can Count On Me*.

The company also is involved in a few theater chains, as well. *Famous Players* was founded in 1920 and currently is Canada's top-grossing chain, with 102 locations with 853 screens. Viacom also shares ownership of *United Cinemas International* (*UCI*) with Universal. UCI operates over 1,000 screens in 120 theaters in various countries and is one of the largest operators of multiplex theaters outside the United States.

## Sony Corp./Columbia Pictures

When the Sony Corporation purchased Columbia in 1989, the theme of synergy boldly emerged. The Japanese electronic transnational paid

TABLE 2.4   *Viacom*
Total Revenue (2001): $23,228 million
Revenue (2001) from Entertainment Division: $2,950 million
Revenue (2001) from Video Division: $5,156 million
Employees: 122,770

### CABLE
#### *MTV Networks*
MTV, MTV2, Nickelodeon, Nick At Nite, TV Land, VHI, CMT, TNN, MTV Films, MTV Europe (nine different feeds), Nickelodeon Movies, Nickelodeon Magazine, Nickelodeon Gas Games and Sports For Kids, Nickelodeon Recreation, Nickelodeon Studios, NickToons, VHI UK, VHI Europa, VHI Classic, Nickelodeon Europe, Nickelodeon Latin America, Nickelodeon Asia, MTV Latin America Joint ventures MTV Italia, MTV Poland, MTV Russia, MTV Brasil, MTV Asia (8 regional feeds), MTV Japan, MTV Australia, MTV Canada, Nickelodeon Australia, Nickelodeon U.K., TV Land Canada,

#### *BET Networks*
BET , BET Jazz, BET Event Productions, BET Books, BET Interactive, LLC (minority interest)

#### *Showtime Networks*
Showtime, Showtime Beyond, Showtime Extreme, Showtime Too, Showtime Showcase, Showtime Next, Showtime Women, Showtime Familyzone, Showtime Event Television (pay per view distributor), The Movie Channel (includes TMC XTRA, FLIX)

#### *Joint ventures*
Comedy Central (with HBO), Gulf DTH Entertainment, LDC (satellite direct-to-home platform in the Middle East), NOGGIN (with Sesame Workshop) non-commercial children's program service (digital cable, satellite and online)

### ENTERTAINMENT
Paramount Pictures, Paramount Classics

Paramount Parks, Paramount's Carowinds (Charlotte, NC), Paramount's Great America (Santa Clara, CA), Paramount's King's Dominion (Richmond VA),

Paramount's King's Island (Cincinnati OH), Paramount Canada's Wonderland (Toronto, Ontario), Star Trek: The Experience (Las Vegas NV), Terra Mitica in Benidorm, Valencia, Spain (joint venture),

Paramount Home Entertainment, Paramount Home Entertainment International Famous Players (853 screens, 94 theaters in Canada),

United Cinemas International (UCI) (50% stake) 1,091 screens in 120 theaters in Europe, Latin America and Asia, Famous Music, Paramount Comedy Channel (UK& Spain) with BSkyB

### TELEVISION
#### *CBS Television Network*
CBS Entertainment, CBS News, CBS Sports

#### *UPN Network*
available in 184 US markets, reaching approx. 97% of the population

#### *Television Production*
King World Productions, CBS Broadcast International, Paramount Television, Spelling Television, Big Ticket Television,Viacom Productions

#### *TV stations (US)*
WCBS (NY), KCBS (LA), WBBM (Chicago), KPSG (Philadelphia), KPIX, KBHK (San Fran), WBZ, WSBK (Boston), KTVT, KTXA (Dallas), KUPA (Atlanta), WKBD, WWJ (Detroit), KSTW (Seattle-Tacoma), WCCO (Minneapolis) with satellite stations KCCO (Alexandria, MN) and KCCW (Walker, MN), WTOG (Tampa), WFOR, WBFS (Miami), KCNC (Denver), KMAX (Sacramento), KDKA, WNPA (Pittsburgh), WJZ ( Baltimore), WNDY (Indianapolis), WWHO (Columbus), KUTV (Salt Lake City) with satellite station KUSG (St. George UT), WTVX (West Palm Beach), WGN

TABLE 2.4 (*cont.*)

| | |
|---|---|
| (Norfolk, Portsmouth, Newport), WUPL (New Orleans), KAUT (Oklahoma City), WLWC (Providence RI/New Bedford, MA), KEYE (Austin), WFRV (Green Bay/ Appleton) with satellite (Escaranaba WI), WHDF (Huntsville, AL) | Westward One, Inc. (15% ownership) Viacom Outdoor outdoor advertising, with operations in the US, Canada, UK, Mexico |
| | **VIDEO** |
| SportsLine.com (minority stake) MarketWatch.com (minority stake) Hollywood Media Corporation (minority stake), Hollywood.com | Blockbuster, Inc. (81%) approx. 6,400 video stores, Blockbuster.com |
| | **PUBLISHING** |
| | Simon & Schuster, Pocket Books, Scribner, The Free Press, Simon & |
| **RADIO** | Schuster Audio, Simon & Schuster |
| Infinity Radio 186 stations in 41 markets CBS Radio Network | Online, Viacom Plus (advertising sales and marketing) |

*Sources*: 2001 Annual Report and Hoover's OnLine (www.hoovers.com)

$3.4 billion for the company – the highest amount paid at that time by a Japanese concern for a US company. At the same time, the company also purchased the Guber-Peters Entertainment Company for approximately $200 million. (Guber and Peters produced a number of profitable films, including *Batman* and *Rain Man*). Sony had previously purchased CBS Records, giving them a strong base in the manufacture of cultural products, as well as audio/video hardware.

It seemed clear that Sony's motivation for purchasing Columbia was the integration of hardware and software. The attraction of rapidly expanding foreign markets for audio/video products also played a big role in explanations of the merger.

As the world's No. 2 consumer electronics firm after Matsushita, Sony makes a wide range of hardware and software products and divides its business into the following areas (with percentages of company sales): Electronics, 64 percent; Games, 12 percent; Music, 8 percent; Pictures, 8 percent; Financial Services, 6 percent; Other, 2 percent (see Table 2.5). Sony's overall sales are truly global: 29.7 percent are from Japan, 32.5 percent from the United States, 21.2 percent from Europe, and 16.6 percent from the rest of the world.

*Columbia TriStar* is the producer of the record-breaking *Spider-Man* (which held the overall single-day box office record of $43.6 million), as well as *Men in Black 2*, and *Stuart Little 2*, while *Sony Classics* is the company's specialty label, with films such as *Sunshine State*, *All About My Mother*, and *Central Station*.

TABLE 2.5  *Sony Corporation*
Overall revenue (2002) 7,578,258 million yen
Pictures revenue (2002): 635,841 million yen
Electronics revenue (2002): 5,310,446 million yen
Employees: 168,000

| | |
|---|---|
| Columbia Records Group | Aiwa Co., Ltd. Sony EMCS Corp. – 50% |
| Columbia House Records Group (owns | partnership with Ericsson), Frontage |
| a 15% stake with AOLTW;remaining | Inc., Sony Information System |
| 85% owned by the Blackstone group) | Solutions Corp., Sony Enterprise Co., |
| Epic Records Group | Ltd., Sony Chemicals Corp., Sony |
| PressPlay (joint venture with Universal | Communication Network, Corp., Sony |
| Music Group; licensing deals with EMI | Computer Entertainment Inc., Sony |
| & BMG) | Siroisi Semiconductor Inc., Sony Life |
| Sony/ATV Music Publishing | Insurance Co., Ltd., Sony |
| Columbia Tri-Star Films | Semiconductor, Kyushu Corp., Sony |
| Sony Pictures Classics | Assurance Inc., Sony Tochigi Corp., |
| Movielink, LLC | Sony Trading International Corp, Sony |
| Sony Pictures Television | Pictures Entertainment (Japan) Inc., |
| Columbia Tri-Star Home Video | Sony PCL Inc., Sony Human Capital |
| | Corp., Sony Finance International, Inc., |
| | Sony Facility Management Corp., Sony |
| | Fukushima Corp., Sony Plaza Co., Ltd., |
| | Sony Precision Technology Inc., Sony |
| | Broadcast Media Co., Ltd., Sony |
| | Broadband Solutions Corp., Sony |
| | Marketing Co., Ltd., Sony |
| | Manufacturing Systems Corp., Sony |
| | Miyagi Corp., Sony Music |
| | Entertainment (Japan) Inc., Sony |
| | Logistics Corp. |

*Sources*: 2001 Annual Report and Hoover's OnLine (www.hoovers.com).

## Vivendi-Universal, S.A.

Universal Pictures has gone through a series of ownership changes since the late 1980s. MCA/Universal was sold to Matsushita in January 1990 for $6.9 billion. The company was owned by Seagram's in the 1990s, but then acquired by Vivendi in 2000.

Vivendi-Universal owns a variety of businesses, as illustrated in Table 2.6, with strengths in communications, media, and water distribution. Unlike the other major companies, the vast majority of Vivendi-Universal's revenues are European in origin (62 percent). US revenues account for 26 percent of the company's total, leaving 12 percent flowing from the rest of the world.

In 2002, Vivendi-Universal consolidated its divisions into three broad areas: Media and Communications, Environmental Services,

TABLE 2.6    *Vivendi/Universal*
Total Revenue (2001): $57,360 million Euros
Total Media & Communication Revenue (2001): $28,115 million Euros
TV & Film Division Revenue (2001): $9,501 million Euros
Employees: 381,504

### MEDIA AND COMMUNICATION
*Music*
Universal Music Group, Decca, Deutsche Grammophon, Interscope Geffen A&M, Island Def Jam Music Group, MCA Records, MCA Nashville, Mercury Nashville, Motown Record Company, Polydor, Universal Records, Universal Classics Group, Verve Music Group, Universal Music Publishing Group, Universal eLabs
Online Music ventures: Pressplay, MP3.com, the JV (with Sony)

*Publishing*
Vivendi Universal Publishing, Houghton Mifflin, Alianza, Robert Laffont, Plon-Perrin, les Presses de la Renaissance, La Decouverte & Syros, Unvers Poche, Larousse, Le Robert, Harrap, Chambers, Vox, Kingfisher, Hemma, Nathan, Bordas, Retz, Cle International, Anaya, Scipione, Atica, Coktel
Software: Knowledge Adventure, Blizzard Entertainment, Sierra Entertainment, Universal Interactive

*TV & Film*
Universal Studios Group, Universal Pictures, Universal Television, Universal Studios Home Video, 13th Street – The Action and Suspense Channel, Studio Universal, The Studio, Sci-Fi Channel, Canal +, Studio Canal+, CanalSatellite (France), CanalSatellite Digital (Spain), Vivendi Universal Entertainment, USA Networks, EchoStar Communications

Universal Studios Recreation Groups: Universal Orlando, Universal Studios Florida, Islands of Adventure, CityWalk, Portofino Bay Hotel, Hard Rock Hotel, Universal Studios Hollywood, Universal CityWalk, Universal Studios Port Aventura (Barcelona, Spain), Universal Studios Japan, Spencer Gifts

*Telecoms*
SFR (France), La Reunion, Cegetel (France), Maroc Telecom (France), Click GSM (Egypt), KenCell (Kenya), V-Fon, V-Net (Hungary), Monaco telecom (Monaco), Xtera (Spain)

*Internet*
@viso, Scoot France & Benelux, CanalNumedia, Allociné Belgium, Allociné France, Allociné Switzerland, Allociné Vision, Canal+ Belgium, Canal+ Denmark, Canal+ Finland, Canal+ France, Canal+ Netherlands, Canal+ Norway, Canal+ Sweden, Cinestore, iTélévision, Zinédine Zidane, Divento, Education.com France, Education.com Germany, Education.com UK, Education.com USA, Flipside France, Flipside Germany, Flipside UK, Flipside USA, Iwin, Uproar UK, Uproar US, Virtual Vegas, MP3.com France, Germany, Japan, Spain, UK, USA), eMusic, Get Music, RollingStone.com, e-brands, Viventurs

### ENVIRONMENTAL SERVICES
Vivendi Water, Generale des Eaux (France), USFilter (US), Culligan (US), Onyx (Waste Management) - Europe, Dalkia (energy) - Europe, Connex (Transportation) - Europe, Fomento de Construccions y Contratas (Spain)

*Sources:* 2001 Form 10-K and Hoover's Online (www.hoovers.com)

and Non-core Businesses. Its Media and Communications Division consists of five smaller sub-divisions: Music, Publishing, TV & Film, Telecommunication, and Internet. TV & Film makes up the largest portion of this division's revenues (33 percent), followed by Telecommunication (27 percent), Music (23 percent), Publishing (16 percent), and Internet (1 percent), respectively.

*Universal Pictures* reported sales of $4.3 billion in 2001 and has produced and distributed a range of feature films, from *A Beautiful Mind* and *Gosford Park*, to action films including *The Mummy Returns* and *The Scorpion King*, to teenage features such as *American Pie 2* and *Forty Days and Forty Nights*.

The speciality arm of Universal is *Focus*, which was formed as a result of the 2002 merger of USA Films (Universal Studios' unit responsible for art house products) and Good Machine (an independent film producer). USA Films was formed when USA Networks (now USA Interactive) purchased PolyGram Home Video and October Films from Seagram (now Vivendi Universal) and merged the companies with Gramercy Pictures.

## MGM/UA

The MGM and UA alliance (MGM/UA Entertainment Co.) formed in 1981, when MGM's owner Kirk Kerkorian took over United Artists. Since then, it's been a complicated saga of unusual buy-outs, aborted deals, and multiple ownership. The company has certainly suffered from this dubious deal-making, sinking to a second-level distribution company. Yet, MGM/UA still holds many valuable assets, including various rights to classic MGM and UA films.

Parent company Metro-Goldwyn-Mayer produces, co-produces, and distributes movies through MGM Pictures (its commercial film division) and is the home of the valuable James Bond franchise (the latest episode, *Die Another Day*). *United Artists* was purchased by MGM in 1981. UA Films serves as a specialized film division for movies with budgets of less than $10 million, plus art house and foreign films. One of UA's resent successes was Bowling for Columbine.

MGM divides its business into the following areas: MGM Pictures; United Artist Films; MGM Distribution, Co.; MGM Television Entertainment; MGM Worldwide Television Distribution; MGM Networks; MGM Home Entertainment; MGM Consumer Products; MGM Music; and MGM Interactive (see Table 2.7).

TABLE 2.7  *Metro-Goldwyn-Mayer, Inc.*

Revenue (2001): $1,387 thousand
Employees: 1,050

    MGM Pictures
    United Artists Pictures
    MGM On Stage
    MGM Movie Channel (Latin America)
    The Independent Film Channel (20% stake)
    Bravo Network (20% stake)
    WE: Women's Entertainment Network (20% stake)
    AMC: American Movie Classics Network (20% stake)
    Z-MGM (stake unclear)
    TeleCine (stake unclear)
    The Film Zone (stake unclear)
    Movie City (stake unclear)
    the Star Channel (stake unclear)
    CineCanal (stake unclear)

**Joint venture:**
    MGM-NBC Media Sales Group

**Alliances with:**
    UPN (in which UPN agrees to broadcast 57 MGM titles during 2002)
    NBC (for distribution for all of NBC Studios)
    Orbit Satellite Television and Radio Network
    Sky Network Television (New Zealand)
    Starz Encore Group (US cable and satellite provider)
    ITV (UK)
    RTL (Germany)
    TF1 (France)
    TVE (Spain)

*Sources*: 2001 Annual Report.

## DreamWorks S.K.G.

The newest of the major players is DreamWorks, which was founded in 1994 by Steven Spielberg, Jeffrey Katzenberg, and David Geffen. The three founders own approximately 66 percent of the company, while Paul Allen, co-founder of Microsoft, owns another 26 percent. Currently, it is a private Limited Liability Corporation, reporting sales of $2.2 billion in 2001.

The company produces films (including Best Picture winner for *Gladiator* and *Shrek*), TV shows (*The Job*, *Undeclared*), and music, including the soundtracks to DreamWorks films. DreamWorks was involved with GameWorks, a video arcade business that it started with SEGA and Universal Pictures, but has withdrawn from that business.

*Speciality divisions.* As noted above, several previously independent or specialty distributors have been acquired by the majors. These include New Line (Time Warner/1995), Miramax (Disney/1992), Gramercy (PolyGram/Universal/1993) and Orion/Samuel Goldwyn (MGM). In addition, a few of the majors have started specialty labels, including Sony Classics, Fine Line (Warner), and Fox Searchlight.

## Independent Production and Distribution

Emanuel Levy (1999) has argued that the concept that best describes independents (or indies) is institutionalization. As Levy points out, independents represent an industry that runs not so much against Hollywood but parallel to Hollywood. In other words, there are two legitimate film industries, mainstream and independent, each with its own organizational structure and its own core audience.

Independent film has become more recognized, with agencies representing independent players, academy awards and other awards going to independent films, and powerful stars and directors working in the independent sector. For instance, Bruce Willis, a Hollywood star who can receive $20 million for his performance in a mainstream film, was involved with an adaptation of Kurt Vonnegut's novel, *Breakfast of Champions*, in 1998. Willis' company, Rational Packaging, bought the book rights and raised independent financing for the $12 million film. However, most major Hollywood stars rarely work in indies.

While the range of independent films and filmmakers is extremely wide, it also has been argued that many in the independent ranks have become much like the mainstream. Several films in the 1980s (*Liquid Sky, Eating Raoul, El Norte, Desperately Seeking Susan*, etc.) demonstrated that independent films can make money and recoup their cost. But more recently, some independents have changed. As one filmmaker explained: "Back then, we used to think a film was a success if it grossed over $1 million. Now, it's not even a success if it grosses over 5 or 10 million" (cited in Levy, 1999). As Levy explains, indies are now no longer content with a modest profit, but instead want the next *Full Monty* or *The English Patient*. In addition, financial backing is becoming difficult for a small film without stars, especially for theatrical and pay-TV markets.

Levy points out that "independent film" since the 1990s has become a euphemism for a small-studio production, and quotes Paul Schrader:

TABLE 2.8  *Independent releases, 1998–2000*

|  | 1998 | 1999 | 2000 |
| --- | --- | --- | --- |
| Artisan | 12 | 12 | 8 |
| Destination Films |  |  | 5 |
| DreamWorks | 5 | 6 | 10 |
| Eros International |  | 15 | 22 |
| Lions Gate Films | 18 | 14 | 20 |
| Trimark Pictures | 9 | 4 | 3 |
| USA Films |  | 10 | 14 |
| Gramercy | 10 | 2 |  |
| October Films | 11 | 4 |  |
| Subtotal | 65 | 67 | 82 |
| Other | 128 | 169 | 173 |
| TOTAL | 193 | 236 | 255 |

*Source*: Grummitt, *Hollywood: America's Film Industry,* 2001

Note: Lions Gate Films acquired Trimark Pictures in October 2000; USA Films formed out of Gramercy and October Films.

> The middle has dropped out. With a few exceptions, there's no place for a $20 to $30 million movie anymore. Hollywood has dropped the ball by leaving social issues to the independents. The movies that studios traditionally made for their prestige value have fallen to the independents, which of course are not so independent. (p. 499)

**Independent distribution.**  True independent distributors are rare, indeed, and have a good deal of difficulty competing with the majors. By the early 1990s, there was little trace of the previously successful independent companies from the 1980s, such as Cannon, New World, and De Laurentiis, and only a few surviving independent distributors at all, as indicated in Table 2.8. A few are outlined here.

*Lions Gate Entertainment* (2002 sales: $267.7 million). Lions Gate is one of the leading independent distributors with successes such as *Dogma* and *Monster's Ball*. The company also produces TV movies, mini-series, and TV series (*The Dead Zone*) through Lions Gate Television, and animated programs (*Kids from Room 402*) through its 51 percent stake in CinéGroupe. In 2002, the company sold its 45 percent stake in Mandalay Pictures (*Enemy at the Gates*).

*Trimark Holdings* (2000 sales: $95.5 million). Lions Gate bought Trimark Holdings for $50 million in 2000 and uses the Trimark Pictures, Trimark Home Video, and Trimark Television properties for film and TV licensing and distribution. Trimark Television licenses movies and TV series to broadcasters, and Trimark Pictures acquires and distributes films not considered cost effective by larger Hollywood companies, such as *Shriek, Saturday Night Live* "Best of" comedy series, and *Held Up*. Trimark's operations also include online film distribution site, CinemaNow.

*Artisan Entertainment Inc.* (2001 sales: $400 million). This company made its mark as an independent distributor with *The Blair Witch Project*, but it has been expanding into television with made-for-TV movies for CBS (*Surviving Gilligan's Island*) and FX (*Sins of the Father*), among other networks. The company has a home video library of more than 7,000 films and is expanding into DVDs. Artisan was formed in 1997 when a group led by Bain Capital acquired home video distributor LIVE Entertainment. Shareholders include former chairman Geoffrey Rehnert, co-founder Alan Gordon, and Canadian broadcaster CTV. In 2001 Artisan acquired Canadian film and TV production company, Landscape Entertainment.

## Issue: Distribution and competition

As will be detailed below, distribution involves a number of different markets where revenues are gleaned for the lease or sale of motion pictures, as well as other related products. According to the MPAA, global revenues for the majors in 2002 totaled $37.3 billion. This included revenues from theatrical, home video, television and other outlets in the US and foreign markets. As a report by Dodona Research recently concluded:

> Most of these revenues, wherever they are earnt, accrue to the major American film distributors, whose attractive flow of product gives them an adequate revenue base on which to support worldwide distribution networks serving theatrical, home video and television markets. Although the practice of selling some foreign rights to subsidise film budget means that the studios' share of the international market is lower than in North America, studio-owned distributors almost certainly command 90 percent of the world market for American films. (Grummitt, 2001, p. 9)

To consider only the domestic market – which Hollywood assumes to be the USA and Canada – the major studios and their affiliates consistently receive between 80–90 percent of the box office (see Table 2.9). One of the factors that helps the majors dominate is the concentration on a small number of films. In the past three years the top 40 films have consistently received more than 60 percent of the (North) American box office – and about two-thirds of this amount was received by the top 20 films each year (ibid., p. 9). As the Dodona

TABLE 2.9   *Studio, affiliate and independent releases and box office, 1998–2000*

|  | 1998 | 1999 | 2000 |
|---|---|---|---|
| NEW RELEASES |  |  |  |
| Studios | 133 | 131 | 109 |
| Affiliates | 81 | 75 | 76 |
| Independents | 193 | 236 | 255 |
| Total | 407 | 442 | 440 |
| BOX OFFICE (IN MILLIONS OF DOLLARS) |  |  |  |
| Studios | 4,612.61 | 5,952.22 | 5,305.25 |
| Affiliates | 971.12 | 610.66 | 1,131.23 |
| Independents | 974.36 | 782.18 | 1,140.71 |
| Total | 6,558.09 | 7,345.05 | 7,577.19 |
| BOX OFFICE PER FILM (IN MILLIONS OF DOLLARS) |  |  |  |
| Studios | 34.68 | 45.44 | 48.67 |
| Affiliates | 11.99 | 8.14 | 14.88 |
| Independents | 5.05 | 3.31 | 4.47 |
| Total | 16.11 | 16.62 | 17.22 |

*Source*: Grummitt, *Hollywood: America's Film Industry*, 2001

report concludes, "The highly concentrated nature of the market not only contributes to the studios' ability to continue to dominate it, their superior resources enable them to attract the best projects and creative talent." Indeed, an oligopoly in motion picture distribution has existed for decades and continues. In typical fashion, the Hollywood oligopoly represents a relatively few large companies that dominate an industry where entry is relatively difficult and collaborative behavior is typical. The majors' dominance is indisputable and undeniable. It is even defended sometimes as necessary for the industry to succeed.

Nevertheless, these corporations are not omnipotent or infallible and are susceptible to economic ups/downs, recessions, depressions, and other problems. The Hollywood companies, in particular, have continually encountered criticism for escalating costs, inefficient and unstable management and luxurious habits and lifestyles. Nevertheless, the majors still remain major.

### Issue: Distribution and conglomeration

Despite some concerns over the limitations of companies actually becoming too big, there are still some clear advantages to large, strong, diversified companies. A recent PBS special focussed on the film industry's role in the large, diversified conglomerates which own

TABLE 2.10  *Film divisions' contributions to corporate owners*

| Parent Corp. | Film division | % revenue | % operating income |
|---|---|---|---|
| Walt Disney | Studio Entertainment | 23.6 | 2.7 |
| AOLTW | Filmed Entertainment | 21.7 | 9.1 |
| Viacom | Entertainment | 13.5 | 8.9 |
| News Corp. | Filmed Entertainment | 27.0 | 15.5 |
| Sony | Pictures | 7.7 | 1.8 |
| Vivendi | TV/Film | 31.2 | 23.6 |

*Source*: PBS (2001), "The Monster that Ate Hollywood."

them. The program's producers specifically asked how much studio revenues contribute to conglomerate owners. The data in Table 2.10 represents the revenues that studios help generate for their parent companies, contrasted with the operating income of the parent companies' business segments. (Operating income is essentially revenues minus expenses, excluding interest and taxes; net income, on the other hand, is what is commonly referred to as the "bottom line" or profits.)

For instance, Disney's 'studio entertainment' – including Walt Disney Pictures, Touchstone Pictures, and Miramax – generated almost $6 billion in revenue for Walt Disney Corp. But after costs were tallied, the operating income was only $110 million. Other companies posted much higher operating revenues. Note, however, that the companies' definitions of the business segments that house their film studios may also include other operations, such as television studios and theme parks, making it difficult in those cases to isolate film contributions.

The conclusion? The role of film for conglomerate ownership is mixed. However, it is important to realize that the major distribution companies are indeed an important part of these larger structures. As Peter Bart, editor of *Variety*, has quipped:

> It's hypocritical for any of the studios to say, or networks to say, [they're] on the brink of bankruptcy, because obviously they live under the very handsome corporate umbrella of gigantically rich companies. I mean, they're not even companies. They're sort of nation-states. AOL Time Warner is a nation-state. So is Vivendi. (PBS, 2001)

## Issue: Corruption and extravagance

Throughout much of its history, Hollywood has been associated with lavishness and excess. Special attention is often given to the "rich and famous" lifestyles of Hollywood stars and celebrity executives. One might wonder if such activities are more extreme than other social groups and that unfair publicity is directed at the film community. However, the industry thrives on publicity, as well as using it deliberately for its own (marketing) purposes, as we shall see in Chapter 5.

More recently, intemperate Hollywood celebrities have been sharing the limelight with corporate executives and accountants. A few corporations involved with the film industry were among those entangled in the wave of corruption and scandal that hit the US corporate world during 2001–02. In addition to the Enron and WorldCom debacles, a plethora of nefarious corporate activities were revealed to the American public. Not that such activities were anything new, but the severity and number of scandals involving criminal accounting and corporate activities at that time served to remind citizens of the potential for lapses in even a minimal corporate ethic.

A few of those stories involved Hollywood companies and tales of extravagance and excess. For instance, Vivendi Universal Chairman Jean-Marie Messier, ousted from the company early in 2001, was reportedly living in a luxury condo in New York that Vivendi bought him for $17.5 million, working on a book that would report his version of the saga. Messier apparently was living rent-free in the apartment (which would typically receive $50,000 a month on the market) while he continued to talk to Vivendi officials about his severance package.

At another troubled entertainment goliath, AOL Time Warner, David M. Colburn, one of AOL's top negotiators, was reportedly fired and locked out of his office at company headquarters in Dulles, Virginia. The press reported that Colburn's departure was related to the ongoing investigation into unconventional accounting practices by the Department of Justice and the Securities and Exchange Commission. The claims were that several of AOL's unusual deals were engineered by Colburn, who is known to be a lavish personal spender. For instance, he reportedly paid $1 million for his daughter's bat mitzvah, which included a performance by 'N Sync.

## The Distribution Process

So how do these companies maintain their domination of the industry through distribution? The rest of this chapter will outline the distribution process, including an overview of distributors' organizations, the different types of distribution deals, distribution procedures, and, most importantly, how the money flows from distribution revenues.

Distributors developed early in the history of the film industry as a separate branch from production and exhibition. As a studio accountant explains:

> It is extremely difficult for the Producer to distribute his own motion picture. This is due to the abilities and investment requirements relative to marketing and the Exhibitor, who may prefer to deal with the Distributor having a track record and handling a number of releases during the coming year. (Leedy, 1980, p. 20)

In other words, motion pictures distributors are wholesalers or middlemen. Most industries have wholesalers, but their role is almost always more narrowly defined than in the film industry.

In other situations, wholesalers are customers of the manufacturers; they buy inventory product at discount prices, add a price mark-up, and resell at a higher price. In other words, wholesalers are intermediaries that are typically not involved in making decisions about the product.

Film distributors, however, have tremendous power and involvement in the manufacturing process. Often, they are totally in control of a film, but even for other projects, they can influence script and title changes, casting decisions, final edits, marketing strategies, and financing of the film.

After a producer has licensed a film to a distributor for a specific length of time, the distributor arranges for its exhibition in theaters and decides on the release schedule. The distributor is in charge of storing and shipping the prints, as well as overseeing the inspection, accounting and collection of receipts from the exhibitors, as well as ancillary fees.

The distributor also conducts market research and develops a marketing strategy for the film. The distributor arranges advertising in various media, as well as building "hype" (word of mouth, promotional events, alliances with special interest groups, etc.).

Distributors typically handle the distribution of a film in all retail outlets, determining when a film will be released (or release patterns) for various markets, including theatrical, home video, pay TV, television and ancillary markets. For instance, the majors usually insist on home video rights for all films that they distribute. (More on these areas in Chapter 3.)

## Distribution companies' organizations

> Theatrical distribution involves a complex web of business rela-
> tionships, market demands and arcane custom and practice.
> (Daniels et al., 1998, p. 85)

As we have seen, the major distribution companies are part of larger
conglomerate organizations that are organized quite differently.
However, the business of film production and distribution itself is
somewhat similar for all of the Hollywood majors. A studio includes a
number of creative executives, who have already been mentioned as
those key players who oversee the development and production of a
slate of films. The story department serves the creative executives by
preparing coverages and keeping track of script development. The
acquisitions department, as mentioned previously, is involved with
the search for scripts.

Production executives are involved with individual productions
(especially budgets) and keep track of the studio's interests. The
production department also assists in casting and other production
needs. Business and legal affairs handles all of the legal negotiations
and records, as noted in the previous chapter.

The marketing department oversees several different activities,
including advertising, publicity, promotion and product placement,
and will be discussed further in Chapter 5. Merchandising is another
area that often is handled under the consumer products division of
the studio.

In terms of distribution, each company operates a home office, as
well as local offices, branches or exchanges. The home office includes
sales managers, print control, and exhibitor relations. Collections and
accounting may be handled at the home office or at branches. The
branch offices are involved in selling, booking, billing and collections
and may deal directly with the managers of large theater circuits. The
branch office prepares paperwork, ships prints, handles advertising
materials, prepares billings, and collects the film rental (Leedy, 1980,
p. 21).

## Distribution deals

One of the most important arrangements in the life of a film is the
distribution deal or agreement. And, not surprisingly, there are a
variety of different types of deals, as well as each agreement being

unique.[1] The basic agreement between a producer/production company and distribution company is a long, complicated document with many boilerplate clauses that are non-negotiable. It includes the assignment of rights for all potential retail markets (theatrical exhibition; home video; cable/pay-cable; television, etc.) The agreement gives the distributor the right to decide how, where and when film is distributed, how it is advertised, promoted, etc.

The agreement also includes important definitions pertaining to revenues, expenses, break-even, etc. These deals vary from film to film, with each representing a unique set of arrangements. And of course, distribution deals also are influenced by the power of the participants. Favored or experienced producers often can arrange especially lucrative deals, especially through their pact-arrangements, as described in the last chapter. For example, the dependent-independent producers, such as New Regency or Morgan Creek, often are able to negotiate advantageous distribution fees since they regularly deal with distributors and provide them with a regular flow of product.

It is important to try to understand the basics of distribution agreements, as they reveal how money flows, as well as power relations within the industry. Because distribution agreement terms are influenced by power and clout, obviously, deals differ widely. But different arrangements also depend on when and how a film commodity becomes associated with one of the major distributors. A few of the typical types of deals are described here.

In-house distribution is applicable when a studio or in-house film is developed and produced by a major. However, production/distribution deals can also be arranged with independents or dependent-independent producers who bring film packages to the studios, which usually provide financing for the production, as well as distribution.

Sometimes a major company will agree to distribute a film, but does not provide production funds. The agreement is called a negative pick-up and the deal is typically made before the film is completed. In this type of deal, the distributor often provides an advance to the producer, finances releasing costs (including advertising and marketing), and then the studio and producer share profits. The advantage to the studio is that the producer risks the production capital, limiting the studio's risk to distribution only. The disadvantage is that when the film is successful, the studio's involvement is limited to the distribution fee (see below).

Although the distributor will often agree to give the producer an advance, as outlined in more detail below, distributors may "creatively" account for profits, thus producers may see few, if any, returns. Thus, a smart producer may try to arrange for a large advance, plus retain foreign rights, as well as avoiding cross-collateralization (when money earned from several markets is pooled).

Negative pick-up deals can be negotiated before, during or after production, but distributors often become interested in a film after screenings at film festivals. The studios and even independent distributors employ acquisition executives to find potential films for negative pick-up deals.

Over the years, co-production/distribution deals have been made between major distributors, although accountants sometimes wonder why. These arrangements are often quite complex and not always successful. A typical deal might be to share the production cost between two distributors, with one distributor handling the domestic territory (USA and Canada) and the other arranging foreign distribution. This was the model used for *Titanic*, where Paramount distributed in the domestic market and Fox handled the foreign markets.

Sometimes independents will pre-sell films to foreign distributors through foreign sales deals, although they still distribute their films in the USA through the majors. Specific film markets exist where films are bought and sold, and will be discussed in a later chapter. A common practice for independent financing is to pre-sell foreign rights through a foreign sales agent, however, this may be problematic with a domestic distributor.

## How Movie Money Flows: Receipts and Expenditures

Breaking down the flow of money that comes in and goes out from the distribution of a motion picture is a good way to understand the distribution process, as well as why the major distributors are the dominant forces in the industry. This section will discuss revenues and expenses for a typical Hollywood film, or, in other words, how movie money flows (as summarized in Table 2.11).

### Gross receipts

All the revenues received from the sale of a motion picture in all markets are considered gross receipts. Table 2.11 lists the potential

TABLE 2.11  *Summary of receipts and expenditures*

| GROSS RECEIPTS | EXPENDITURES |
|---|---|
| THEATRICAL EXHIBITION | – Distribution Fee (30% US, 35% Canada & UK, 40% rest of world) |
| | – Distribution Expenses |
| HOME VIDEO | P&A: |
| | • Prints |
| PAY/CABLE TV | • Advertising and publicity |
| | (+ 10% advertising overhead) |
| TELEVISION | Collections |
| (NETWORK + SYNDICATION in the US) | Dubbing, foreign versions, any copyright or licensing fees |
| NONTHEATRICAL (airlines, military, schools, hospitals, prisons, etc.) | Shipping/transportation |
| | All forms of taxes |
| | MPAA dues |
| MERCHANDISE | Theater checking |
| | Royalties/residuals |
| MUSIC | Misc. (charitable contributions, legal fees . . .) |
| MISC. | Overhead (10%) (fixed costs of marketing dept.) |
| | – Interest on negative cost |
| | – Negative cost (can include budget, overhead (12–25%), interest) |
| | – Deferments & gross participations |
| | NET PROFIT<br>– Net Profit Participations<br>– Producer's Share (50%?) |

sources of gross receipts. While more discussion of these retail outlets and sources of revenue will be presented in the next chapter, it is important to note that each market operates differently. For instance, even the domestic theatrical market has different business practices than foreign theatrical markets. In other words, there is no consistency from market to market.

*Theatrical exhibition.*  Box-office receipts are only one source of revenues for a Hollywood film, but the theatrical release usually precedes release in other outlets and sets the value for the markets that follow. The distributor's share of the total box office receipts (the gross) is called the film rental and can be as high as 90 percent of the box office gross after exhibitor's expenses. It is often claimed that distributors receive 50 percent overall of the total box receipts, however, this amount actually may be underestimated. A more detailed discussion of the division of box-office receipts is included in the next chapter.

*Home video.* The sale of videocassettes and DVDs often represents larger revenues than the theatrical box-office. While previously, the distributor did not receive revenues from video rentals, a direct revenue-sharing model has been adopted since the late 1990s, with tapes sold at a lower cost to retailers (around $8–10) for 45–50 percent of the rental fees. The major studios have made these kind of arrangements with the leading retail chains, Blockbuster and Hollywood Entertainment.

However, when stating home video revenues in profit participation deals, the studios only report 20 percent of their wholesale sales. In other words, "the studio includes only 20% of videocassette revenue in gross receipts and puts most of the remaining 80% in its pocket" (Baumgarten, Farber, and Fleischer, 1992, p. 53). While the reason for this dubious practice may be historical, the practice is one of the most controversial in motion picture accounting.

Furthermore, additional fees reduce the reported revenues even more. From the 20 percent reported, the studio takes a distribution fee (typically 30 percent in domestic markets and 40 percent in foreign markets), plus additional expenses. Thus, rather than a 20 percent royalty, the amount available to profit participants is actually closer to 10 or 12 percent.

As Daniels et al. (1998, p. 68) conclude:

> The upshot is that at some studios, what begins as a supposed pure 20% royalty is reduced by fees and expenses to approximately a 10% to 12% royalty. There is always a legal, contractual basis for this reduction. Still, the end result is that the participant loses the benefits of between 80% to 90% of a major portion of the motion picture's revenue.

*Pay television.* License fees for domestic pay-TV usually are based directly on the theatrical box office gross of the film. In these deals, a film must have appeared in a minimum number of theaters for a minimum number of weeks with a minimum amount of advertising expenditures. Studios have "output deals" with the major pay-TV channels (HBO/Cinemax and Showtime/Movie Channel), thus every major feature film eventually airs on one of these channels. Also, remember that the same companies that own these pay-TV outlets own the major distributors. Output deals specify base license fees paid by pay-TV services according to the box office gross of a film. For instance, if a film received $5 million at the box office, the base license fee might be 50 percent or $2.5 million. For wildly successful films, however, the fee would not exceed a certain amount. For instance, *Batman* received over $200 million at the box office, but its pay-TV license fee was $15 million. Other variations are more complex and include other factors, such as the number of pay-TV subscribers, etc.

*"Free-TV"*. Although the industry sometimes refers to advertising-supported television as "free," the term is misleading as advertising represents a form of financing television that is not entirely "free." Consumers ultimately pay higher prices for products and services, to which advertising expenses have been added. Be that as it may, when reporting revenues from "free" television, the industry is usually referring to network, syndicated and cable television, and foreign television.

In the USA, networks pay negotiated license fees to broadcast motion pictures, with prices varying from $3-12 million. At issue is whether or not Fox, and perhaps eventually, the other fledgling networks, Paramount and Warner, are considered true networks, which influences the amount of the distribution fees applicable.

The domestic syndication market involves individual stations in the USA and Canada, which purchase packages of around 12–20 films, with a single license fee negotiated for the entire package. For purposes of profit participation, each film is assigned a specific amount of the overall package according to a complicated ranking system that is based on US theatrical film rental, running time, genre, talent, and network rating.

*Non-theatrical.*    The largest non-theatrical market is the airlines, although Hollywood films also are licensed to the military, schools, hotels, hospitals, prisons, colleges, public libraries, railroads, churches, oil companies, etc. Non-theatrical sales are typically negotiated flat fees or a specific amount per viewer, and represent a relatively minor source of revenue.

*Foreign markets.*    As noted earlier, foreign revenue sources are increasingly significant for Hollywood features and are generated from theatrical, television, and home video markets. In foreign theatrical markets, distributors may use their own subsidiaries, a foreign affiliate or a subdistributor. But here again, controversial accounting practices prevail. Even though various expenses (the foreign distributor's fees and expenses) are deducted before a studio receives foreign revenues, the US distributor usually reports 100 percent of the film rental as revenue. In other words, the studio is reporting more revenue than it actually receives so that a larger distribution fee (discussed below) can be charged. Foreign television markets are similar to syndicated television, where films are sold in packages and the license fees allocated among various films in the package in a variety of ways.

*Merchandising, videogames, music, publishing.*  Not all films generate additional revenues from these sources, however, some box office hits are able to profit handsomely from additional commodities which flow from the film commodity. Many different kinds of deals are involved with licensing the rights to characters, stories, and music, that flow from the initial film product. And it may come as no surprise that distributors add fees to manage these markets, as well.

*Interest income.*  Distributors sometimes collect interest from those revenue sources that are slow to pay (exhibitors, airlines, etc.). How and if this interest income is to be shared between distributor and outside participants is another potential area of dispute.

*Miscellaneous.*  A wide variety of additional revenues are possible from the marketing opportunities created by a Hollywood film. For instance, the sale of advertising materials (posters) may bring in some additional funds, as well as the sale of the making-of-the-movie programming created for television outlets.

It may seem obvious that the classification of income is important to all the players involved in a film. Profit participants want all income included, whereas distributors try to argue that some revenues are due to their special efforts. It also might be argued that additional income from some sources should be applied to a reduction in production cost, and thus a distribution fee (as discussed in the next section) should not apply.

## Expenditures

*Distribution fee.*  The distribution fee is "the film-rental amount retained by the distributor in accordance with the contractual provisions of its agreement with the outside participants" (Daniels et al., p. 103). The

TABLE 2.12   *Typical distribution fees*

|  | % |
|---|---|
| Theatrical distribution |  |
| US and Canada | 30 |
| Foreign | 40 |
| Television distribution |  |
| Network | 25 |
| Syndication | 30–40 |
| Pay/Cable | 30–40 |
| Non-theatrical | 30 |
| Home Video | 30 |
| Merchandising | 50 |

fee is intended to cover the costs of the distributor's operations or "fixed-distribution overhead costs," in other words, its offices, corporate expenses, etc. Furthermore, the fee is charged for the distributor's efforts in soliciting play dates, booking the picture, and collecting rentals.

How and when distribution fees are charged, as well as what expenses are included, are highly disputable issues. Distribution fees are typically paid before any distribution expenses, production costs, or other charges, and before most profit participants.

The distribution fee is usually a non-negotiable percentage of revenue from a specific source and varies according to geographic area and market. Although there are slight variations between the majors, the typical distribution fees (some of which have been discussed previously) are summarized in Table 2.12. For instance, distribution fees are 25 percent for network television revenues and 30–40 percent for syndication revenues (although independent distributors may charge as much as 50 percent).

While many observers consider the distribution fee relatively high, it is defended because of the (supposedly) high risk nature of film distribution, where it is claimed that distributors often do not recoup distribution expenses.

**Distribution expenses.**   While there are numerous expenses involved in distributing a motion picture, distribution expenses are one of the most controversial issues in motion picture accounting. Determining how charges should be covered and whether they are appropriate can be a real problem, especially for producers and profit participants. Some of the typical expenses are discussed in some detail in the next sections, followed by a discussion of profits and profit participation.

*Prints and Advertising (P&A).* With expanded release of Hollywood films, the costs of prints and advertising (or P&A) have increased. These costs will be discussed separately below, although they are sometimes discussed in unison.

*Prints.* The cost of each print can be as much as $1,000. Thus, for a typical release in the USA, print costs can amount to over $3 million. Release print costs also may include reels, inspection, cases, rewinding, replacements and shipping.

Printing and dubbing of foreign release prints sometimes are required to be prepared within a specific country. However, those costs are added to distribution expenses, in addition to shipping and transportation.

At issue is whether print costs are considered a production cost or a distribution expense. In addition, some film laboratories may give distributors discounts and/or rebates. While these amounts logically would seem to be applied to a reduction in print costs, it is possible that a distributor may argue that the discount should be given to the distributor because their overall business has prompted the discount. The distribution of films by way of electronic or digital means may mean substantial reductions in these expenses in the future, as discussed in the next chapter.

*Advertising.* Marketing strategies and advertising will be discussed more thoroughly in Chapter 5, however, it is necessary at this point to distinguish between several different types of advertising for accounting purposes. Again, there are questions as to how to account for such expenses. Whether these costs are distribution expenses or sales costs covered by the distribution fee is a matter of contractual interpretation and potential dispute.

Trade advertising. Initially, advertising may appear in the trade press (*Variety*, *Hollywood Reporter*, etc.), as a way of attracting talent, potential distributors and exhibitors, or even for ego gratification.

Television advertising. Network advertising has some advantages especially for blockbuster films that open nationwide. Despite the high costs involved, network advertising has grown dramatically in the last few decades.

Cooperative advertising. All local advertising is called cooperative advertising, but is shared in different ways depending on the market and the distributor. Local newspaper advertising is still quite important for theaters, as it is a major source of information for audiences.

Sneak previews.    Different kinds of sneak previews include a preview of the director's cut, trade sneak (for sales purposes, especially for exhibitors), and "word-of-mouth sneak" (for publicity near the release date).

Theater advertising.    Different forms of advertising take place at the theater, including stand-up cut-outs, posters, banners, buttons and clothing worn by theater staff, etc. Another form of advertising at the theater is trailers. Distributors usually sell this material to theaters, and thus, there are issues over the accounting for the cost and income. Whether or not these marketing costs should be counted as distribution expenses or part of the distribution fee is a regular controversy.

Furthermore, most studios add 10 percent of the total advertising costs as an overhead charge. This amount is in addition to advertising expenses and is said to cover salaries and indirect operating costs of distributor's advertising and publicity personnel. It has been argued that this amount should be covered in the distribution fee and the distributor is adding overhead-on-overhead or double-billing.

A making-of-the-movie program or featurette may involve additional cost, but may also attract additional revenues. The determination of how such revenues are distributed is another thorny issue.

**Taxes, copyright and licensing fees.**    Various types of taxes are involved with film distribution and are included in a film's expenses. Sales taxes and remittance taxes (taxes on money remitted to the USA from a foreign country) are usually included, but rarely are any kind of income taxes. Foreign taxes are especially tricky in that it may not be clear which taxes apply to the specific film and not to the distributor's other business ventures. Other expenses may involve copyright and licensing fees which are involved with the distribution of the film.

Royalties/residuals.    Residuals are paid to contracted workers for films released in supplemental markets. The royalty and residual rates are specified by the industry trade unions and guilds and are often quite complex. However, they are significant sources of income for Hollywood players, especially for highly successful films. It might be noted that residuals only came into existence after 1960, when labor organizations began to negotiate for a share of revenue from television markets.

MPAA dues.   For each film distributed by one of the majors, an amount is assessed to cover annual dues to the distributors' trade organization, the Motion Picture Association of America (MPAA). Generally, this assessment is based on the theatrical performance of each picture released during the year. The dues assessment is claimed to cover various activities of the MPAA in promoting and protecting the industry, as discussed in Chapter 5. Tricky issues pertain to this expense as sorting out the charges for a specific film from other parts of a distributor's MPAA dues assessment is a difficult process.

Bad debts.   Again, this is a controversial deduction, but the distributors sometimes attempt to include uncollectable rentals in the accounting process at this point. As expected, film accountants have expressed concern about this policy, explaining: "Regardless of the accounting method used, a bad debt due to the uncollectability of film rental should not be reported as a distribution expense. Instead, the film rental previously reported should be reversed, as well as the amount of the distribution fee computed thereon" (Daniels et al., 1998, pp. 168–9).

Miscellaneous.   A wide range of other expenses are typically included in a film's expenses, including theater checking or audits, costs of foreign censorship, special titles, legal expenses and settlements. Distibutors will also sometimes deduct charitable contributions and legal fees, expenses which are typically problematic with unhappy profit participants.

Overhead.   A 10 percent overhead charge is included in distribution expenses for the fixed costs of the distributor's marketing department. Again, this practice is controversial.

Interest on negative cost.   As in most lending situations, interest on a production loan is paid before the principal, thus, the interest related to negative costs are paid before the actual costs of production. Interest charges are accounted for in a more or less "normal" way, which means that the charges are paid before net profit participants (or net profit). If the studios are involved in financing, the rates are determined based on the prime rate of the studios' main banks. For example, Warner Brothers charges 125 percent of the prime rate of the First National Bank of Boston.

Negative cost.  Although it would seem that the determination of production costs would be relatively simple, of course, it is not and there are often claims and dispute between the distributors and profit participants. Typically included in negative costs (for accounting purposes) are actual production costs, overhead, interest, deferments and gross participations.

Actual production costs typically involve pre-production, production and post-production costs, including material, equipment, physical properties, and labor, in addition to costs associated with copyright and title searches, clearances and registrations, royalty and license fees, etc.

Daniels et al. (1998, p. 185) report that, "Studios will often insist or advise, or at a minimum, strongly hint that filmmakers use production facilities owned by the studio." These facilities not only include the studio lot, but also any production services that the distributor may own, even though the rates for these facilities may be higher than other companies.

In addition, many (if not all) the studios add an overhead charge – anywhere from 12–25 percent, but usually 15 percent of the direct production costs, no matter where the film is produced. Various costs are (or are not) covered by this charge, but the intent is to "absorb all of the studio's costs that are not directly charged to a picture." If studio facilities are used, this (again) may lead to double billing.

Both production and distribution salaries charged to a picture are accompanied by an add-on for supplemental labor costs. This "fringe" amount is intended to cover the employer's share of payroll taxes, health, pension and welfare costs, plus workers' compensation insurance and holiday and vacation pay. However, it may also include a profit for the studio: "the studios are known to turn fringes into a profit center by always calculating at the highest rate, even if the actual rate paid is less. . . . the supplemental payroll cost or fringe-benefit rate is somewhat sacred and downward negotiation will be difficult" (ibid., p. 187).

**Gross participations and deferments.**  Frequently, stars and other power players are able to demand profit participation in a major motion picture. Profit participations are calculated in terms of "points" – or percentages of defined or calculated profits, either gross or net. Here, there is an extremely wide variation in terms used that can become unbelievably confusing.

Profit participations seemed to originate in the 1950s when Lew Wasserman, Jimmy Stewart's agent at the time, argued for the star to receive part of the profits from the Universal film, *Winchester '73*. With the breakdown of the studio system in the 1950s, profit participations became more common, especially as distributors attempted to reduce risk. With more profit participations, distributors began insisting on terms that increased the amount of revenue necessary to reach "breakeven" in the computation of "net profits" (see below). For example, distribution fees were increased and interest charges added on production funds borrowed or advanced.

By the early 1960s, gross participant deals emerged as a reaction to these moves. Major talent demanded not only increasingly larger up-front payments, but more often a share of the receipts *before* the studio deducted its distribution fee. By 1983, the major stars and director were commanding anywhere from 5 percent to 15 percent of a film's rentals.

Some argue that this represents a kind of control by talent, as well as a justification for why budgets keep increasing. Only a few power players (mostly top actors) are able to negotiate gross participations, while other lesser talent, such as directors and producers, receive some diluted form of gross participation. Most writers and other players without a track record (in other words, without clout) become net participants, and often receive nothing.

Gross participations are rarely "first-dollar gross" (or participations directly from the distributor's revenues), but are computed after certain "off-the-top" expenses. These can include conversion expenses, checking, collections, residuals, trade dues, licenses, taxes, and theater level advertising. While some of these costs are defined by "boilerplate" contract definitions, they can be amended by negotiation.

Gross participations are deductible as production costs, which means that the overhead charge by the studio applies to these amounts. With more and higher gross participants, there are more problems (and less money) for lesser participants, such as net profit participants.

In addition, talent may arrange deferments instead of receiving salaries during production. Deferments involve an amount paid upon an agreed event. For instance, $100,000 is paid when the film reaches $10 million in domestic box-office gross. Depending on the type of deferment and other contractual arrangements, these amounts are paid out of the first net profits, but before any net profit participants are paid (see below).


## Profits?

### Net profits/breakeven

After all fees and expenses are paid, a film is said to "break even" or begins to produce "net profits." However, there are incredibly complex definitions for the point at which a film begins making a profit. Breakeven has been described as a "magical number with a myriad of definitions." For instance, there are various kinds of breakeven, such as artificial, actual and rolling, each with its own complex explanation.

Generally, net profits have been defined as: "Gross Receipts, less 1. Distribution fees, 2. Distribution expenses, and 3. Production costs (which may include overhead, interest, and gross participations); plus, deferments out of first net profits or participants in gross receipts before breakeven" (Daniels et al., 1998, p. 227).


### Net profit participations

Even more complex are the arrangements for net profit participations. Studio accountants explain that "the participation in net profits is a *contractually defined* formula by which a participant might obtain additional compensation if various criteria are met" (ibid., p. 225; emphasis added). Some accountants claim further that 3 to 4 times the negative cost must be taken in at the box office for a film to reach net profit, and that most pictures *never* generate a net profit – at least for the participant. For instance, witnesses in one lawsuit testified that "twenty-nine of the motion pictures released by Paramount from 1975 to 1988 achieved significant net profits – an annual average of more than two of the studio's fifteen releases. These films paid out to over eighty-four profit participants more than $155 million" (cited in ibid., p. 226). However, in recent years, net profit participants reportedly have received much less because stronger players have been taking larger gross profit shares.

## Producer's share

The producer's share of a film's revenues is negotiated differently from these other participants. Often, a producer splits 50 percent of the net profits with the distributor. However, because the producer is responsible for the production of the film, it is claimed that he/she should share the cost of talent. Thus, third-party participations are included as a deduction in computing the producer's net profit. These amounts may be taken directly out of the producer's 50 percent share of net profits or deducted before the producer's 50 percent share is computed.

The producer also may be penalized if the production went over budget, again according to different formulas used by different studios. If the producer has a multi-picture deal, there may be a cross-collateralization arrangement where the producer's share of one film's losses may be taken out of the producer's share of a successful film's profits. Sometimes bonus payments may be tied to some objective measure of a film's success, in addition to a net or gross participation.

In general, some standard definitions that pertain to the distribution of profits can be negotiated and others cannot. For instance, the 20 percent royalty on home video, distribution fees, and interest charges remain immovable at all the major studios.

## Issue: Creative accounting

A good deal of controversy that is often highly publicized surrounds the accounting methods used by Hollywood. Creative accounting is especially controversial when it pertains to profit participants. As experienced accountants explain: "Hollywood has evolved a profit participation system that is so arcane even the experts are sometimes left with more questions than answers" (Daniels et al., 1998, p. 288).

*The accounting process.* It is obvious that accountants play key roles in Hollywood. The big five accounting firms (Arthur Andersen, Deloitte Touche Tohmatsu, Ernst & Young, KPMG, and PriceWaterhouse-Coopers) maintain offices in Los Angeles and are involved with Hollywood business.

The industry uses highly unusual procedures including reporting accounts differently for profit participation and other purposes (tax accounting, etc.). Thus, the claim that Hollywood keeps "multiple sets of books for the same picture" is technically true. For profit participants, studios regularly report revenue when it is collected (cash accounting) and expenses when they occur (accrual accounting). In all other industries, either one method or the other is used, but not both. While claims are made that this policy is necessary because of the nature of the industry and that profit participants are not cheated, it is a highly controversial issue which even accountants disagree on. As one accountant concludes, "Generally accepted accounting principles for financial reporting have little effect on reporting motion picture results to outside participants" (Leedy, 1980, p. 14). Meanwhile, the studios defend some of these practices and definitional creativity by arguing that "ultimately, they need to earn a certain return on their investment no matter how they reach that number" (Daniels et al., 1998, p. 54).

Other problems involve the definition of terms that change from contract to contract. While specific terms are delineated in talent agreements and employment contracts, profit participation agreements are extremely complex documents. Generally, participants or their representatives attempt to negotiate the best deal, however, some terms are "off-limits for all but the most powerful players." As one experienced accountant explains:

> there is a great lack of precise definition or consistent usage of terms within the motion picture industry. Many contractual provisions utilize the definition: "as that terms is generally understood in the motion picture industry." TERMS ARE NOT GENERALLY UNDERSTOOD IN THE MOTION PICTURE INDUSTRY. [Emphasis in original] They vary from Distributor to Distributor and from one geographic location to the next. (Leedy, 1980, pp. 34–5)

Generally there are potential problems that involve allocation, reporting, and timing of revenues and expenses, or arbitrary price allocations; the timing of reporting revenues; the classification of revenue; and the amount of revenue.

As Daniels et al. explain, accounting errors may be classified as errors of omission (failure to include something which should be included) and errors of commission (including something which should not be included). Often errors found in audits are either in recording information (mechanical errors), contract interpretation or ambiguity in language, or pertaining to fairness and equity. Again, experienced accountants explain that "History tells us that when distributors err in calculating whether a participant is due additional compensation under a profit participation agreement, the error usually favors the distributor, not the participant" (Daniels et al., 1998, p. 271).

Sometimes, contracts are renegotiated when successful talent take advantage of the "subject to review" clause to obtain better deals. Audits have become basically a normal part of the business and often result in claims from profit participants. As accountants explain:

> Although each claim is discussed individually, no single claim, other than errors that have been agreed to, is ever settled. No distributor wants to set a precedent for other participants and future audits. A flat payment, referred to in a general release and settlement that acknowledges no wrongdoing on the part of either party, resolves all issues raided in the audit. (ibid., p. 275)

In very rare cases, litigation follows, however, usually cases are resolved before going to court. One lawsuit that did proceed, however, claimed that "the entire participation system amounts to nothing more than a price-fixing conspiracy by the major powers in a company town."[2]

The most widely publicized case involving profit participants was Art Buchwald's plagiarism suit against Paramount in 1988, when he claimed that the film *Coming to America* earned a sizable profit and he deserved to participate in those funds (see O'Donnell and McDougal, 1992). The issue is usually whether there is a net profit and how it is defined. However, in general, all terms involved with profit participants are defined terms.

A former Hollywood studio executive offers further comments:

> It's like trying to trace a phone call – revenues mysteriously come in and just as mysteriously go out. Only a few individuals (such a big-ticket talent) can afford to do an audit to verify the income they're due, and in most cases, the audit will invariably find something amiss.[3]

Audits and lawsuits are common, especially when a film is a box-office hit. While Buchwald won his suit against Paramount, another case involving *Batman* had the opposite result. Other challengers to the distribution of film revenues quietly disappear without their day in court. Thus, creative accounting continues to haunt Hollywood.

## Issue: Distributor clout

Despite the risky nature of the film business and the "inflated" demands of stars and others to share in profits, the major distributors remain in control. They often set the terms of deals and are in dominant positions. An industry insider explains it this way: "the pervasive market power of the major studio/distributors in the US (the MPAA companies, generally) has been gained and is maintained by engaging in numerous questionable, unethical, unfair, unconscionable, anti-competitive, predatory and/or illegal business practices" (Cones, 1992).

The distributors argue that the film business is risky; others argue that the movie-making business is out of control with inflated production budgets and outrageous marketing expenses. It's also important to realize that about 5 percent of movies have earned about 80 percent of the industry's total profit over the past decade (De Vany and Walls, 2001). Thus, success propels more success and a few movies, mostly the major studios' movies, make most of the profit.

Furthermore, the context of the distribution business needs to be understood. As Larry Gerbrandt, chief content officer and senior analyst for Kagan World Media, explains:

> it's not unusual for a studio to have invested a billion dollars and to generate less than a 10 percent return on that. So on a stand-alone basis, it's not a very good business. However, if they didn't make movies, you wouldn't be able to run theme parks. You wouldn't be able to run or create TV networks. You wouldn't have libraries against which you can create cable networks. The movies really provide the economic foundation and much of the leverage that these companies have in terms of being able to do other businesses.
>
>     . . . Having a blockbuster film allows you to charge more for almost everything else you do that year, because of the way movies are packaged in with other business deals and other films. So the hits are really the locomotives that drag the rest of the train down the tracks. (PBS, 2001)

Having encountered the distribution locomotive, it is time to turn to the tracks, or the retail outlets where the film commodity is offered to consumers. The next chapter will outline the exhibition business, as well as providing some detail on other markets for Hollywood products.

## Notes

1   Good sources for the distribution process are Daniels et al. (1998), Leedy (1980), and Cones (1997).

2   Garrison v. Warner Bros., Inc. et al., US District Court, Central District of California, Case No. CV-95-8328, filed January 18, 1996. Cited in Daniels et al. (1998), p. xxi.

3   M. Amdur, "H'w'd Burns as Feds Fiddle," *Variety*, 29 July 2002, p. 51.

# Exhibition/Retail 3

## Introduction

Motion pictures are sold in many retail markets, including theaters, home video, cable, and television. The Internet and video-on-demand also are looming as new retail markets (see Table 3.1). These various markets interact in building consumer awareness and contribute to the overall revenues for a film. In other words, Hollywood films continue to make money for the major studios in various platforms, known as "windows of exhibition," years after their theatrical release. These markets have unique attributes and characteristics, which will be discussed in this chapter, although more detail will be offered on theaters because of their role as the traditional retail sector of the film industry.

## Theaters/Cinemas

The introduction of new outlets for motion pictures has continuously been accompanied by predictions that theaters or cinemas were doomed. Nevertheless, most films are still released first in theaters, which still attract sizable revenues each year. (See Table 2.9 for total US box office revenues.)

Despite other markets that sometimes attract more income, theaters are still considered the key film market for a number of reasons. While some significance may be given to filmmakers' attachment to the silver screen, the importance of building consumer interest in a film at the box office is primary and, correspondingly, sets the value for other markets. As one marketing executive explains:

> A bad opening will usually kill a movie and kills all the potentials of the movie. Because while the preponderance of income and the revenue

strings in the movie business today are no longer from that domestic box office – the money really is coming in from worldwide box office – sales to television, home video, DVD, and all those other revenue strings on a global basis are so driven by that success or failure in the domestic box office. (PBS, 2001)

TABLE 3.1 *Release patterns and markets*

| through 1950s | through 1980s | Currently | Future? |
|---|---|---|---|
| Theaters | Theaters | Theaters | Theaters |
| • First run | Net. TV | PPV | Internet? |
| • Re-release | Syndication | Pay cable | VOD? |
| | Non-theatrical | Home Video | Home Video? |
| | | Net. TV | Net. TV |
| | | Cable/Syndication | Cable/Syndication |
| | | Non-theatrical | Non-theatrical |

Non-theatrical markets include 16mm, schools, universities, hotels, hospitals, prisons, military, etc.

VOD = video-on-demand
PPV = pay-per-view

The following sections will discuss theatrical release patterns, the film booking process, exhibitors' revenue sources, and US theater companies.

## Theatrical release patterns/runs

Decisions on when and where to release a film are made by the distributor and are influenced by various factors, including other films' release dates, and the time of year. Often, studios will arrange for surveys of prospective moviegoers that provide pre-release tracking data, as well as (sometimes) word of mouth. An example is an announcement about Revolution Films in *Variety*, November 13, 2002: "Gearing up for a busy 2003, Revolution has shuffled its summer release slate, most notably shifting Jack Nicholson/Adam Sandler comedy *Anger Management* from June to April 11. . . . A positive test screening Tuesday in Thousand Oaks, however, convinced Revolution it could get out in front of the summer."

A former marketing executive compares the box office to a contracting and expanding pie. "It's different week in to week out. . . . That expansion and contraction is what leads you to start to think about when you want to release the movie" (PBS, 2001). One significant development is the importance of the opening weekend. It is claimed that about 70–75 percent of a film's revenues are earned during the weekends, and nearly 85 percent of all films open on the first day of the weekend, Friday.

Summer and holiday releases also have become especially important, as many films make the majority of their revenues during these times. Previously, summer was considered the worst time to open a movie, however, it has become a key playing time for major films, as the prime audience is off from school and theaters offer cool locations for entertainment. While summer-wide releases tend to run for a longer period, the summer season is being pushed further back each year. Distributors want to get their movies on the screen early so that if they are successful, they can run through the entire summer. Another particularly busy period is Christmas, although most Christmas releases often open two or three weeks before the actual holiday.

Motion picture release patterns are highly variable and are affected by changes in the market. Usually, after a movie opens in theaters, demand is revealed, and then adjustments are made. It is estimated that about 65–70 percent of all motion pictures earn their maximum box-office revenue in the first week of release. The exceptions are those that gain positive word-of-mouth and thus enjoy long runs. The point of widest release for most movies is the second week, but the maximum revenue is still in the first week.

Furthermore, for the huge majority of films, the opening weekend is the high point for ticket sales. Thus, the strategy is to book a huge number of screens for the all-important first weekend. A film that holds up week after week, is said to have "legs," while one that has unexpected box-office success is called a "sleeper."

There are various strategies for the number of theaters where a film is booked. Sometimes a distributor will try a pre-release to test marketing campaigns and the viability of wide release. Pre-releases are used to gauge the appeal of a movie and to test different campaign approaches. As discussed in Chapter 5, most market research is conducted with a recruited audience. The audience's reaction to the film guides the final editing and directs the marketing campaign. However, it is not the same as testing the product at the point-of-sale with a paying audience.

Currently, the most common release pattern used for big Hollywood films is a *wide release*, which involves 600 to 2,000 playdates in the US market. One source claims that wide releases account for three-quarters of the total domestic box-office revenue. However, more recently, it is not uncommon to find big films booked for over 3,000 playdates. For instance, 3,182 playdates were booked for *I Spy* during Christmas 2002, and double-screening in many venues boosted the screen count to more than 4,200. Meanwhile, Disney arranged 3,350 engagements for the *Santa Clause* sequel, following the usual practice of introducing family pictures as wide as possible. *Santa Clause II* attracted $29 million during its opening weekend, while *I Spy* brought in a "disappointing" $14 million.

Wide release strategies are typical for major films with blockbuster potential. But they are also used when a film may not be able to sustain a long run (or probably won't have legs). The distributor books the film in a huge number of theaters to obtain maximum results. It may be possible to advertise the large weekend grosses to lure more moviegoers into the theaters before they hear any bad word of mouth. This also has been called a *hit and run*, when a film opens on as many screens as possible to achieve first week results with an anticipated negative word of mouth and strong drops in the second week. On the other hand, if the film does well, a wide release allows the film to develop legs and continue at many locations.

The *modified wide release pattern* is also used. A movie can open with a few hundred prints and then expand week-by-week so that it has time to build awareness and a positive reputation through word of mouth. Because the modified wide release may not cover all the markets, spot television advertising is generally used for the first wave. The distributor may also start with a few prints to fund the copying of more prints as well as more advertising out of the revenues from the first few theaters.

Wide release patterns have become standard practice because of the high cost of television advertising, which is thought to be the most effective advertising medium for selling Hollywood movies. As we have seen, other costs have increased, so if the product gets into the marketplace sooner, funds may become available to pay off debt sooner.

In addition, it is argued that it is beneficial to complete the theatrical release as quickly as possible to take advantage of the potential income from videocassette and DVD sales and rental. It is also possible that when distributors are not confident in a film's appeal, a broad theatrical release can set up a window for the home video market. The theatrical release makes the movie title familiar to those who rent videocassettes and buy DVDs. Some movies that are disappointing in theatrical release become top sell-throughs and rental videocassettes and DVDs.

However, a wide release makes it difficult for anything other than a big movie with a popular cast to do well at the box office. Some films may need time to build awareness and positive word of mouth. The thousand-print release puts tremendous pressure on films that are not supported by a big campaign and do not gross well in the first week.

*Limited releases* are those that include 11 to 599 playdates, while *exclusive releases* involve under 10 playdates (1 to 3 per major market) and are used for specialized and foreign films. These films may open, wait for favorable reviews, and then move slowly to additional theaters. Reputations for specialized films are also built at festivals, which is especially important for international markets. (More on festivals in Chapter 5.)

A film that needs critics' positive reviews to draw an audience may utilize a *platforming* strategy, opening first in a limited number of theaters, primarily in New York and Los Angeles, then spreading slowly around the country to increasingly more theaters. Other strategies may involve *regional releases* or *territorial saturation*, especially for movies tailored for specific markets. Such efforts include saturating a territory with lots of prints and heavy advertising and promotion.

*Four walling* – or renting and/or operating theaters in specific markets for a particular film – is rarely done nowadays. However, as noted above, sometimes a film may open in only a few markets where the distributor rents a theater for a flat weekly fee and takes all receipts.

**Adjustments.**    There is a good deal of flexibility in booking films, as a distributor tries to adjust playdates according to the market. It is possible for the release of a film to expand, with a significant increase in playdates, but still stay within bounds of the previous pattern.

The exhibition contract will usually call for a minimum run of from four to eight weeks. On a widely released movie, the number of screens on which it is shown will typically decline during the run. However, some widely released movies become so popular that the number of screens may not decline and might even increase during the run.

In the past an exhibitor operating a larger (eight- to ten-screen) multiplex often sets aside one or two screens for smaller, specialty or foreign-language films. But because of the nature of typical agreements between distributors and exhibitors (which will be discussed shortly), an exhibitor may be inclined to drop a new release after the first or second weekend, unless the film develops legs.

The distributor may pull a film earlier than expected because the movie isn't drawing audiences, even though a producer or others associated with the film may not agree. The trick is to figure out whether or not it is possible for a film to build a reputation, even though the box office is slow at first.

**Box office data.**   Box office decisions these days are based mostly on data gathered and distributed by one company. AC Nielson's Entertainment Data Inc. collects box office results each evening from more than 50,000 movie screens across 14 countries. The data is compiled and delivered before dawn to the major movie studios and theater circuits using electronic and hard copy reports. Similar operations are online in major territories in Europe, Australia and Latin America.

Nielsen EDI provides information for decision-makers in the industry, as well as to the press. The revenue data are used to guide marketing expenditures after, or even during, a film's opening weekend, as well as in making the various decisions mentioned above (Davis, 2002).

Nielsen claims to have created the first centralized source for box office information over 25 years ago. The idea for Nielsen EDI came from a former theater booking secretary at the Mann circuit whose responsibilities included daily phone calls to her counterparts at studios and competing circuits in order to share box office information. In 1976, she saw the opportunity to streamline the process by creating a central clearinghouse for box office data and convinced the studios and major exhibitors of the benefits of sharing competitive information through a third-party service.

In 1997, Entertainment Data Inc. was acquired by ACNielsen, which was itself acquired by VNU in 2001. Nielsen EDI is a member of VNU's Media Measurement and Information Group, together with Nielsen NRG, Nielsen VideoScan, Nielsen SoundScan, Nielsen EMS, and Nielsen Media Research.

The company claims to have been an early adopter of faxes, electronic data interchange, the Internet, and wireless communications. The company's online multi-language system is called BOFFO, and reports box office performance to domestic and international clients. Nielsen EDI also introduced "real time Friday matinee reporting" of over 500 North American screens, stressing the growing importance of first day and weekend grosses. Box office statistics include per-screen averages and weekend-to-weekend percentage changes.

In addition to collecting revenue data, EDI tracks other aspects of the industry. In particular, they perform regular price surveys of theaters and gather locations, prices and scale of theaters, producing such publications as the *Release Schedule*, *Theater Atlas* and *School*

*Holiday Calendar.* Nielsen also issues an Academy Award Guide using statistical analysis in assessing Oscar hopefuls' chances.

And finally, fitting for a company concerned with reporting box office receipts: "Nielsen EDI shows its support for the commercial film industry through its annual Reel Awards, granted to the distributors of films that reach the milestone of $100 million in domestic grosses. The Reel Awards are the only industry honors recognizing film box office achievement" (http://www.entdata.com).

## Film booking process

Distributors lease or license films for exhibition in theaters through direct negotiation or a bidding process. Since the Paramount decrees, block booking (or selling groups of films together) is illegal and motion pictures are required to be booked "picture by picture, theater by theater." Thus, a licensing agreement is required for each theater, even though deals are still made with theater chains.

A bidding process is sometimes used that involves a bid request letter from a distributor and written or oral bids from exhibitors. The process is supposed to be competitive and usually includes commitments for minimum playing time, clearances, guarantees (an upfront amount required by the distributor and not returned to the exhibitor), advances (possibly returned if a film is not successful), film rental terms, and advertising terms. Of course, as might be expected, the bidding process varies with distributor and region. The exhibition contract is usually negotiated and even if there is competitive bidding, it is not binding (see Squire, 1992).

Closed bidding is when the distributor opens exhibitor bids privately so that the exhibitors do not know the particulars of the bids submitted by their competitors. While distributors favor the practice, many exhibitors consider it unethical (Cones, 1992, p. 83). Some distributors will wait until the exhibitor bids for a film are in, then call an exhibitor to whom the distributor would like to award the film and report the highest bid received for the film to that point from the favored exhibitor's competitors. The distributor then allows that exhibitor to come in late with a higher bid and awards the first-run of the movie to the late (and highest) bidder. The practice, which is called the "five o'clock look," obviously favors the financially stronger theater chains" (Cones, 1992, p. 199).

Distributors often request exhibitors to submit bids on a film without screening it, or a process called blind bidding. Independent distributors rarely engage in this practice, as many of them realize that retailers in any business should not be expected to sell a product without seeing it first. Some would argue that the larger chains are favored in this process as they have the resources to accept the risks involved. Meanwhile, the exhibitor's trade organization, NATO, has supported the passage of laws prohibiting blind bidding, which have been adopted in some states. However, distributors have not sat idly by while states adopted such laws. For instance, one entertainment lawyer reports that the studios have threatened to avoid shooting on location in states which pass anti-blind bidding statues (ibid., p. 287).

*Box-office split.* Once a bid is accepted, a Distributor/Exhibitor Agreement is arranged, which includes the period of time that the film will play at the theater, advertising arrangements, and how film rentals are to be determined, or in other words, the box office split. An important point to understand about this process is that the distributor's motive is to maximize the film rental and the exhibitor's motive is to minimize it.

The most common box-office split is a 90/10 deal, where 90 percent of the box-office revenues go to the distributor and 10 percent to the exhibitor, after the house allowance or the house nut, which is an agreed-upon amount that represents the exhibitor's operating expenses. These expenses are negotiated for each film and vary according to the clout of the exhibitor.

Current distribution/exhibition deals also often include a minimum for the distributor, which is called a floor. In other words, regardless of the house nut, the distributor must receive an absolute minimum share of the box-office receipts. For instance, a theater may have a 90/10 deal with a 70 percent floor and a $10,000 house nut. If the box office receipts are $40,000, the distributor would receive $28,000 (the 70 percent floor), rather than the $27,000 that would have been due without the floor. The floor usually diminishes each week during a theater run, so the floor may be 70 percent the first week, 60 percent the second week, 50 percent the third week, etc.

An exhibitor's contract also specifies advertising arrangements, including how much is to be spent and who will pay. Typically, exhibitors will pay a certain amount of local advertising, often called cooperative advertising. In a typical deal, exhibitors will contribute 20 percent of the aggregate local marketing expenses.

Given this brief look at these deals, it may be hard to see how exhibitors can survive, much less make a profit. However, most distributors are willing to renegotiate when a film does particularly poorly at the box office. The deal includes the phrase "selling subject to review" and usually favors the exhibitor. Renegotiation occurs mainly because distributors want to maintain good relations with exhibitors. And while there is a mutual dependence between distributors and exhibitors, it might be argued that the power of the distributors is greater.

There are a number of other ways that exhibitors attempt to even the score with distributors. One way is to take their time with payments, not only film rentals but also advertising expenses. But there are other sources of revenue, as well.

## Exhibitors' revenue sources

Theaters do not survive merely on box office receipts, but earn revenue from a variety of sources and attempt to cut costs in many ways.

*Admissions.* Ticket prices are set by the theaters, although exhibition deals certainly have some bearing on these prices. Over the years, ticket prices have increased gradually, as indicated in Table 3.2. After all the negotiations and renegotiations, theaters are said to claim overall 50 percent of the total box office. Whether this amount is industry myth or actually verifiable, however, is another matter (see Vogel, 2001).

*Popcorn and soda.* Concession sales are central to exhibition, since profits are not shared with distributors. Thus, theaters benefit from anything that increases the traffic past the concession stands. For instance, lower priced matinees or other special screenings mean (potentially, at least) more concession sales. Industry estimates suggest that concession stand sales make up anywhere from 50 percent to 80 percent of a theater's profits. In 1998, concession sales for US theaters were reported to be around $2.5 billion.

What is even more significant is the profit margin on concession items. The mark-up on popcorn approaches 75 percent, even factoring in staffing, equipment, oil, salt, butter – or "butter flavoring" – and the popcorn itself. Candy bars, by comparison, represent a profit margin somewhere between 20 and 30 percent (Smith, 2001).

The concession supply business has been mostly a trucking business, but it has changed dramatically recently, becoming highly centralized and automated. In earlier times, regional concessionaires were the norm. Today many exhibitors turn to national companies,

TABLE 3.2 *Average US ticket prices and admissions,
1987–2002*

| Year | Average Ticket Price ($) | Total US admissions (in billions) |
|---|---|---|
| 2002 | 5.80 | 1.63 |
| 2001 | 5.65 | 1.49 |
| 2000 | 5.39 | 1.42 |
| 1999 | 5.06 | 1.47 |
| 1998 | 4.69 | 1.48 |
| 1997 | 4.59 | 1.39 |
| 1996 | 4.42 | 1.34 |
| 1995 | 4.35 | 1.26 |
| 1994 | 4.08 | 1.29 |
| 1993 | 4.14 | 1.24 |
| 1992 | 4.15 | 1.17 |
| 1991 | 4.21 | 1.14 |
| 1990 | 4.22 | 1.19 |
| 1989 | 3.99 | 1.26 |
| 1988 | 4.11 | 1.08 |
| 1987 | 3.91 | 1.09 |

*Source*: MPAA, NATO

based on their ability to truck supplies from regional warehouses to theaters (Squire, 1992, p. 356).

The trade organization for the concessions industry is the National Association of Concessionaires, founded in 1944. The organization generally represents the recreation and leisure-time food and beverage concessions industry which includes (in addition to movie theaters) stadiums and arenas, convention centers, theme parks, zoos and aquariums, and a wide range of other facilities. The association represents companies that provide products and services to these facilities, such as suppliers, equipment manufacturers, popcorn processors, etc.

**On-screen advertising.** Advertising in cinemas has been routine in Europe for years, however, it is relatively new in the USA. In 2001, US movie theaters received between $200 million and $300 million in on-screen ad revenue, according to industry estimates. Although revenues are growing, it is revealing to contrast this amount with the $19.4 billion spent on network TV advertising during the same year.

One company, Screenvision Cinema Network, has been packaging advertising for theaters since the late 1970s, although the ads were no comparison to the hard-sell commercials that started to appear at the end of the 1980s. By 1989 the company produced commercials for 5,700 screens and sold approximately $25 million annually in ad time.[1] Screenvision charges advertisers $20,000 per thousand viewers for a one-time 60-second spot, or $600,000 to $700,000 for a 28 day run that carries the guarantee of 31 million viewers. Screenvision is a New York-based movie-ad joint venture of Carlton Communications PLC and Thomson Multimedia SA.

Advertisers are willing to commit such sums for two basic reasons: (1) They believe that commercials specifically designed to run in theaters are effective; and (2) moviegoers are, in general, relatively light viewers of television and therefore are exposed to fewer ads than the majority of the American populace. Moviegoers thus represent a prime (untapped) target for advertisers, especially the younger audience that (supposedly) does not watch as much television.

Late in 2002, Regal Entertainment announced plans to create 20 minutes of "pre-show" ads and program shorts prior to the advertised start time of feature films at its theaters. Regal's plan was to create a mix of "rolling stock" commercials and other pre-movie programming. The head of the theater chain explained, "I hope that the line between entertainment and advertising will begin to blur. There is no other medium that delivers a message on a 30-foot-high screen with digital sound." The executive also noted that the additional ads and entertainment would not affect showtimes, but "it also allows more time for the concession stand."[2]

*Lobby-marketing.*   In addition to lobby attractions such as video games and merchandise sales, another form of advertising also has appeared in the form of lobby marketing. Although such tactics began several years ago, they were used mostly by local businesses until recently. After Calvin Klein made headlines by placing ads on popcorn bags, other advertisers became interested. For instance, Target Corp. supported its sale of back-to-college supplies with branded popcorn bags at 104 theaters in ten major cities. The bags featured a woman and her Target blanket, with Target's red bull's-eye logo in the middle of the bag.

Lobby promotions experienced double-digit growth in 2001 and generated roughly $40 million to $50 million, according to industry estimates. Popcorn-bag ads are bought for set time periods, and prices vary seasonally. A national buy for a medium bag for four weeks in June would have a cost-per-thousand of about $118. The price is steep, considering that advertisers typically pay about $20 to $30 per thousand viewers for ads on national TV shows aimed at 18-to-34 year olds. However, the ads target a very specific audience.

Loews Cineplex Entertainment has three staff members dedicated to luring such sponsors. John McCauley, vice president of marketing at Loews, says he can get as much as $1 million from a company for an annual sponsorship agreement that typically entitles it to theater signage and access to the theater lobby. Companies such as Coca-Cola Co. and General Mills Inc. are also using theaters for their ad pitches.[3]

National Cinema Network is another company involved in theater advertising. Founded in 1985, NCN introduced ads and promotions in theaters and is now a unit of the AMC Entertainment Inc. theater chain, which represents about 10,000 screens. NCN acts as a broker between advertisers and theater operators such as AMC, Carmike Cinemas Inc. and National Amusements Inc.

National Cinema Network's NationalCinema.net is an advertising network specializing in online advertising sales for movie and entertainment-related web sites, including Hollywood.com and MovieTickets.com. NCN represents the web sites of several theatrical exhibitors including AMC Theaters (amctheaters.com and Movie-Watcher.com) and Marcus Theaters (marcustheaters.com).

NationalCinema.net differs from similar ventures, as advertisers reinforce their online campaigns with ads, promotions, and sampling conducted in theaters that the company services. Through the use of information entered by consumers when accessing local showtime information, an identifiable channel is created for advertisers. The company boasts "integrated cinema media (film, slide and audio advertising), lobby marketing and Internet opportunities (CineMarketing Solutions) that reach moviegoers everywhere they go."

*Labor issues.* While there are many ways that theaters can increase profits (raise ticket prices, increase attendance, sell more popcorn), another way is to reduce expenses. Theaters do this by employing part-time workers for low pay, as well as turning to automation for projection, ticketing, etc. The number of US theater employees reported in 2001 was 137,700. In the same year, 50 percent of theater ushers, lobby attendants and ticket takers were paid an hourly wage of less than $6.61, according to the exhibition industry's trade organization.

*On-line ticketing.* Online movie ticket selling sites grew significantly during the blockbuster-filled year of 2001. Sites included AOL Moviefone.com, Fandango.com, Hollywood.com (owned by Hollywood Media Corp.), and MovieTickets.com (owned by AMC Entertainment, National Amusements, Famous Players, Hoyts Cinemas Corporation, Marcus Theaters and Viacom). MovieTickets.com offers the online sale of movie tickets with additional content designed to assist users with their moviegoing plans.

**Theater operations.**   The main theater organization is the National Association of Theater Owners (NATO), which is the largest exhibition trade organization in the world. The association claims to represent more than 26,000 movie screens in the USA and in more than 20 countries worldwide. The membership includes the major cinema chains as well as independent theaters. NATO's expressed purpose is "to preserve, enhance, and promote the magic of going to the movies." It accomplishes this through various activities, including lobbying for the industry, gathering statistics on the theater business, and promoting quality theater operations.

It is interesting to note that at least one film company, or filmmaker, has recently become personally involved with theater standards. Lucasfilm Ltd. has issued a set of "Recommended Guidelines for Presentation Quality and Theater Performance for Indoor Theaters," that covers film presentation, digital image presentation, theater environment and presentation, sound quality and theater maintenance and operations. Perhaps this is not surprising considering Lucas' sound business. But this also represents the commitment of at least one Hollywood power player to upgrading the theater experience.

Another company involved with theaters is the National Cinema Service, which offers nationwide motion picture projection and sound equipment sales, installation and repair. The company features projection and sound equipment maintained by a staff of theater technicians who are members of IATSE.

## Theater companies

Rather than the disappearance or even decline of movie theaters, the exhibition sector of the film industry has experienced extensive growth over the last few decades. Between 1990 and 2000, NATO estimated that the number of theater screens grew 50 percent from 23,814 to 36,264 (see Table 3.3). During the same period, real box office receipts grew by only 16 percent from $6.61 to $7.67 billion. In 2001, there were 34,490 screens, 663 drive-in screens, for a total of 35,153 screens (see Table 3.4).

The most significant trend in the theater market in the USA is the increasing size of the multiplex (or multi-screened complex.)

TABLE 3.3   *US cinema sites, 1995–2001*

| Year | Indoor | Drive-In | Total |
|------|--------|----------|-------|
| 2001 | 5,813  | 433      | 6,246 |
| 2000 | 6,571  | 408      | 6,979 |
| 1999 | 7,031  | 520      | 7,551 |
| 1998 | 6,894  | 524      | 7,418 |
| 1997 | 6,903  | 577      | 7,480 |
| 1996 | 7,215  | 583      | 7,798 |
| 1995 | 7,151  | 593      | 7,744 |

*Source*: NATO

TABLE 3.4   *US movie screens, 1987–2001*

| Year | Indoor | Drive-In | Total  |
|------|--------|----------|--------|
| 2001 | 34,490 | 663      | 35,153 |
| 2000 | 35,627 | 637      | 36,264 |
| 1999 | 36,448 | 737      | 37,185 |
| 1998 | 33,418 | 750      | 34,168 |
| 1997 | 31,050 | 815      | 31,865 |
| 1996 | 28,905 | 826      | 29,731 |
| 1995 | 26,995 | 848      | 27,843 |
| 1994 | 25,830 | 859      | 26,689 |
| 1993 | 24,789 | 837      | 25,626 |
| 1992 | 24,344 | 870      | 25,214 |
| 1991 | 23,740 | 899      | 24,639 |
| 1990 | 22,904 | 910      | 23,814 |
| 1989 | 21,907 | 1,014    | 22,921 |
| 1988 | 21,632 | 1,497    | 23,129 |
| 1987 | 20,595 | 2,084    | 22,679 |

*Source*: NATO

Duplexes were created in the late 1950s, but until 1970, most theaters still had only one screen. The first multiplex theaters were created by partitioning existing theaters into smaller ones, and by the mid-1970s, exhibitors were building new theaters with up to four screens.

In 2000, the MPAA reported that 32 percent of theaters in the USA had a single screen, 43 percent were "mini-plexes" with 2–7 screens, 20 percent had 8–16 screens and 5 percent, known as "mega-plexes", had more than 16 screens. The largest megaplexes, however, offered over 40 screens. Megaplexes can be as big as 150,000 square feet, seating 12–15,000 people on a weekend day. While many of the typically older and much smaller theaters still operate in towns and niche locations, theaters that have recently closed have typically been small, while newly constructed theaters are much larger. As a result, the average number of screens per theater rose from 3.6 to 4.9 between 1995 and 2000 (see Davis, 2002; Acland, 2003).

TABLE 3.5   *Top 10 circuits in the USA (as of June 1, 2002)*

| Circuit | Headquarters | Screens | Sites |
|---------|-------------|---------|-------|
| 1.  Regal Entertainment Group | Knoxville, TN | 5850 | 552 |
| 2.  AMC Entertainment Inc. | Kansas City, MO | 3308 | 235 |
| 3.  Carmike Cinemas, Inc. | Columbus, GA | 2333 | 323 |
| 4.  Cinemark USA, Inc. | Plano, TX | 2241 | 191 |
| 5.  Loews Cineplex Ent. Corp. | New York, NY | 2161 | 226 |
| 6.  National Amusements, Inc. | Dedham, MA | 1087 | 96 |
| 7.  Hoyts Cinemas Corp. | Boston, MA | 922 | 102 |
| 8.  Famous Players, Inc. | Toronto, Ontario | 841 | 91 |
| 9.  Century Theaters | San Rafael, CA | 822 | 76 |
| 10. Kerasotes Theaters | Springfield, IL | 532 | 81 |

*Source*: NATO

But the exhibition business in the USA has recently gone through some troublesome times. This period of overbuilding during the 1990s led to serious financial instability, in addition to the usual business deals that theaters often encounter with the Hollywood majors. Between 2000–2001, a dozen major circuits faced bankruptcy reorganizations and various restructuring. Subsequently, some of the companies sought (with mixed results) public capital to finance prospective acquisitions, thus prompting a wave of consolidation in the exhibition business.

Finally, in mid-2002, Regal Entertainment was formed from three smaller chains, creating an unprecedented circuit of nearly 5,900 screens. Other circuits, including AMC, Cinemark and Loews, were left to try to compete with this new dominant force in the exhibition sector. Whether publicly or privately owned, most exhibitors were in much better shape in 2003 than a few years earlier. Since the exhibition sector is heavily concentrated, more attention is given below to the major chains, as summarized in Table 3.5.

**Regal Entertainment Group.**   This company is the largest theater owner in the USA and owns over 5,800 screens at over 550 theaters in 36 states through Regal Cinemas, Edwards Theaters, and United Artists Theater Company. Regal's sales for 2001 were over $556 million and the company reported 23,815 employees.

The company also operates Regal CineMedia, which sells in-theater advertising, and The Satellite Theater Network, which rents out theaters for business and social functions. Regal Cinemas also operates a handful of IMAX 3-D theaters at select multiplexes and several FunScapes entertainment centers, which house movie theaters, miniature golf courses, video games, and other family-oriented entertainment sites.

Regal Cinemas, United Artists, and Edwards Theaters were all in bankruptcy proceedings before investor Philip Anschutz, CEO of Qwest Communications, bought controlling interests through his company, The Anschutz Corporation. Anschutz controls the majority of the voting power of Regal Entertainment.

The company also operates the Regal CineMedia unit, a $67 million project to install digital distribution and projection technology in two-thirds of Regal's 550 theaters, covering three-quarters of its total screens. Regal aims to boost pre-show capabilities and facilitate the occasional videocast of concerts and sporting events as an alternative to movie programming during slow times during the week.

**AMC Entertainment Inc.**    With reported 2002 sales over $1.3 million, AMC is the second-largest movie theater chain in the USA (behind Regal Entertainment). The company's 235 theaters with more than 3,300 screens are located in 29 states and the District of Columbia, as well as in Canada, France, Hong Kong, Japan, Portugal, Spain, Sweden, and the UK. The company also has teamed up with CBS, Famous Players, Hollywood.com, Marcus Theaters, and National Amusements to launch online movie ticket seller MovieTickets.com. A charitable trust created after the death of former CEO Stanley Durwood owns 10 percent of AMC.

**The National Cinema Network.**    As discussed previously, NCN sells theater advertising. It is a subsidiary of AMC Entertainment, but operates in most major markets through partnerships with Carmike Cinemas, Mann Theaters, and Pacific Theaters, among others.

**Carmike Cinemas, Inc.**    This company has more than 2,300 screens at more than 300 locations in 35 states. The company traditionally has been the only exhibitor in small to mid-sized markets, but has made a move into bigger markets with the introduction of multiplexes that average 14 screens apiece. The company also owns a few family entertainment centers called Hollywood Connection, featuring rides and games alongside multiplex theaters. In 2000 Carmike filed to reorganize its business under Chapter 11 and has since sold more than 100 of its theaters, emerging from bankruptcy in 2002. The Goldman Sachs Group owns about 47 percent of the company.

**Cinemark USA, Inc.**    Cinemark is the fourth-largest movie exhibitor in the USA and has more than 2,200 screens in 191 theaters in the USA and

13 other countries, mostly in Latin America. Cinemark's sales for 2001 were over $853 million. The company operates multiplex theaters (the ratio of screens to theaters is about 11 to 1) in mid-sized cities and in suburban areas of major metropolitan markets. Some larger theaters operate under the Tinseltown name and about 11 percent of their theaters are "discount" theaters, as opposed the houses which exhibit first-run movies. Chairman and CEO Lee Roy Mitchell owns about 91 percent of the company's voting stock.

**Loews Cineplex Entertainment Corp.**   This company is the fifth largest US movie chain and owns more than 2,100 screens in about 226 theaters in the USA and other countries. Sales reported for 2002 were over $856 million and the company reports around 16,500 employees. The company operates under the Loews and Sony names in 19 US states and Washington, DC, as well as the Cineplex Odeon name in Canada. Loews Cineplex also owns 50 percent stakes in theaters in Spain (Yelmo Cineplex) and South Korea (Megabox Cineplex). In the USA, however, Loews' growth has slowed down because of the over-building in the industry.

Sony Pictures Entertainment owned about 40 percent of the company, while Goldman Sachs owned about 26 percent. However, an investment group led by Onex Corporation acquired the firm in 2002 in conjunction with its emergence from Chapter 11 bankruptcy protection. The chain planned to file an IPO later that year, but pulled back for various reasons. Onex is a diversified Canadian conglomerate that also operates the smaller Galaxy circuit in Canada, and recently took a 7 percent stake in AMC.

### Issue: Competition and ownership

The theater industry has been a relatively concentrated area for much of its history. Theater chains continue to dominate the theatrical market, while independent exhibitors struggle to survive. As noted above, the industry has experienced a new round of consolidation, which may continue. Regal is well-positioned to add additional screens, while the other large chains may do the same in an effort to compete.

The exhibition market also has a long history of anti-trust activity. The most famous anti-trust action resulted in the Paramount consent decrees in 1948, which still affect the structure of the industry today. In particular, the Paramount decrees resulted in the forced vertical disintegration of the industry after the five major studio-distributors (Paramount, Warner Brothers, Twentieth Century Fox, Loew's and Radio Keith Orpheum) were found guilty of restraint of trade including vertical and horizontal price fixing (see Conant, 1978).

While the major distributors seemed to be moving back into theater ownership during the 1990s, they seem to have stepped back from their recapture of the exhibition end of the film business at the end of the decade. Although a few of the majors still have some interests in theater chains, most of these investments are outside of the USA. Certainly, one might think there would be concern in those countries over the control of film markets, including exhibition, by foreign interests. (Further discussion of these issues will be presented in Chapter 4.)

## Ratings and Classification System

The theater business is also charged with trying to enforce Hollywood's system of rating and classification of films (see Appendix A). The rating system was developed in the early 1960s as a form of industry self-regulation to avoid censorship.[4] The system is sponsored by the MPAA and NATO and remains a voluntary system (with no force of law) that aims to provide parents with advance information about films.

A specially designed committee called Rating Board of the Classification and Rating Administration views films, and, after a group discussion, votes on the ratings. While the Rating Board claims to use the criteria that parents use when deciding what is suitable for their children, the decisions are inevitably controversial. The process involves assessing theme, language, violence, nudity, sex and drug use and how each of these elements is employed in the context of each individual film.

The awarding of a rating has certain economic implications, as potential audiences will be attracted by the different rating designations. The system allows producers to re-edit films and re-submit them in hopes of receiving another rating. In addition, producers may appeal against a rating decision to the Rating Appeals Board, which is made up of representatives from the industry organizations that sponsor the rating system. A two-thirds secret ballot vote of those present on the Appeals Board may overturn a Rating Board decision.

While the process is voluntary, the majority of Hollywood films are submitted to the rating process. The rating symbols used in the process have been trademarked, thus producers cannot use them without going through the classification process. Furthermore, the decision to enforce the rating system also is voluntary, although it is claimed that the overwhelming majority of theaters follow the guidelines and "diligently enforce its provisions."

## Electronic or Digital Cinemas

Another potential change for the exhibition sector is the shift to electronic distribution. The next few sections discuss this looming development and its significance for the industry as a whole.[5]

After years of speculation, the technology and support for electronic or digital distribution of films to theaters are developing rapidly. E-cinema or digital cinemas involve film prints converted to electronic form, digitized and encrypted, then transmitted from a central server to cinemas via DVD, satellite or fiber-optic link, and projected on electronic projectors.

In the past few years, various demonstrations have shown that the quality is improving and is finally acceptable to the film industry. Digital versions of major films have been demonstrated at trade shows, including a screening of *Star Wars: The Phantom Menace* at Showest '99. (Around that time, George Lucas vowed to release the next *Star Wars* installment only in a digital format.) In addition, a few theaters screened digital versions of Disney's *Mission to Mars*, *Dinosaur* and *Toy Story II*, as well as *Final Fantasy*, during the summer of 2001.

The industry is making progress in establishing technical standards through organizations such as the SMPTE (Society of Motion Picture and Television Engineers) and the MPEG (Motion Picture Experts Group), as well as NATO and the MPAA. Several e-cinema systems seem to be emerging but the one most often mentioned is Texas Instruments' Digital Light Processing (DLP) system, which uses a digital micro-mirror device. The company has three major licensees (Barco, Christie Digital and Digital Projection), and is seen by some as the industry leader. Meanwhile, Hughes-JVC (a company owned by the Victor Company of Japan) is developing a system based on Direct Drive Image Light Amplifier (D-ILA), using liquid crystals on a chip. Another contender is Technicolor's Digital Cinema, developed in conjunction with Qualcomm. By mid-2001, 31 sites were participating in a demonstration program that included Technicolor, Texas Instruments, and Disney.

As noted above, distribution of digital films is possible by DVD, satellite or fiber-optic link. Ultimately, satellite distribution may be the most efficient method, and has been demonstrated with technology developed by the Boeing Company. The system is supported by the company's military satellite experience, presenting interesting potential alliances. Miramax participated in early tests, offering its feature film *Bounce* for a trial run of the system in March 2000, and *Spy Kids* for another demonstration in March 2001.

Both Disney and Sony have shown enthusiasm for e-cinema, as well as other industry sources. According to a *Screen Digest* report, there are likely to be an estimated 10,000 digital screens worldwide by 2005 and a complete transition within 20 years. The enthusiastic report also predicts that almost 100 per cent of the major Hollywood studios' films will be available both in digital and conventional (35mm) format by the end of 2004 (von Sychowski, 2000).

Many of the advantages cited by e-cinema's supporters are apparent. The most obvious is the elimination of film prints, which cost on the average of $3 million for a major film, or around $1,500 per print. Often 3–4,000 prints are produced for each film, with total global cost of prints estimated at $5 billion each year. Digital versions of films also eliminate wear and tear that is common with film prints, with fewer scratches and less dust. In addition, multi-language audio tracks become possible, as well as simultaneous worldwide release dates. Distributors would be able to more easily move poorly performing films or possibly alter or re-edit films during their theatrical runs.

E-cinemas are envisioned as multi-format outlets featuring movies, live concerts and other special events, corporate meetings, etc., which could help some theaters earn desperately needed extra revenues. This type of activity is already happening in Canada at Viacom's Famous Players cinemas, which feature live pay-per-view wrestling from the World Wrestling Federation, utilizing Bell ExpressVu satellite operations. Another additional source of income might be advertising from local sources, which may be enthusiastically welcomed by some, while dreaded by others. With digital projection, individual theaters might also be able to schedule screenings more easily to accommodate public demand, as well as saving on less labor-intensive projection.

Although theater projection is already often automated, further reductions in labor costs may be possible.

While there are clear advantages and most believe that digital cinema is inevitable, there are some formidable questions that will need to be answered before widespread digital exhibition is a reality. Again, security and control are key issues. Even with encryption systems, the potential for pirating theater-quality versions of new films is more ominous than current piracy practices, which often involve videotaping projected films in theaters.

With a number of companies developing digital cinema technology, there are likely to be compatibility issues. It is still unclear whether there will be one standard or "open architecture" allowing more than one system to be used. In addition, questions prevail regarding the compatibility of encryption and compression equipment.

Another issue that e-cinema enthusiasts seem to overlook has to do with the advantages of film projectors that are not only less expensive, but also more rugged and universally adaptable. Even if the costs come down for electronic systems, e-cinema equipment may quickly become obsolete, given the constant development of digital technology.

And then there is the critical issue of cost. Though prices for digital projectors are dropping (from $220,000–$240,000 to $160,000 in just one year), they still are major investments compared to a 35mm projection system which is currently priced at around $30-40,000. Most analysts agree that digital systems must be around $100,000 to be viable. With the total cost of converting 100,000 screens around the world at an estimated $25 billion, the big question is, who will pay?

In a recent trade paper article, one exhibitor expressed the sentiments of many other theater owners, explaining: "We know exactly what we are prepared to pay to move to digital: nothing." Many of the major US theater chains will be hard-pressed to make such substantial investments, as recent theater upgrading has left a number of them in or near bankruptcy. One proposal has suggested that a consortium of the major studios fund the new projection systems, but it remains to be seen if the majors will agree. More than one studio executive has explained that it is up to the exhibitors to fund the new technology, as one of the costs of doing business. Another option is from Technicolor Digital: the company will install systems at no cost to exhibitors or distributors, but will charge exhibitors 12.5 cents per customer, as well as charging studios to distribute films electronically. Clearly, this is a crucial issue that will need to be resolved before e-cinemas become the norm.

Furthermore, even though the distributors seem to be the most obvious benefactors of the new systems, it is unclear whether they will be willing to give theater owners any breaks in new exhibition licensing arrangements, where many would argue that the distributors now have the upper hand.

Still, the enthusiasm over e-cinema is growing, with glowing reports and claims by industry spokesmen, who anticipate major changes and increased opportunities. Patrick von Sychowski, author of the previously mentioned *Screen Digest* report, comments: "Electronic cinema is an entirely new medium and as yet the industry hasn't had the opportunity to grasp its full impact." E-cinemas may be commonplace sometime in the future, however, it is unlikely that these thorny issues will be sorted out in time for an all-digital first run of *Star Wars – Episode 3* when it is scheduled to open in 2005.

While the newly enlarged and recently enriched cinema companies, such as Regal Entertainment, may find it easier to introduce electronic systems, it still remains to be seen how long it will take for "D-cinema" (as *Variety* calls it) to actually emerge as a standard in movie theaters.

## Home Video

By the end of the twentieth century, home video represented a far more lucrative source of income for feature films than theaters. By 2001, video sales and rentals totaled $118.7 billion, and the proliferation of DVD technology promised further rises in revenues. This section will briefly outline the historical background of the home video business, as well as the current industry, followed by a brief discussion of the DVD phenomenon.

### Historical background[6]

The history of video technology is part of the history of television, as efforts to record television signals began as early as television itself. These developments divide roughly into three chronological stages: first, mostly professional video recording, followed by various

attempts at consumer video systems, and finally, the successful introduction of consumer systems, after the introduction of Betamax.

While magnetic tape was developed in the 1950s to record images,
it was mostly used for professional broadcasting. Although some
US companies produced professional video technology, it was the
Sony Corp. that successfully introduced a system for the consumer
market. Sony's Betamax system went on sale in 1976, priced at
$1,295, and was an immediate success. Betamax was promoted at first
for time shifting, a term attributed to Sony head, Akio Morita,
referring to the process of recording programs off television and
playing them back later.

Meanwhile in 1976, Matsushita and JVC introduced a competing
format – VHS (video home system), which developed as the primary
competition to Sony's Betamax. VHS was a smaller machine, with a
different loading system, but offered a longer tape running time.
Although there was competition for a few years, by 1979 twice as
many VHS systems were selling as Betamaxes and by the late 1980s,
Betamax's share of the US market was quite small.

Home video technology became popular relatively quickly and was
called a revolution at the time. As the costs of machines dropped,
sales and penetration rates increased. The total number of machines
in the USA increased to 4.8 million in 1984. In 1983, only 7 percent
of US homes owned either videocassette recorders or videodisc
players, but 62 percent of TV homes were reported to have machines
in late 1988.

Early promotion of VCRs by manufacturers emphasized time-
shifting. So it may not be surprising that for the first few years, taping
programs from television was the most popular use of home video
technology. However, the emphasis on taping programs off-the-air
did not escape the attention of the Hollywood majors, some of the
most important suppliers of television programming.

The Universal vs. Sony/Betamax case (filed in 1976) pitted the
electronic companies, such as Sony, against the Hollywood majors,
who argued that time-shifting was a copyright violation and that
revenue would be lost from the sale of movies to network TV. Yet, by
the time that the Universal/Sony case was settled, the time-shifting
novelty was gradually wearing off. By 1986, studies showed that the
primary reason most people gave for purchasing a VCR was to view
movies. According to another estimate, only 30 percent of VCR viewing by 1987 was watching tapes recorded from television or cable,
and the majority of VCR activity centered on watching pre-recorded
videos – and, mostly, Hollywood movies. By mid-1988, it was

reported that the average VCR owner spent only 2.5 hours recording tapes, but almost four hours playing tapes.

While the first pre-recorded videos were relatively expensive pornographic or X-rated material, an outside entrepreneur began obtaining the rights to sell Hollywood film on tape and the deluge was on. In the late 1970s, the sale of films on tape started rather slowly, followed by some attempts by entrepreneurs to rent copies of purchased movies. The right to rent these tapes was covered by the First Sale Doctrine, a provision of the Copyright Act of 1976 that allows the legitimate buyer of a copyrighted work to dispose of the copy as he or she wishes. In other words, after a cassette has been *sold* to a retailer, no further royalties can be claimed, and the copyright owner loses control of that copy.

While the studios philosophically supported a rental system, they certainly didn't care for the First Sale Doctrine, and, thus, tried to prevent rentals via contractual restrictions, as well as pushing direct sales rather than rentals. From 1978 on, a rental system emerged, despite the reluctance of the major distributors. While the majors even tried to prohibit rentals in their contracts, they eventually yielded to the popularity of the rental system, and released more of their films on video. By 1981 all of the large Hollywood distributors had their own video divisions or combined with another company to distribute their films in video form.

Meanwhile, the majors turned to legislative efforts to change the First Sale Doctrine, especially after the Supreme Court's Betamax decision. Several bills were introduced as the Hollywood lobbyists tried to get the copyright law changed, as well as introducing a royalty tax on rentals and sales of copyrighted movies and pushing legislation that would require manufacturers to install anti-copying devices in all VCRs. However, all of these efforts failed. A series of attempts to get video retailers to share rental revenues followed, but the retailers resisted. Meanwhile, rentals grew and direct sales diminished. The majors gradually dropped their retail prices to encourage the sell-through market. However, they also increased their prices to wholesalers thus raising retailers' prices.

Thus, home video became popular in the USA because of the availability of software, or pre-recorded tapes, especially Hollywood movies, and the development of a popularly accepted distribution system (rentals). In other words, home video became another successful market for theatrical motion pictures, representing not only another outlet for their films but an extremely profitable one, with low distribution expenses involved.

### Home video in the twenty-first century

The home video industry in the US attracted sales of $18.7 billion in 2001. Home video consumers spent $7 billion renting VHS tapes and an all-time-high $1.4 billion renting DVDs. Consumers spent an additional $5.4 billion purchasing DVDs and $4.9 billion purchasing VHS tapes. DVD hardware penetration rose to 36.4 percent of all US television households by the end of 2002. At the same time, VCR hardware penetration reached 91 percent.

Consumer demand for most rentals historically peaks in the first three weeks of availability and then drops off sharply. There are claims that a good deal of the profits from the home video business is from late fees, although this is difficult to substantiate.

As discussed in Chapter 2, home video revenue is reported by distributors as a standard 20 percent royalty on wholesale sales. In other words, "the studio includes only 20% of videocassette revenue in gross receipts and puts most of the remaining 80 percent in its pocket" (Baumgarten et al., 1992, p. 53). The origin of the 20 percent fee can be traced back to the initial arrangement that Magnetic Video (the first company to sell Hollywood film on video) made with Fox. Ultimately, all of the studios adopted the 20 percent wholesale royalty. In addition to counting only 20 percent of the wholesale revenues, distribution fees and other expenses are extracted from this amount. Thus, rather than 20 percent royalty, the amount available to profit participants is actually closer to 10 or 12 percent.

Home video rights are typically arranged as part of the initial production/distribution deal and represent an important source of revenues for film producers. By 1986 it was claimed that 45 percent of all revenue received by a film producer was from the video marketplace. By 1990, US and foreign video revenues accounted for 35–50 percent of a typical film's total income. By the end of the twentieth century, it was even higher.

In the early years, home video was described as a new competitive arena, attracting new players and companies. However, the field narrowed rather quickly to a smaller number of key players. By the end of the 1990s, the video business looked similar to the recording industry, with the majors handling sales for independent production companies.

In the early years of home video, seven of the major Hollywood film distributors held over 90 percent of the market share for home videos (Twentieth Century Fox, Paramount, Warners, MCA, MGM, Columbia, and Disney). And while the percentages have shifted over

TABLE 3.6   *Top DVD/VHS distributors' market shares (%)*

| Company | % |
| --- | --- |
| Buena Vista Home Entertainment | 19.0 |
| Warner Home Video | 18.9 |
| Other | 12.1 |
| Universal Studios Home Entertainment | 11.8 |
| 20th Century Fox Home Entertainment | 8.8 |
| Columbia TriStar Home Entertainment | 8.6 |
| Paramount Home Entertainment | 7.9 |
| DreamWorks Home Entertainment | 5.9 |
| MGM Home Entertainment | 4.4 |
| Artisan Home Entertainment | 2.6 |

*Source*: *DVD News*, January 21, 2002

the years, the majors have continued to hold substantial portions of the business (see Table 3.6).

## Home video distribution

The Hollywood majors are still the key forces in home video distribution, which has its own industrial structure. Video distribution is handled by distributors or wholesalers, who buy products from manufacturers and sell to retailers. Manufacturers or suppliers are companies that own the video rights to titles. They produce and market videos to wholesalers, distributors and large retailers. Duplicators make video copies for manufacturers. And retailers are businesses that deal exclusively with consumers, although some large retailers also may do wholesale business.

There may be some confusion over the term distributor, or whether one is referring to *home video distributors* – wholesale companies buying from suppliers, selling to retailers – or to *film industry distributors* – companies that distribute and sometimes produce films for release in many markets, but sometimes called manufacturers or suppliers, in the home video business.

Since the evolution of a rental system in the early 1980s, the structure of video distribution involved either a two-step process including wholesalers, or a direct distribution method with suppliers distributing directly to retailers and other outlets. The two-step process dominated the business through the 1980s, although the second method of direct distribution has prevailed since then.

Program suppliers/manufacturers are companies with video rights to a title. However, a large part of the business is dominated by companies affiliated with, in joint ventures with, or subsidiaries of,

Hollywood's major distributors. In other words, the major video suppliers are the major Hollywood distributors.

By the beginning of the 1990s, the studios had started distributing their products directly to large retail accounts, and very often, used direct distribution in many foreign markets. Not only were there consequences for wholesalers, but retailers experienced more inconvenience and higher prices (and thus more concentration has characterized the retail end of the business, as discussed below). At one time there were over 100 video wholesalers in the USA, however, only a few major wholesalers remain. Thus, home video wholesaling represents yet another sector of the media business that began as a relatively differentiated activity, but became concentrated rather quickly.

*Ingram Entertainment Inc.* is the largest distributor of video rental and sell-through products, including DVDs, video games and related products. Ingram had total revenues of $871 million in 2001, of which approximately 55 percent represented rental revenue and 70 percent sell-through products sold through video distribution. Ingram also serviced over 10,000 retail accounts including video specialty stores, Internet retailers, drugstores and supermarkets.

Another smaller wholesaler is *Video Products Distributors, Inc.* (VPD), founded in 1980 and based in Folsom, California. The company distributes pre-recorded videocassettes, DVDs and related products to over 3,500 video retailers and other sellers of video from ten facilities located throughout the USA. VPD is a privately-held company.

## Home video retail[7]

The business of video retailing has gone through several stages: a period of direct sales at high prices, to one of mostly rentals. Then, with lower prices for direct sales, a mix of sales and rentals evolved. In the early 1990s, however, the suppliers were pushing more and more towards sell-through, by continuing to offer cassettes as low as $14.95, yet increasing the price to retailers for rental copies.

Currently, the major retail outlets arrange deals with the major distributors to share revenue for rentals, but also benefit greatly from the sell-through business. From 1997, a direct revenue-sharing model has been adopted, with tapes sold at a lower cost to retailers ($8-10) for 45-50 percent of the rental fees. The major studios have made such arrangements with the leading retail chains, Blockbuster and Hollywood Entertainment, both outlined below.

Some independent video distributors, such as LIVE Entertainment, produce their own product, as well as distributing a broad range of products (audio CDs, tapes, and video products), plus specialized merchandise to mass merchandisers (such as Target, Kmart, etc.).

About 77 percent of the movies ordered each month by video store owners are A-titles or Hollywood films that have appeared in movie theaters. Another study has indicated that 56 percent of a video store's inventory will never have appeared at a local theater, and 40 percent may have never appeared on television, however, A-titles still accounted for 75 percent of videos rented by 1987. So, the retail end of the business has evolved as a "hit-obsessed market," with video stores, especially, stocking and promoting hit movies over other titles, and the smaller, non-blockbuster film facing the problem of lack of exposure in many video outlets.

In 1983, there were over 25,000 video stores in the USA. While the independent or "mom & pop" video store characterized the early video industry, many of these retailers experienced increased competition from video chains, mass merchandising outlets, and convenience stores in the late 1980s and early 1990s. By the mid-1980s, the video retailing sector started showing distinct signs of intense concentration. During the following years, however, there was even further concentration (see Table 3.7). These days, the video store business in the USA is dominated by primarily one, possibly, two companies, which will be discussed below.

**Blockbuster.**    Blockbuster is the world's leading renter of videos, DVDs, and video games with over 8,000 stores throughout the Americas, Europe, Asia, and Australia. It is claimed that more than 3 million customers visit a Blockbuster store each day.

TABLE 3.7   *Top video retailers by estimated revenue, 2001*

| Firm | Revenue (in millions of dollars) |
| --- | --- |
| Blockbuster | 5,374 |
| Wal-Mart | 2,713 |
| Kmart | 2,114 |
| Hollywood Entertainment | 1,801 |
| Musicland Stores | 1,336 |
| Target | 1,055 |
| Circuit City | 632 |
| Sam's Club | 500 |
| Best Buy | 478 |

Blockbuster has been the leader of the video store pack since the early 1990s, and is now part of the Viacom empire. The first Blockbuster store was opened in 1985, but only one and a half years later, the Fort Lauderdale-based company owned 800 stores and has been growing steadily. By the beginning of 1991, Blockbuster owned over 2,000 stores and dominated the business. The company received $1.25 billion in revenues out of $2.3 billion received by the 100 largest video chains.

After extensive expansion in the 1980s and 1990s, Blockbuster remains dominant. The Blockbuster style has been similar to the successful McDonald's formula: standardization and consistency. Blockbuster is also reported to arrange exclusive deals for films from suppliers, a charge that has definite anti-competitive implications.

**Hollywood Entertainment Corp.**   This company is another home video player, however, much less dominant than Blockbuster. Hollywood owned and operated around 1,800 Hollywood Video retail superstores in 47 states and the District of Columbia as of July 2002. In 2001 it was estimated that Hollywood held a 20 percent share of the US market, with its average store generating approximately $766,000 in annual revenue. Total revenue increased from $302 million in 1996 to $1.4 billion in 2001, with a total of 22,660 employees.

In 2000–2001, Hollywood Entertainment reported a change in its business strategy, from one of high growth in revenue through new store openings to one of revenue growth and cash generation from existing stores. After opening an average of 306 stores annually from 1996 through 2000, the company opened only six stores in 2001.

The company's superstores average approximately 6,800 square feet and typically carry over 7,000 movie titles, featuring a combination of new releases and catalog movies on both videocassette and DVD. Approximately 83 percent of the company's 2001 revenue were received from movie rentals and games; the remainder was generated from the sale of new and previously-viewed movies and video games, and concessions.

**Mass merchants.**   Traditional video stores have increasingly had to compete with non-video outlets and mass merchants in the rental business, as well as in sell-through activity, which has been favored by distributors. The real competition developed when rack-jobbers started placing videos on shelves at mass merchants, such as Wal-Mart, Target, Federated, Fedco, and Sears, as well as supermarkets, drug stores, and sometimes, even video stores. By 1985, 25 percent of mass-merchandise discount stores were carrying videos. By the mid-1990s, nearly 45 percent of the supermarkets in the country carried videos.

Rack-jobbing companies place videos on a consignment basis in these outlets. The Handleman Company and Lieberman Enterprises have dominated the rack-jobbing business for a number of years. Another example, is Video Channels, owned by the Rank Organization, which is also involved in video duplication.

**VSDA.** Established in 1981, the Video Software Dealers Association (VSDA) is a not-for-profit international trade association for the home entertainment industry. VSDA represents more than 1,700 companies throughout the United States, Canada, and a dozen other countries. Membership includes video and video game retailers (both independents and large chains), as well as the home video divisions of major and independent motion picture studios, and other related businesses.

### DVD (digital versatile disc).[8]

The DVD "revolution" started in 1997 after the price of players fell from $500–$200 in three years. In 2002, consumers bought 25.1 million DVD players; by the end of 2002, the technology represented the fastest selling consumer electronic product ever, having reached sales of 30 million units within five years. In 2001, American homes had more DVD players than computers (one out of four homes, as noted previously).

DVD technology boasts several advantages over laser discs and video discs. In addition to numerous playback possibilities (computers and DVD players), the discs themselves are nearly indestructible, plus additional material about a film can be added. In addition to the improved quality over VHS, it is no wonder that Hollywood's creative-types are enthusiastic about DVD's possibilities for adding previously-cut material and featuring other background about a film.

DVDs in some cases account for 30 percent of a studio's retail revenue from home video sales and rentals. The discs wholesale for only $10–$15 each (compared to $45–$65 apiece for videocassettes) and are sold to consumers at $18–$30. One studio head explains that the studios make $15 in profit on the sale of one DVD. Meanwhile, the major video chain, Blockbuster, pays an average of $20 wholesale for each DVD, but $70 for video, plus no supplementary fees are involved with DVD rentals.

The release of *Gladiator* opened Hollywood's eyes to the DVD goldmine and pointed to young men as the major purchasers. Yet other releases attracted even more diversified buyers: *Crouching Tiger, Hidden Dragon* had gleaned $50 million in DVD sales by August 2001, while *Pearl Harbor*'s first day release on DVD supposedly attracted $67.5 million compared to an opening weekend box office of $59.1 million.

Then, *Monsters, Inc.* was released in mid-2002, with consumers buying more first-day copies than any other title up until that time. DVD sales of *Monsters Inc.* exceeded 3 million copies. Although many retailers were selling the title at loss leader prices, Disney's wholesale revenue was at least $85 million for only one day's sales. Consumers purchased 5 million VHS and DVD copies, with a far higher percentage – 60–65 percent – being purchased on DVD than the 50 percent the studio expected.

Then, at the end of 2002, *Spider-Man* broke the record again, selling 7 million copies on one day, with 11 million copies sold over one weekend, generating about $190 million in retail revenue. More than $125 million was spent buying and renting the title on DVD and videocassette on its opening day alone, with more than $200 million netted by the superhero over the weekend.

Between 75–80 percent of the copies purchased – or roughly 8.5 million units – were on DVD, setting a record for a major release. Sony's wholesale cut of each DVD was in the range of $18, regardless of the price the title sold for in stores. The studio shipped more than 26 million DVD and VHS copies of the movie to retailers in the USA and sold 40 percent of them during one weekend. Over 14 million units were shipped overseas, while around 1.8 million copies were sold to rental stores.

It is interesting to note Blockbuster's position that there should be an exclusive window for DVD rentals and sales. A "DVD rental window" would mean that video stores would have an opportunity to offer the discs to customers exclusively, preventing discount retailers like Wal-Mart Stores – which accounted for 18 percent of consumer spending on video purchases in 1999 – from grabbing a piece of that market until the exclusive rental window expired.

### Issue: Recycling and commodification

The rapid introduction of DVDs points again to the potential for ongoing revenues from the recycling of Hollywood commodities.

Again, films that have seemingly run their course in terms of attracting profits can be dragged (again) from the vaults and offered in a new form. There is no doubt that the new digital technology has been, and will continue to be, immensely profitable for the major studios, as well as other film companies with attractive products.

Meanwhile, many consumers have responded with their purchases of DVD players and discs, anxious to add the latest technology, albeit a technologically superior one, to their entertainment collection. While everyone seems happy, questions might be raised regarding the ongoing commodification of the cultural sphere, as well as the continuous recycling of cultural fare.

## Cable Television

### Historical background

While cable television can be traced back to the 1950s with early CATV systems, the boom in cable came in the 1970s when HBO started offering something that the commercial television networks did not: relatively new, uncut Hollywood films. In September 1975, HBO became the first cable service to shift from microwave to satellite delivery of its programming simultaneously to the entire nation of cable systems.

Despite initial problems and intense opposition from the Hollywood majors and exhibitors, HBO and several other movie channels, such as Showtime and the Movie Channel, became quite successful. The majors found that pay-cable, especially, offered another lucrative outlet for their products after theatrical release.

Despite claims to the contrary, Hollywood was involved with cable in various ways from its very beginning. However, the studios either pursued dead-end technology, became involved in pay television too early in its history or used their typical monopolistic style. As cable television evolved, the studios withdrew to their own concerns only to find others moving in during key periods of cable/pay-cable's development in the mid-1970s.

Again, the film industry reacted to others' success with moaning, resentment, and hostility. But, cable and pay cable were here to stay, and indeed offered film distributors additional markets for their product via basic and pay channels, pay-per-view services, as well as over-the-air stations carried on cable systems. By the 1990s, the film industry was intimately involved with cable, pay-cable and pay-per-view – if not in terms of ownership, then through a valuable customer relationship.

## Cable ownership

At least one of the largest US cable systems and many of the most successful cable channels are owned by the majors. Cable systems in the USA are operated almost always by private companies granted franchises from municipalities. These companies typically have a monopoly in a specific location and there is considerable concentration in the cable industry, especially through chains of cable systems, or MSOs (multiple-system operators). Cable systems, cable channels, and program producers have been combined in one company, sometimes connected with one of the Hollywood majors (see Table 3.8). Currently, the primary example is AOL Time Warner, the second largest cable operator in the USA, and, as we have seen, the owner of pay channels (HBO, Cinemax, etc.), and several major production companies.

Cable systems arrange to carry pay channels through contracts (usually from 3–5 years in length) which specify fees paid by the operator plus other provisions. Typically, the cable operator keeps 50 percent of pay revenues, while the remainder goes to the program supplier. While the operator chooses which pay services to carry, there may be specific incentives and/or restrictions that favor the system carrying only one service, rather than two competing services. Indeed, there have been claims that systems affiliated with MSOs that own pay services typically carry the parent company's pay channel.

Pay channels can be found on most cable systems, attracting over 51 million subscribers by 2001. The average monthly rate for typical pay-cable service was $15.00 in 1995, while revenues for the cable industry amounted to $49.4 billion in 2002.

Early studies indicated that the main reason subscribers wanted pay cable (or even cable) was to view uncut, relatively recent movies. Thus, it is not surprising that the mainstay of pay channel programming in the USA is Hollywood films, which is often touted as the basis of cable's diverse programming. This proliferation of films on pay cable is more understandable when you consider that ready-made Hollywood movies still represent extremely economical programming.

Despite the slight decline in pay subscribers in the late 1980s due to home video and the emphasis by operators on basic cable, pay

TABLE 3.8  *Leading US cable networks and conglomerate ownership (ranked by number of subscribers, in millions)*

| Rank | Network | Subscribers | Parent Corp. |
|------|---------|-------------|--------------|
| 1 | TBS Superstation | 87.7 | AOLTW |
| 2 | ESPN | 86.7 | Walt Disney* |
| 3 | C-SPAN | 86.6 | Cable operators |
| 4 | Discovery Channel | 86.5 | Walt Disney* |
| 5 | USA Network | 86.3 | Vivendi |
| 6 | CNN (Cable News Network) | 86.2 | AOLTW |
| 6 | TNT (Turner Network Television) | 86.2 | AOLTW |
| 8 | Lifetime Television (LIFE) | 86.0 | Walt Disney* |
| 8 | Nickelodeon | 86.0 | Viacom |
| 10 | A&E Network | 85.9 | Walt Disney* |
| 11 | The New TNN | 85.8 | Viacom |
| 12 | The Weather Channel | 85.3 | Landmark |
| 13 | MTV (Music Television) | 84.9 | Viacom |
| 13 | QVC | 84.9 | Comcast |
| 15 | ABC Family Channel | 84.8 | Walt Disney |
| 16 | The Learning Channel (TLC) | 84.7 | Walt Disney* |
| 17 | ESPN2 | 84.5 | Walt Disney |
| 18 | CNBC | 84.1 | General Electric |
| 19 | AMC (American Movie Classics) | 83.9 | Cablevision |
| 20 | VH1 (Music First) | 83.7 | Viacom |

*Source*: Subscriber data from *Cable Program Investor*, 28 February 2003, p.16, by Kagan World Media. Online at http://www.ncta.com/industry_overview/top20networks.cfm? indOverviewID=59

* Represents partial ownership.

NOTE: Subscriber figures as of 28 February 2003, and may include non-cable affiliates and/or subscribers. Broadcast viewership is not included.

cable is still a lucrative endeavor dominated by only a few companies. As discussed in Chapter 2, AOLTW and Viacom dominate this market through their ownership of HBO, Showtime, and several other important pay cable channels.

## Pay-TV deals

Cable programming comes from a wide array of sources, including original productions for cable and sports presentations. However, as noted previously, feature films and television programs are overly abundant on pay, as well as basic, channels. And this type of recycled programming is supplied by a relatively small number of companies, most often connected in one way or another to the Hollywood majors.

The sale of feature films to pay cable represents a profitable activity for these companies, as these outlets offer additional revenue for a feature film. Pay cable release of major motion pictures usually follows home video release. Basic cable channels typically purchase feature films after independent broadcast stations (or the syndicated market), although in the late 1980s film distributors started by-passing the syndicated market by sometimes selling first to basic cable.

Studios have "output deals" with pay-TV channels (HBO/Cinemax, and Showtime/Movie Channel, and a few others), thus every major feature film eventually airs on one of these channels. Output deals specify base license fees paid by pay-TV services according to the box office gross of a film. For instance, if a film received $5 million at the box office, the base license fee might be 50 percent or $2.5 million. The average is claimed to be approximately $6 million to $8 million per picture. But for wildly successful films, the fee is considerably higher. For instance, even though *Batman* received over $200 million at the box office, its license fee was reported to be around $15 million. Foreign pay-TV deals are even more varied, but are important outlets for Hollywood films.

Thus, film companies generate a good income from selling their films to pay cable. In 1984, it was estimated that the film business received $600 million from the pay cable market. Around the same time, pay cable revenues were said to contribute about $3 million to an average Hollywood film's revenues. These revenues have increased considerably since that time.

There also are exclusive deals arranged by the pay channels for film packages (although these practices smack of anti-trust violations). The efforts to obtain exclusive contracts have enhanced the competition between major pay services – that is, HBO/Cinemax vs. Showtime/TMC. But the competition also has led to arrangements that tie other pay services to specific studios.

Another trend affecting pay cable has been the proliferation of Hollywood blockbusters. It still takes big bucks to get the big films on pay cable, as mentioned above. Such deals also often include an arrangement for the production company to shoot footage for a making-of-the-movie featurette which will run on the pay cable channel to promote the film.

But there are other consequences of exclusive arrangements, long-term contracts, and blockbuster prices. New cable channels find it difficult to compete, with Time and Viacom still holding onto their "suffocating oligopoly."

## Pay-per-view

The possibility of viewers paying for individual programs or special events has been around for a while, in one form or another. Subscription television (STV) is the oldest of the pay TV approaches, in existence for the past 40 years. Coinciding with the cable boom in the late 1970s, several companies operated STV stations using over-the-air scrambled signals, a service that had been authorized by the FCC in 1968. By 1984, STV attracted 1.7 million subscribers. But it faced stiff competition from pay cable, as well as rising operating costs, subscriber complaints, and piracy problems.

Meanwhile, another option was offered called pay-per-view, with several services offered in late 1985. Viewer's Choice was started by The Movie Channel/Showtime, and Request TV was organized by former Showtime President, Jeffrey Reiss. Movies available on Viewer's Choice were to be offered at the same time as videocassette release.

Ultimately, STV couldn't compete with the growing cable systems, which increasingly offered some of these pay-per-view options. Addressable cable systems allowed customers to order specific programs or events for an extra fee beyond their monthly basic or pay cable charges. Overall, pay-per-view services garnered revenues of $2.5 billion in 2002.

Most often, when the exclusive home-video window closes, studio films are then made available to pay-per-view venues on both cable and satellite TV systems. At this stage, the movie is available exclusively for two to six weeks on PPV. (Note that the film will always be available on video after its initial availability, so "exclusivity" does not take into account the home video window.) Generally, studios will get anywhere from 45-55 percent of the revenues generated from PPV, depending on the individual movie and the number of PPV channels on which it can be exhibited.

While some pay cable companies have been viewed by the majors as formidable obstacles over control of an important distribution outlet, Hollywood has been more excited about pay-per-view. The film companies especially like pay-per-view's potential of bringing in as much as $40 million in one night for a blockbuster film. An example was *Star Wars* on PPV, which attracted 1.5 million customers at $8 each.

For the studios, pay-per-view represents an "unbundled" method of pricing, as opposed to the "bundled" pricing of pay-cable. In other words, it allows more direct pricing of a given film or supply of films.

While feature films have played a key role on PPV, there has been heavy competition from home video. Cable operators have been reluctant to add the addressable feature to systems as long as home video first receives feature films. Consequently, sporting events are currently more prevalent on PPV. For instance, Direct Ticket Pay-Per-View features a good deal of sports and pseudo-sports such as wrestling. However, films are also featured through Blockbuster Pay-Per-View Movies, a direct connection with the dominant home video retailer.

Hollywood films also are distributed via DBS or direct broadcast satellite systems, which attracted 19 million subscribers in 2002. DirecTV currently dominates the US market with 11 million subscribers and was finally purchased by Rupert Murdoch in 2003, adding to his worldwide network of satellite broadcasting, which already included BSkyB in Britain, Star TV in Asia, Foxtel in Australia, SkyTel in Latin America, and Stream in Italy. The other dominant DBS company in the US is EchoStar Communications Corp., which offers pay television services on its DISH Network to over 8 million subscribers.

### Issue: Concentration and integration

Concentration and integration are well established in the US cable industry. Concentration is especially strong in cable system operations, as well as in pay cable and program suppliers. And there is considerable integration between cable system operations, basic and pay cable ownership, as well as with program suppliers. Because of these integrated activities, it is increasingly more and more difficult to distinguish between cable, television and film industries, although the industries and the government still insist on these distinctions.

Industry lines continue to be blurred with HBO, once the "nemesis" of Hollywood, part of a company that incorporates one of the Hollywood majors. AOLTW's production activities are integrated with important cable television channels, while Viacom presents similar vertical integration. Integration of programming services makes it possible for cable operators to withhold programming from rival cable companies or new outlets, but also provide opportunities to expand profits from these companies' film commodities, as well.

## Television

Since the mid-1950s, television has provided another market for Hollywood films. This area includes broadcast TV (sometimes called "free" TV, a term that was questioned in the previous chapter), but also refers to advertiser-supported cable.

After a film reaches the premium cable or pay TV market, it may appear on network television about 12–18 months later, for one to two runs. Increasingly, the top-rated cable channels – USA Network, TBS, TNT – have been able to outbid the networks to obtain rights to broadcast movies. In some cases, the network or cable channel may even buy future runs at five- or ten-year intervals. (Note that many of these channels are owned by the majors, as indicated in Table 3.8)

The network or cable channel negotiates with distributors for each movie, typically paying the studio a fixed amount ranging from $3–15 million, depending on the movie and the number of runs. Television revenues were often higher before video and pay cable.

While network TV has often been a movie's penultimate revenue stream, it was a minor coup when Fox TV arranged for the television premiere of *Star Wars: The Phantom Menace*, immediately after it appeared in home video formats. (Recall that Fox also was the film's distributor.) The film was not the only one to bypass both the PPV and premium cable windows, as Disney decided to do the same with *Toy Story* by broadcasting the movie on its own network, ABC.

Following the broadcast premiere and second run (or however many runs the network or cable channel has bought the rights to broadcast), the movie then moves into the syndication market.

Films are sold in packages of 15–20 films to individual television stations, groups of stations, and advertiser-supported cable channels, usually 2–3 years after theatrical release. Films are licensed to the highest bidder on a title-by-title basis, and a single license fee is paid for the package. Still, for the distributor's profit calculations, a single film in the package is allocated a percentage of the total package license fee using a point system, based on factors such as theatrical revenues, running time, genre, talent, and network audience ratings. Sometimes films are sold to local television stations and groups on a cash-plus-barter system.

While television still represents a lucrative market for Hollywood films, it remains to be seen what will happen when (and if) any of the forms of Internet, video-on-demand or other new forms of distribution take hold. (More on these developments at the end of this chapter.)

## Non-theatrical markets

The largest non-theatrical market is the airlines. But films are also licensed to the military, hotels, schools, hospitals, prisons, colleges, public libraries, railroads, churches, oil companies, etc. Non-theatrical sales are typically negotiated flat fees or a specific amount per viewer, and represent a rather minor source of revenue.

### Airlines

In flight entertainment (IFE) has been around longer than many people may think. It began on air transport aircraft more than 35 years ago with film projection to the front of the passenger cabin. Needless to say, IFE has come a long way and continues to advance rapidly, both technologically and in terms of its economic potential.

The first inflight movie was in 1925, when a WWI converted Handley-Page bomber showed the black and white, silent film *The Lost World* during a 30-minute flight near London. It wasn't until 1961, however, when a company called Inflight Motion Pictures developed a 16mm film system for commercial aircraft, that feature films began to be exhibited on regularly scheduled commercial flights. An 8mm film cassette was developed in 1971, making it possible for flight attendants to change movies inflight. By 1978, an industry organization was formed, Airline Entertainment Association (AEA), later becoming the World Airline Entertainment Association (WAEA). The first VHS system was made available for airline use in 1978.

Obviously, the market for airline films has grown with the growing airline business. Annual airline expenditures on inflight entertainment and communication were $2.1 million in 2000, although this amount declined in 2001 ($1.5 million) and 2002 ($1.8 million) because of various problems in the air transport industry. Some of the companies involved in this market are Entertainment in Motion, Emphasis Inflight Entertainment and InterAct.

*Entertainment in Motion* was founded in 1988 and provides entertainment to over 130 airlines around the world. The company offers first-run theatrical films from Hollywood as well as first-run Chinese and French films. In addition to distributing films in their native language, the company distributes dubbed and subtitled versions in more than 12 different languages.

Another ancillary market is the sale of films for cruises. *Sea Movies*, a California-based company owned by Entertainment in Motion, sells movies to cruise lines around the world, representing yet another market for Hollywood films.

## Internet Film Distribution

Even though there has been a good deal of attention given to the Internet and digital media, models of film distribution and exhibition are evolving relatively slowly for these new media outlets. The final sections of this chapter consider unfolding developments in film distribution via the Internet and video-on-demand (VOD) utilizing either cable or telephone lines (or DSL).[9]

Some of the excitement over the Internet has been prompted by the possibilities for distributing new and interesting entertainment forms. Short films and some independent movies have been distributed via the Internet at sites such as Atomfilms, iFilms, CinemaNow, CinemaPop, and Hypnotic. Of course, Hollywood has always looked to such independent and experimental alternatives for innovative ideas, thus, everyone seems to be looking for the next *Blair Witch Project*. Nevertheless, the major Hollywood companies mostly have been unsuccessful in developing Internet sites with new content.[10]

Another possibility is the direct release of feature films via the Internet. On May 5, 2000, SightSound.com released *The Quantum Project*, billed as the "first direct-to-Internet movie," with a $3 million budget, known actors, and relatively high production values. Still, major Hollywood films continue to be released first in theaters, with little discussion of changing this release pattern.

Hollywood seems mostly concerned with the Internet as an additional outlet for the distribution of films sometime after they have appeared in theaters. In March 2001, MPAA head Jack Valenti announced that within a year, Hollywood features would be available for download via the Internet. "The studios have a history of watching, waiting and studying. They would have preferred to be able to do that, but the experience with Napster has told them that option is not available," explained Skip Paul, a former Universal executive who is now chairman of iFilm.

But even though the studios are reported to be formulating serious Internet strategies, it is still unclear as to how the online distribution of Hollywood films will unfold. Several scenarios might be possible:

(1) independent sites or middlemen; (2) each major with its own site; (3) one site for all majors; or, (4) several jointly-owned sites. The only option that does not seem likely is one jointly owned channel, because of obvious anti-trust violations.[12] While many may consider the distributors' ownership of any exhibition outlets to be problematic, it seems likely that the majors will gather additional revenues from distribution to a number of different sites – that is, after issues of control are settled (as will be discussed below). A few examples of existing services (or plans for future sites) will be discussed briefly in the next sections.

### Independent sites

*SightSound Technologies* claims to have rented the first full-length film download over the Internet in 1999. In January 2001, the service also offered Miramax's 1999 feature film, *Guinevere*, to be downloaded (not streamed) for a 24-hour viewing license at $3.49. The claim is that it was the first Hollywood movie offered online in a legal, non-pirated way. The Disney-owned Miramax also made a deal to offer 12 full-length features on SightSound, which offers other films (mostly porn and cheap indie films) for downloading.

During the summer of 2001, the company appeared to be struggling to stay afloat, cutting its workforce and complaining that

> For the last 10 years, the major motion picture studios and the major record labels have maintained an unnatural prohibition with their content on the Internet. And it is their unwillingness to utilize this new and useful way to distribute movies and music that has forced Sight-Sound Technologies to where it is today.[13]

*MovieFlix.* A company that seems to make some money by offering feature films online is MovieFlix. The site offers public-domain and independent movies that cost very little to acquire. Movieflix has two employees and has sold films such as *Femalien* and *Bruce Lee in New Guinea*, plus some soft-core adult content. The site makes a comfortable profit, with 6,300 subscribers paying $5.95 per month.

### Minor studio-owned sites

*CinemaNow* started streaming independent films both for free and for a fee in November 1999. The site is partly owned by Lions Gate

Entertainment, but also has received funding from Microsoft and Blockbuster. CinemaNow offers fee-based films in their traditional pay-per-view window and a subscription service. The company provides highly encrypted digital movies that make it difficult for pirates to copy. In June 2001 Hollywood.com joined CinemaNow, which offers pay-per-view films for $2.99 each, available for streaming at any time during a 48-hour window from the time of purchase. CinemaNow's library includes more than 1,200 films, mostly from independent companies. In 2002 the company arranged a deal with Warner Brothers, claiming that it was the first major Hollywood studio to offer video-on-demand services over the Web.

## Major studio-owned site

*Movielink.* Movielink was formed in 2001 and is owned equally by Sony Pictures Entertainment, Universal Studios, Paramount Pictures, Metro-Goldwyn-Mayer and Warner Bros. The project was finally launched November 11, 2002, representing the first time a large supply of recent, popular films were available legally on the Internet.

The site allows downloading of films over a high-speed Internet connection, with individual titles available for $1.99 to $4.99. The compressed files average about 500 megabytes in size and take about an hour to download with a high-speed DSL or cable modem connection. The films can be watched using media players from RealNetworks Inc. and Microsoft Corp. While the full-screen quality is roughly equivalent to that of a VHS tape, the image becomes worse when enlarged. Viewers can pause, fast forward and rewind the films. The movies can be viewed an unlimited number of times, but only during a 24-hour period. The movies delete themselves after the one-day license expires, and will sit on a computer hard drive for 30 days if not watched. The files are encrypted and will not play the movie if it is sent to another computer. A small program called "Movielink Manager" tracks downloaded files and how long a user has to watch them.

The company planned to test the service to determine consumer preferences, such as whether people want films in letterbox or full-screen format. Movielink started with about 170 titles, including recent films such as *A Beautiful Mind* and *Harry Potter and the Sorcerer's Stone*, but also offered classic films, as well. The studios provide films to the service about six weeks after they are released on DVD and home video.

Of course, a joint effort of five studios would seem to have anti-trust implications. In fact, The Walt Disney Co. and Fox Entertainment Group had formed their own rival video on demand service but it was disbanded early in 2002 after Fox pulled out, citing regulatory concerns. But even though the Movielink venture was reviewed by the anti-trust division of the Justice Department, the site's launch went forward.

Shortly following the launch, however, the following message was posted by the Chairman and CEO of another independent site called Intertainer:

> To The Intertainer Family:
> As many of you already know, on September 24th we filed a Federal Anti-trust suit against AOL Time Warner, Sony, Universal and Movielink. On October 21st we plan to take the site down until we can work out a fair business model with the defendants, who control more than 50 percent of the theatrical motion picture business and more than 60 percent of the music business. To the 147,000 broadband users who became Intertainer members and to our friends and colleagues in the trade, we appreciate your continued support. We promise to return when there is an environment in which the independent company such as ours is allowed to compete for your business. Whether the current environment of increasing media concentration is good for our Democracy is of course, the ultimate question.

It also might be noted that around this time, Intertainer went through nearly $125 million in venture capital and attracted only 147,000 customers. The site offered films via streaming, charging a $7.99 per month subscription.

Others were not impressed with the launch of Movielink, either. As one Internet observer commented:

> Fortunately for the movie studios, they probably don't care that they've greenlighted HudsonHawk.com. In fact, they almost certainly know that Movielink won't make them any money. The site, and the tens of millions of dollars that have been spent on it, are pure PR: The studios have seen how music executives have been vilified as greedy Luddites, and they want to avoid that fate. Movielink's primary purpose, as some people involved in the project admit, is to demonstrate that the studios are providing a legal alternative for Internet movie pirates.[14]

*Internet issues.* While the Internet continues to attract a good deal of attention, technological and economic questions continue. The technology has developed rapidly, with broadband Internet connections and compression technology making it possible to transmit large amounts of data relatively quickly. According to the US General Accounting Office, more than 100 million Americans were online in some way in 2000, however, only about 12 percent had high-speed or broadband access. Just over 10 percent of the 103 million US television households – or 10.9 million homes – had high-speed Internet access (cable, satellite, DSL, fiber, or wireless), while 39 percent or 43.2 million were running on dial-up modems.

Thus, for most people, receiving feature films via computers still is a relatively slow and cumbersome option and will remain so for the near future. For instance, several reporters reported numerous obstacles before managing to download *Guinevere* when it became available in early 2001. One writer reported that even at optimum speed, it took approximately 24 hours for the actual download. Another noted that, "Watching a film . . . while leaning forward staring at a computer isn't exactly a bring-out-the-popcorn kind of experience. Fifteen minutes into the film I gave up and took my dog for a walk."[15]

Besides the gnawing question of whether there are enough people who will pay to watch movies on computers, the other pressing issue, of course, is piracy. In a world where digital copies of films do not deteriorate with each copy, Hollywood is obviously concerned that digital pirates can easily produce huge quantities of copies, quickly, inexpensively, and from anywhere. With the industry already claiming $2 billion loss each year from the piracy of audiovisual products, digitized versions of Hollywood films present serious problems.

One estimate is that Hollywood films are traded online nearly 500,000 times each day from hundreds of sites. MediaForce, an online company that tracks pirated digital content, claimed that a million pirated downloads occurred during the month of June 2001, including box office hits, such as *Lara Croft: Tomb Raider, Shrek* and *Pearl Harbor.*

The industry's anti-piracy efforts are led by the MPAA, which is working on political solutions, trying to convince governments to enact strong legal protections, such as the Digital Millennium Copyright Act of 1998. Like the music labels, the studios have chosen to challenge piracy first in court. The industry took on iCraveTV, an online rebroadcaster based in Canada, and RecordTV, an online video recorder made available to the public by an Agoura Hills, California, company. Then they crippled another company, Scour Exchange, which went bankrupt within months of a suit being served.

In January 2000, the majors won a major battle when a US District Court found in favor of the studios in a suit that challenged the public posting of programming code that makes it easy to copy DVD movies. Most Hollywood movies on DVD include CSS (Content Scramble System), which has been used since 1996. With the code-breaking system, called DeCSS (Decrypt the Content Scramble System), DVDs can be played on any system. The code was published in *2600: The Hacker Quarterly*, considered the bible of hacker publications, and posted on its website (www.2600.com). One report summed up the court's decision on the case, noting that "The trial was a rout. The US District Court judge ruled in favor of the eight studios on every point."[16]

While technological issues ultimately may be sorted out (with some obvious help from the government), there are still economic questions to be answered. A major concern is how to profit from this new form of distribution. While other distribution outlets have provided additional profits with little added costs (for example, television, cable, videocassettes, DVDs, etc.), Internet distribution may be different. Content providers, such as the major film studios, may have to pay per-stream licensing costs to software companies (such as Real Networks or Quicktime) so customers can view videos, as well as per-stream charges to Internet service providers (such as AT&T). As one analyst recently explained, "The early model for broadband has been TV. But broadband is exactly the opposite of the broadcast world. Your costs go up as your audience grows."[17]

This also explains why advertising may not be in the picture. The size of audience needed to support advertising may not be possible without prohibitive costs. Still other analysts assume that the majors will solve these issues by distributing their films from their own servers, with relatively low distribution costs.

If revenues are forthcoming from some kind of Internet distribution, other questions remain about the timing (or "window") of a film's Internet release, and whether it ultimately will replace video and/or pay-TV. Rights to Internet distribution will have to be negotiated (especially for past films where such rights have not been imagined, much less specified), including issues relating to territoriality, and payments to talent and licensors. Certainly, Internet distribution rights will have to become (if they aren't already) an essential part of Hollywood deals (see Moore, 2000).

As for the reaction from audiences, film critic, Roger Ebert predicts:

> People won't stay away from the theater. They like to be in a crowd, get out of the house, go on dates – they like the whole movie-going experience. I do see online and theaters as different release patterns.

The online films will not be considered as good as what's in the theaters. Today, if a movie is released directly to video, or on cable, it is seen to be subtly inferior. That's not always the case, but that's the way people see it. If you made a really good movie, you wouldn't release it online. Theatrical releases will still be the way filmmakers want to get their films out.[18]

*Other Internet uses.* While the Hollywood majors are fighting digital pirates and sorting out ways to officially distribute their wares via the Internet, they also are using the technology in other ways. In addition to sites that offer industry news and information, all of the majors have web sites that promote their various businesses, as well as sites for individual movies, as will be discussed in Chapter 5.

## Video-on-Demand

### Cable

Some commentators believe that the majors would prefer an Internet/television combo, moving from a personal computer platform to a television-like platform. In other words, they would prefer getting the potatoes back to the couch for "lean back" rather than "lean forward" technologies. A television setting, with more sophisticated remote control devices and interactive electronic TV program guides, will allow not only movies to be delivered on demand, but pizza and other merchandise, as well.

VOD revenue was $192 million for 2001 and is predicted to grow to $4.75 billion by 2005. Furthermore, enthusiasts predict that VOD households will reach 27.8 million by 2005. But these estimates are made with the assumption that these services will be able to offer Hollywood movies. If 44 million homes are using VOD by 2010, the market may be worth anywhere from $2 billion to $6 billion a year. One report estimates that at least $1 billion in additional revenues may be forthcoming for the studios, which generally get about 50 percent of pay-per-view revenues from cable and satellite companies.[19]

But VOD delivered by cable also is dependent on the huge multiple-system operators (MSOs), such as Time Warner Cable, Insight Communications, Cox, and Comcast. Also involved are the companies producing the technology that will aggregate and store the content, companies such as Concurrent, Demand Video, DIVA, nCUBE, and SeaChange. When VOD on cable finally takes off, sales for such equipment is expected to reach $1-2 billion per year within the next five years.

One of the services that could become a major player is iN Demand, the industry pay-per-view consortium, owned by AT&T, Time Warner, and Comcast – three of the largest cable operators in the USA. But cable systems also are developing their own VOD services, as well.

Another version of film distribution via cable is Subscription VOD (or SVOD). For a single monthly fee, usually between $6-10 above basic subscription fees, subscribers have access to a list of titles that change monthly. The movies are available during the usual pay TV window.

Early efforts to implement a version of SVOD included HBO and Time Warner's Full Service Network (FSN) trial in Orlando, Florida, in the early 1990s, and Viacom's Showtime Anytime, tested in Castro Valley, California, in 1993. The services experienced technical and economic challenges, but have contributed important consumer research and business modeling for these companies' current plans.

HBO has tested an SVOD service called HBO On Demand, in Columbia, South Carolina, which allows subscribers to watch original HBO programming, including *The Sopranos* and *Sex and the City*, as well as films from Warners, DreamWorks, and Fox. The service is set up similar to pay-per-view, although subscribers can watch films whenever they want. Showtime planned to begin trials sometime in 2001, with a service that would offer movies from Paramount and MGM, plus original programming.

A similar service is offered by Starz Encore, a subsidiary of Liberty Media, which claims that it is the largest provider of cable and satellite-delivered premium movie channels in the USA. Starz Encore owns 15 domestic channels and offers various themed movie packages, including films from Disney, Sony and Universal.

## DSL

Another VOD option is delivery by way of high-speed telephone lines. An example is Intertainer, a service that sends its signals over private computer networks, connecting to homes either by digital subscriber line (DSL) or digital cable. Consumers buy a device that switches the signal from their computer to their TV set. Most customers receive the service via DSL, which involves going to the Intertainer icon on the DSL provider's home Web page that gets them into the computer network. After typing in a password, customers choose a movie, and get billed either through their credit card or their DSL provider. Intertainer may eventually be available as an added feature of digital cable, available through a set-top box with remote control.

Originally formed in 1996, the project includes a range of investors, including Comcast, Intel, Microsoft, NBC, Sony and Qwest. The service offers recent motion pictures from a number of major studios (Universal, Warner Bros, Dreamworks, Fox, New Line Cinema, Columbia/TriStar), and pricing options include pay-per-view and package options. While Intertainer currently offers films after their home video release like other VOD services, it is unclear how much of its program fees go to content providers. Also, Comcast is the only cable operator that is testing the service, so it will likely have to continue to rely mostly on telephone companies' DSL services.

It is unclear how successful Intertainer will become, as much depends on relationships with both the Hollywood content providers and eventually, cable operators. A similar service was planned between Blockbuster (the video store giant) and Enron (a telecommunications company). EBEntertainment was to be a "high-speed, closed phone line VOD service." But without much support from the Hollywood majors (only MGM agreed to offer its film archives), the project folded in mid-2001. While Hollywood's lack of cooperation may have represented a wait-and-see attitude, it also seems likely that the studios intended to prevent Blockbuster from gaining an edge in yet another lucrative outlet for their products.

**VOD issues.** Even though many feel that VOD, in one form or another, is an inevitability, there are still some unresolved issues. It seems clear that cable companies want VOD – and they feel that they need Hollywood movies – to better compete with satellite services. However, one of their big problems is the reluctance of Hollywood companies to supply content. As the head of Viacom explained at a cable industry convention in 2001: "Paramount wants to make money with its films, and video-on-demand could end up displacing existing revenue from video rentals and sales."[20] Of course, home video is the single largest revenue source for the Hollywood films, attracting over $15 billion in 2000. Thus, for Hollywood companies, any form of VOD will need to supplement, but not detract from, home video revenues, or completely replace those revenues.

Another possibility, however, is the simultaneous release of films on DVD and VOD, which would replace the current pay-per-view business. Others feel that VOD can replace the video rental business where the studios are dependent on a highly concentrated retail business (Blockbuster).

Clearly, the timing of VOD releases, as well as the licensing arrangements between the studios and VOD companies, are key issues. According to some sources, the studios are demanding around 70 percent of the revenue from VOD, although Universal's deal with iN Demand was said to be a 60 percent deal.[21] Until some of these technical and economic wrinkles are ironed out, video-on-demand may continue to be (as many observers have already noted) video on delay.

This chapter has presented a brief overview of some of the current and newly developing outlets for Hollywood films. As new markets become viable and profitable, older outlets either decline or adjust. In addition, the industry continues to expand with the production of additional commodities and the expansion of existing markets. These developments are discussed in Chapter 4.

## Notes

1 *Advertising Age* is the general source for these developments, although *Variety* and *Box Office* provide relevant information on theater advertising, as well.
2 C. Diorio, "Regal Ramps up Pre-show Push: Hall Looks to Blur Line Between Entertainment, Advertising," *Variety*, 13 November 2002, p. 17. It might be noted that these announcements were made after Regal's consolidation of two other theater chains, discussed further in the next section of this chapter.
3 S. Vranica, "Marketing at the Movies," *Wall Street Journal*, 5 September 2002.
4 Much has been written on the history of censorship (see especially Lewis, 2000). This section is drawn especially from natoonline.com, and mpaa.org.
5 This section is a version of J. Wasko, "The Future of Film Distribution and Exhibition," in Harries, 2002, pp. 195–206.
6 This section is adapted from J. Wasko, 1994.
7 This section relies on information from industry trade publications, such as *Video Marketing Newsletter*, *Variety*, and *Billboard*, as well as Lardner (1987), Moret (1991), and Wasser (2001).

8 Most of this discussion relies on reports in *Variety* and other trade publications.

9 This section is based on Harries (2002).

10 Examples include Digital Entertainment Network, Warner's Entertaindom, and pop.com.

11 Cited in L. Rich, "Hollywood Braces for 'Napsterization'," CNN.com, 20 January 2001, <www.cnn.com/2001/TECH/computing/01/10/hollywood. napsterization.idg/.

12 The majors tried a jointly-owned channel (called Premiere) to distribute their films on pay-cable, but could not get away with the blatant disregard for anti-trust law. See Wasko, 1994, pp. 78–9.

13 P. Sweeting, "Sight Sound Shrinks Workforce." *VideoBusiness Online*, 9 July 2001, <www.videobusiness.com/news/070901_sightsound_layoffs. asp.

14 B. Fritz, "HudsonHawk.com: Movielink Will be Another Internet Flop," *Variety*, 11 November, 2002, p. 9.

15 C. Tristram, "Broadband's Coming Attractions," *Technology Review*, June 2001, p. 72.

16 J. Shprintz, "Hack to the Future," *Premiere*, March 2001, http:// www.premiere.com/Premiere/Features/301/hackers.html.

17 C. Tristram, "Broadband's Coming Attractions," *Technology Review*, June 2001, p. 72.

18 Quoted in D. Ferris, "Roger Ebert on Digital Movies," CNN.com, 2 August 2000, <www.cnn.com/2000/TECH/computing/08/02/ebert. interview.idg/ 7.

19 J. Black, "Video-on-Demand: Hollywood is Missing the Big Picture," *Business Week*, 26 March 2001, p. 71.

20 P. Sweeting, "Vod is MIA at NCTA," *Video Business Online*, 13 June 2001, http://www.videobusiness.cothem/news/061301_ncta_VOD_no-show.asp

21 P. Sweeting, "Universal Opens Window on iN Demand Cable VOD Deal," *Video Business Online*, 20 July 2001, http://www.videobusiness.com/news/ 072001_universal_vod_indemand.asp

# Expanding the Industry 4

Hollywood and the film industry are constantly changing, and usually expanding, due to the continual search for profit. Some of the industry's expansion strategies have involved efforts to commercialize various areas, to produce additional products, to connect to other diversified activities, and to seek additional retail markets. This chapter will discuss these trends, namely, commercialization, commodification, diversification, and globalization, as they apply to the US film industry.

## Commercialization/Commodification

In the past few decades, the Hollywood industry has become more explicitly commercialized through the practice of featuring products in films. In addition, more commodities are being produced in conjunction with feature films in the form of merchandise, as well as the production of media products that flow out of the primary film commodity. The next sections will discuss commercialization in the form of product placement and commodification in terms of merchandising.

### Product placement

The latest James Bond film, *Die Another Day*, features over 20 branded products that were not included in the film by accident. Bond drives an Aston Martin, the bad guy (Zao) drives a Jaguar, and the heroine (Jinx) is assigned a Thunderbird. Meanwhile, Range Rovers are used extensively as utility vehicles. Bond drinks Finlandia vodka, sips Bollinger champagne, and shaves with the latest Norelco electric shaver.

All of these products were deliberately "placed" in the film. While some of the companies paid specific fees for their products to appear in the film, most placements were arranged on a barter basis with the companies supplying products and technical assistance to the production company. But, more importantly, 007's "partners" coughed up over $120 million in advertising that featured the film as well as the products. The campaign included global television, print, radio, and outdoor advertising, plus various sweepstakes and other promotions. No wonder *Time* magazine suggested that the film might have been called, *Buy Another Day*.

During the 1980s, product placement evolved into a full-fledged industry. By the end of the decade, the major studios included departments specifically dedicated to product placement and the process began to gain widespread recognition (Turcotte, 1995).

> We've moved from an unstructured era of product placement – where products got into movies because $50 was put in the pocket of the prop master if he would put that soft drink in front of the camera – to where companies are professionally reading scripts, looking for opportunities for their clients, and paying fees directly to the production to have that product in the movie. (PBS, 2001)

This section will consider different types of product placement, the various players involved in the process, and some of the implications of this development.

**Product placement types.**  Three basic types of product placement are often discussed: visual, spoken and usage. A visual placement occurs when a product, service, or logo can simply be observed. A spoken placement occurs when an actor or off-screen voice mentions a product, service, or corporation. A usage placement occurs when an actor or actress actually handles or interacts with a product, service, or corporation. A placement that involves usage often includes both a visual and spoken element as well (Turcotte, 1995). More recently, of course, products have moved into important narrative roles with entire movies revolving around specific products, as in the case of *Cast Away* and *You've Got Mail*. Branded products and services played major roles in these two films, with narrative elements structured around the products. At least in the case of *Cast Away*, the two products featured (Federal Express and Wilson Volleyballs) reportedly appeared without direct payment. However, the major narrative role given to these products was significant and pushed the product placement phenomenon to a new level.

It is difficult to estimate how much is generated overall or even from specific product placement deals, as they vary tremendously. While huge amounts have been claimed from key placements, as noted above, no payment is made for some product appearances. On the other hand, arrangements often involve a barter deal, as in the case of *Die Another Day* above. In addition to paying for the placement of a product in a film, the process also increasingly involves promotion and marketing campaigns. An earlier example was the $100,000 that Nabisco paid for Baby Ruth candy bars to be shown in *The Goonies*. But the company also agreed to provide $1.5 million dollars in network advertising and to give away movie posters with the purchase of its candy at displays in 37,000 stores. Although a producer may benefit from payment received for placing the product in the film, distributors may find that promotional campaigns are often the most alluring aspect of a product placement deal.

Product placements with promotional tie-ins are invaluable for a film's marketing campaign, as explained by a successful marketing executive:

> The value of a promotion to the marketing department is if you can have other people supporting the movie – and it's their money, not the studio money – it just adds to the pressure in the marketplace. It adds to the awareness of the movie. . . . It's not only the studio that's talking about it. It's on the front page of *Time* magazine. *Dateline* had it on last night with the star. I go to my 7-Eleven, the soft drink I buy is doing it. It's everywhere. (PBS, 2001)

In addition, some deals are developing into more elaborate corporate partnerships. For instance, in July 2001, Vivendi Universal and Toyota arranged a marketing and promotion partnership that they claimed was the biggest deal ever between a show business conglomerate and a major automobile company. The agreement covers all of Universal's businesses, including theme parks, motion pictures, TV, consumer products, online ventures, video games and music. The arrangement builds on an already existing multi-year deal in Japan between Toyota Motor Corp. and Universal Studios Japan.

The deal provides for Toyota to receive first-look opportunities for product placement and promotion in Universal-produced films, home video, and DVD releases. In addition, Toyota is allowed to use various Universal properties, including characters and film and music library products, in its advertising and sponsorship opportunities on

Universal's channels overseas, as well as placement in interactive video games. At the end of 2002, Toyota was planning exclusive sponsorships of theme park rides and attractions based on films such as *Back to the Future*, *Men in Black* and *Spider-man*.[1]

Not every placement situation is ideal, however. This was exemplified by the well-publicized incident involving the placement of Coca-Cola in *Natural Born Killers*, where the product was associated with "violent images of psychotic mass murders" (Turcotte, 1995). Other examples might be cited, as well.

Product placement also is not universal in that identifiable products do not appear in all Hollywood films. Yet, the practice is still common and seems to be growing. While it is possible that placements are a potential source of production funding for some films, it might be stressed again that product placement is probably more important as it contributes to the advertising and marketing of a film.

A specific process for product placement in Hollywood films has evolved over the years, involving the studios, corporations and advertisers, and product placement agencies.[2]

**The studios.** At least one executive at each of the major studios is assigned to product placements. Some of the companies refer to this responsibility as "production resources," while others refer to it directly as "product placement." This department serves as an intermediary between the filmmakers and the corporate marketers or their agents. The studio executives who are dedicated to product placement frequently interact with film producers, prop masters, and other production people, as well as with executives from other studio departments, particularly those involving clearances and promotions.

The studio executive's first step is to read and analyze scripts for upcoming films that are scheduled to go into production and to prepare a breakdown of potential product placement opportunities. In addition, the production team (producer, director, prop master, set decorator, set designers, etc.) generally develops two lists of items needed for the film, which are then forwarded to the production resources department.

The first list includes items required to shoot the film, which may or may not involve specific brands. The second list includes additional items that the production team would like to have. The studio executive compares notes with the production team and then attempts to find the products and make the deals. The first call is frequently to the numerous product placement agencies that represent many of the corporations that have established an interest in this specialized method of promotion. The next calls are usually to the corporate marketers who have established offices specifically dedicated to serving their product placement or entertainment marketing needs.

The role of prop masters within the business of product placement has changed considerably over the years, as decisions made about what props are used are significant for potential placement deals. However, it is also important to point out that decisions about product placement are made not only by producers and other management personnel, but also by "above-the-line" talent, in other words, writers, directors, and the stars.

Talent agencies also are becoming involved with product placement deals. Not only are agencies aware of film projects from their conception, they represent writers who can add a product or company name to a script in the first draft and then sell that placement to corporate clients. In addition, directors represented by the agencies can be encouraged to feature the product prominently in the film.

**Advertisers.**   Major consumer companies such as Anheuser-Busch, Ford, Kodak, AT&T, and Coke (the "brands", as *Variety* calls them) have made a major commitment to product placement and other forms of entertainment marketing. AT&T, for instance, had 500 clear placements in 1993, while Ford had nearly 350 placements worldwide that same year.

Corporations sometimes arrange their own placements, thus following an "in house" model. Some corporations, particularly large consumer goods companies, operate entertainment marketing offices, usually based in LA, which deal directly with the studios. Deals are arranged individually or through long-term deals, as in the example of the Universal/Toyota arrangement discussed previously.

Advertisers also are becoming more directly involved in creating entertainment, or as *Variety* calls it, advertainment. Companies participating in such original, reality-based or scripted entertainment have included BMW, Chrysler, Ford, General Motors, Home Depot, Nike, and Quicksilver, among others.

In fact, in late 2002, Universal Pictures formed a Brand Group that, among other things, would be involved in creating branded entertainment around the studio's films. One project was to produce a reality car-improvement show for a cable network like TLC that would be based on *The Fast and the Furious* sequel (*2 Fast 2 Furious*), which could be sponsored and paid for by auto repair chain Pep Boys.

Numerous problems emerge with such projects, which means that they can become stuck in development hell. While producers and studios are anxious to find co-financing partners for films, they are sometimes viewed as only interested in a brand's money without a promotional partnership. Advertisers have their own impression of how the industry works and are often surprised at film costs. In addition, deals can become complicated with too many power players involved. As a *Variety* writer explains:

> Film creatives behind projects don't want to be dictated to by a brand who wants more shots of its car's front grille or thinks the tires are too muddy. Then there are the egos. Although Hollywood's tenpercenteries have partnered up with Madison Avenue's ad agencies, a clash of egos on both coasts exists, creating a power struggle that focuses discussions more around clout than on creativity.[3]

Meanwhile, some advertisers are sponsoring short films featuring their products shown on the Internet. Examples include BMW, Skyy Vodka, Ford, Chrysler, and Perrier.

*Product placement agencies.* Most of the corporations interested in product placement opportunities use a placement agency to deal with the studios. Companies may pay a fee of $7,500 to $100,000 per year, although the average is around $24,000. Agencies usually ask for one- to two-year contracts. Most of the successful product placement agencies today were started less than 15 years ago and many of them even more recently. The vast majority of agencies are located in the Los Angeles area. (See Table 4.1 for a list of product placement agencies.)

As an industry analyst observes: "The product placement agent doesn't represent people; he represents products. One agent might represent several non-competing products: Mar's bars for candy, Dr. Pepper for soda, Coors for beer, Ford for cars, and so forth" (Litwak, 1986). In other words, the product placement agent spends his time looking for suitable scripts and placements for products.

Placement agencies often offer more than product placement, however, with many offering a full array of entertainment marketing services, ranging from coordinated promotions with entertainment themes to seeking licensing opportunities with entertainment companies. One of the top agencies is actually a public relations firm that specializes in the entertainment business.

Agency executives work similarly to the studio executives in that they receive scripts, which they review for product placement and other entertainment marketing opportunities for their clients. They

TABLE 4.1   *Product placement agencies*

| Firm | State |
| --- | --- |
| Feature This! | CA |
| Vista Group | CA |
| Norm Marshall & Associates | CA |
| Hollywood International Placements | CA |
| Hero Product Placement | CA |
| Cine Promotion Germany | |
| Creative Entertainment | CA |
| Dave Brown Entertainment | CA |
| Aim Promotions | NY |
| Prime Time Marketing | ILL |
| ICM | CA |
| Rogers & Cowan Inc | CA |
| Product Placement New Zealand | |
| Showcase Placements | CA |
| Rave Revues | CA |
| Promo & Props | CA |
| International Promotions | CA |
| UPP | CA |

then contact the studios and their clients with these ideas. Next, they negotiate the deals on behalf of their clients. Finally, they present their clients with "visibility reports" which detail the results of their product placement efforts.

The advantages of using a product placement agent may seem obvious. As a product placement company boasts on its website: "They need you. You need them. We make it all happen" (PropStar Placements). Agents handle the negotiations for cash payments and/ or promotional campaigns for products connected with a film. At the minimum, agents arrange for release forms for the product's use in a film. While including a product in a film without permission is not necessarily a violation of a manufacturer's rights, written permission avoids a possible lawsuit.

Agents also can obtain samples or "freebies" that can be used as props or by the production company during a shoot, obviously lowering production costs. Other more costly items (such as cars, jewelry, etc.) can be loaned during a film's production.

**ERMA.**  Product placement has grown so much that there is a trade organization to promote the business. The Entertainment Resources & Marketing Association (ERMA) was founded in 1991, with membership including the major film studios, production companies, product placement agencies, and corporate marketers. One of ERMA's executives explains:

We've encouraged people to come out of the closet about product placement. Whereas only five years ago people were hiding. They thought what they did was wrong and that the public was against it. They found out the public is actually for it. The production people are for it. The companies are for it. There is really only a very small segment of people who are opposed to product placement. (cited in Turcotte, 1995)

It's not clear who is referred to as that "very small segment of people," but it is clear that there is far more commercialization going on in Hollywood films these days. Before we turn to the implications and issues of these developments, another strategy for expanding Hollywood companies' profits will be presented in the next section.

## Merchandising

While Hollywood films historically have helped sell some products, the deliberate production of additional commodities associated with the film commodity has accelerated tremendously over the past few decades. Until the 1960s/1970s, relatively little merchandising activity took place in Hollywood, except for Disney. Merchandising started for the Disney brothers with the tremendous success of Mickey Mouse's *Steamboat Willie.* In 1929 the company was offered $300 to put Mickey Mouse on writing tablets. Then, during the 1930s, a wide range of Disney products appeared in markets around the world, everything from soap to ice cream to Cartier diamond bracelets. The extra income helped to finance expensive production at the Disney studio. Mickey is still claimed to be the most popular licensed character in the world and appears on thousands of merchandise items and publications.

Yet the Disney Company has been the exception, rather than the rule. The motion picture industry may have been relatively slow to pick up on merchandising, but this type of activity has accelerated dramatically. The current phase of film-based licensing can be traced back to the merchandising successes of *Star Wars* and *E.T.* in the 1970s, but has continued with blockbuster, action-figure based films (*Batman, Spider-Man,* etc.), and the successful franchise films early in the twenty-first century (*The Lord of the Rings, Harry Potter*).

Further interconnections between products and films were presented in *A Bug's Life* and *Toy Story,* films that were about toys or particularly toyetic characters. As one industry observer notes,

"Rarely has such synergy between movies and products been so fully realized" (Litwak, 1986). Perhaps another plateau will be reached when the film *Food Fight* is released – it is set in a supermarket where products on the shelves come to life at night.

The distinction between tie-ins and merchandise is often blurred, as some merchandise is produced for tie-ins. Merchandise here is defined as commodities based on movie themes, characters, or images which are designed, produced and marketed for direct sale, and not connected to other products or services as with tie-ins. An example of a tie-in is represented by the promotion of Disney films at McDonald's.

Licensing is the legal act or process of selling or buying property rights to produce commodities using specific copyrighted properties. On the other hand, merchandising can be thought of as the mechanical act of making or selling a product based on a copyrightable product.

There is an extremely wide variety of movie-based merchandise, including items based on a specific movie, character or theme, or ongoing movie characters and themes. While there has been a strong emphasis on children's toys, games and other such items (lunch boxes, school supplies, etc.), movie-based merchandise also includes home furnishings (clocks, towels, bedding, mugs, telephones), clothing, jewelry, stationary items, print material (novelizations, posters, etc.), food (especially cereals and candy), and decorations (such as Christmas ornaments).

There are also more unusual, less mass-produced items that sometimes accompany (or follow) movie releases, including "art objects" such as prints, sculptures, ceramic figures, and animation sets. Other merchandise is based on the celebrity status of Hollywood stars, or generic movie or studio merchandise.

While movie-based merchandising can be viewed as part of the proliferation of commercialization in Hollywood, this type of activity is part of a larger merchandising and licensing trend. While licensed products represented $66.5 billion in retail sales in 1990, according to the trade publication *Licensing Letter*, such products now generate more than $73 billion dollars a year, of which $16 billion is derived from entertainment such as movies. Exact estimates of the film industry's merchandising revenue are difficult to find, however, an international licensing group estimated that $2.6 billion was generated from movie licensing royalties during 2002.

This type of business is also quite concentrated with just a few large players dominating the licensing activity. Again, the major players in character and entertainment licensing are the big movie studios and broadcasting companies.

Entire TV programs and characters – especially those aimed at children – are an obvious and prevalent form of merchandising, while sports teams and players, rock stars, and musical groups have long histories of licensing and merchandising activities. Movie-based merchandise is enhanced by the proliferation of such activities, as well as the massive, coordinated merchandising campaigns – often started months before a film's release – associated with a few blockbuster films. Again, this merchandising bonanza continues to grow. The first *Batman* set numerous records when it grossed $250 million and earned $50 million in licensing fees. And then along came *Spider-Man* . . .

*Spider-Man*, the wildly successful film released in spring 2002, represents an interesting case of movie merchandising[4]. The character of Spider-Man has existed for almost 40 years, created by Stan Lee at Marvel Comics in the early 1960s. Prior to its film debut in 2002, the character had been seen in comic books, multiple cartoons, and briefly, a live action television show. The comics alone are sold in more than 75 countries and in 22 different languages. In spite of this, it took more than 15 years for a movie on the character to be made. With such a long history, it isn't surprising that the film was highly anticipated, and that Sony went into overdrive to promote and prepare merchandise for the blockbuster. *Spider-Man* was to be, as *Business Week's* Hollywood reporter put it, "the holy grail" for Sony: a film which would create opportunities for endless fast-food tie-ins, video games, toys, and sequels.

The character's history was a troubled one. Marvel Comics was facing bankruptcy, and, in 1985, sold the film rights to Cannon Films, owned by Menahen Golan, for $225,000. Golan then spent $2 million on a number of unworkable scripts for the project. Cannon Films itself was bought by Pathe Communications, which then also went bankrupt. Golan, however, took the film rights with him to his new company, 21st Century Films, as part of his separation deal with Pathe Communications. However, he was still unable to finance the film, and sold the TV rights to Viacom in 1988, while theatrical rights were sold to Carolco for $5 million. Carolco signed James Cameron to write the script, and overnight, the film's budget went from $15 million to $50 million. However, multiple lawsuits in 1993 – combined with the bankruptcy filings of Marvel Comics, Carolco, and 21st Century Pictures – left the film in limbo.

Ultimately, the rights sold to Golan were said to have expired and Marvel, emerging from bankruptcy in 1998, settled the previous suits, and sold the film rights to Sony for $7 million. The film, which debuted in May 2002, earned almost $115 million in its opening weekend and over $400 million by the end of 2002, making it the highest grossing comic book adaptation as well as the highest grossing movie of the summer. Such numbers are particularly impressive in light of estimates that as much as 80 percent of a film's revenue now comes from the sale and rental of videos and DVDs as well as merchandising.

The film, which cost $139 million to make, cost $50 million to market, a process that began long before the film came out. Sony is reported to have spent upwards of $5 million alone for a package of commercials during Super Bowl XXXVI. During the 13 30-second spots, Sony aired commercials for *Spider-Man*, as well as *Men In Black II*, *Stuart Little II*, and *XXX*.

Not surprisingly considering the long, convoluted history that brought Spider-Man to the big screen, the licensing deals for the film have been complex as well, with Marvel Enterprises and Sony sharing the royalties in a 50/50 deal managed by the newly formed Spider-Man Merchandising, LP, created in early 2002 to manage the character.

*Spider-Man* also benefited from a number of important tie-ins including deals with Reebok shoes, Wal-Mart, Nokia, Kellogg, Dr. Pepper, Hershey, and CKE-owned food chains Hardee's and Carl's Jr. Perhaps most impressive, however, was the addition of Cingular Wireless to the mix, bringing the sizable budget of a telecom company into the merchandising stream. And, of course, there were the toys. Some estimates place the value of the market for licensed children's toys at $27 billion, a sizable fraction of the $132 billion market for all licensed children's products. Rights to produce *Spider-Man* video games were sold to Activision, which produces games not only for Sony's Playstation 2, but also for the Microsoft-owned rival Xbox system and for home computers as well.

**Merchandising process.**   As demonstrated in this case, film producers and distributors rarely manufacture film-related products themselves, but license the right to sell these products to other companies (called the licensees). In most instances there is no risk to the producer or distributor (or, the licensor) because the licensee incurs all manufacturing and distribution expenses. The producer/distributor typically receives an advance payment for each product, as well as royalty payments, often between 5–10 percent of gross revenues from sales to retailers (i.e., the wholesale price). If the movie does not succeed and the products don't sell, the manufacturer is responsible for the loss (Cones, 1997).

The owners of licensable properties are most often the major entertainment companies discussed previously. Special licensing divisions often are organized to handle the company's own copyrighted properties, and sometimes, those owned by others, as well, e.g. Warner's Licensing Corporation of America (LCA) and Disney's Consumer Products division. But even smaller, successful film producers sometimes become involved in licensing, as represented by Lucasfilm Licensing.

The proliferation of movie merchandising is related to the sales of general merchandising, as well as the increase in animated features and the re-release and remakes of films with readily identifiable, ongoing characters and themes. The major studios realize that not only can the sale of movie-related products generate substantial revenue, but these products can be used effectively to promote films. Typically, 40 percent of movie merchandise is sold before a film is released.

The benefits for studios are the increased profits that may contribute to production costs. Although movie-related merchandise often is popular, products based on films are sometimes considered risky for merchandisers, as they ultimately may not be successful and often have short life-spans. Licensees may have to take further risks initially by sinking money into a film that is not completed (or sometimes not even started). On the other hand, a studio may need to change a release date, especially to coincide with the lucrative Christmas season or to avoid other competing films. But for the most part, licensing represents a potential source of income to film companies and merchandisers.

It might be noted that many movies have limited merchandising potential. While *Star Wars* and *Harry Potter* films will produce additional revenues from a seemingly endless stream of merchandise, films like *Saving Private Ryan*, *Elizabeth* and *Life is Beautiful*, have much less merchandising potential. Musicals, such as *Saturday Night Fever*, *Grease*, *Flashdance*, and *Dirty Dancing*, can earn substantial revenues from soundtrack recordings. Moreover, a hit song can promote a film. In fact, music videos have become important marketing tools (see Cones, 1992). The ideals, of course, are film franchises such as *Star Wars*, *Harry Potter*, and other similar films that continue to produce additional commodities, and thus, additional profits.

## Video games

The businesses of film and video games have become increasingly intertwined over the past two decades and deserve some additional attention here.[5] One of the obvious links is Sony Corp.'s dominant role in the video hardware business through its PlayStation system and its ownership of one of the major studios, Columbia Tristar. Sony commands at least 50 percent of the market share for the sale of video game hardware in the USA. The video game industry had close to $10.4 billion in total sales at the end of 2002. Software sales accounted for more than half of these revenues. According to the Video Software Dealer's Association, Americans spent $633.6 million renting video games in 2001.

The videogames industry has relied heavily on Hollywood films for inspiration in the creation of products and has profited from this relationship. One estimate is that between $1 and $1.4 billion was earned by the major studios from movie-based games, representing one of Hollywood's biggest source of licensing revenue. From the standpoint of video game makers, the stronger a film's brand, the better it will probably do as a game. Among the most profitable games of 2002 were those based on *Harry Potter*, *Lord of the Rings*, and *Star Wars*. Not surprisingly, as the profitability of video games has risen, the greater the interest and, hence, involvement by Hollywood. Currently, every major studio either owns or has long-standing license agreements with video game producers.

However, this was not always the case. Not surprisingly, in the early days of film/video game synergy, it was the producers of video games who came knocking. Uncertain about the future of video games, the majors preferred a wait-and-see attitude. Rather than participate in the creation of their own games, the majors tended to license their brands, such as Indiana Jones or James Bond, to video game producers who would attempt to adapt the film's story onto a basic video game prototype (Kent, 2001).

One of the first interactions between Hollywood and the gaming business was Warner's purchase of Atari in 1976 during the early years of game development. Although Warner owned Atari until 1996, the first cross-overs between films and games didn't really occur until the early 1980s, just as the home video game business hit a major slump. Just as Atari reached its peak in 1982, it released *E.T. The Extraterrestrial* based on the blockbuster movie. Within a year, the company had to destroy more than 6 million copies (Sheff, 1993). Video games based on the successful Indiana Jones films met a similar fate that same year. The market for home video games did not improve until around 1990.

But while the home video game was in distress, arcade games offered another area for experiment. At the same time Atari was faltering, arcade games based on films were coming into their own. In the same year that Atari debuted the first movie using computer-generated effects, Disney also launched a popular arcade game based on its film *Tron*, in conjunction with Bally/Midway. The game did so well that the company ultimately created a second game based on the film, *Disks of Tron* (Kent, 2001).

Other industry players experimented with video games as well. Don Bluth, former Disney animator, helped create the arcade sensation *Dragon's Lair*, which featured graphics much closer to an animated cartoon than to any existing video game. The game was so successful that the company releasing it was saved from Chapter 11, selling more than 16,000 machines at a price of $4,300 each (ibid.).

However, while the relationship between Hollywood and the video game industry continued, it did so slowly. It was not until the early 1990s that Hollywood began to try and reverse the flow of synergy. In 1993, Disney released the first movie based on a video game, *Super Mario Brothers*, based on the hit Nintendo video game. The main character, Mario, may in fact be the best example of synergy in the video game industry, having been created in 1983 as a part of the then best-selling game *Donkey Kong*. The combined successes of the video game and the film spurred Hollywood to test the waters further, creating an increasing number of films based on video games, including Paramount's *Lara Croft: Tomb Raider*, Sony's *Final Fantasy: The Spirits Within*, and Warner Brothers' movies based on Pokemon (see Table 4.2).

Ultimately, synergy between the two industries has proven lucrative for both, with estimates of cross-licensing earning more than $1 billion for each industry during the year 2000. In part this may be due to the video game industry's recognition that games can be targeted at many more audiences, in particular older, more affluent groups. Thus, it seems likely that the Hollywood/videogame relationship will continue.

### Issue: Movies and consumption

While product placements, tie-ins and merchandising are not characteristic of all Hollywood films, it is clear that these commercial

TABLE 4.2  *Top ten video game-based films*

| Film Title | Studio | Adjusted Gross | Release Date |
|---|---|---|---|
| *Lara Croft: Tomb Raider* | Paramount | $131.2 million | 6/15/2001 |
| *Pokemon: The First Movie* | Warner Brothers | $ 95.5 million | 11/10/1999 |
| *Mortal Kombat* | New Line | $ 91.7 million | 8/18/1999 |
| *Pokemon: The Movie 2000* | Warner Brothers | $ 45.9 million | 7/21/2000 |
| *Street Fighter* | Universal | $ 45.3 million | 12/23/1994 |
| *Mortal Kombat: Annihilation* | New Line | $ 44.3 million | 11/21/1997 |
| *Final Fantasy: The Spirits Within* | Sony | $ 32.1 million | 7/11/2001 |
| *Super Mario Bros.* | Disney | $ 28.6 million | 5/28/1993 |
| *Resident Evil* | Sony | $ 17.7 million | 3/15/2002 |
| *Pokemon 3: The Movie* | Warner Brothers | $ 17.1 million | 4/6/2001 |

*Source*: Boxofficemojo.com
*Note*: Gross adjusted for ticket price inflation.

activities have accelerated dramatically over the last decade. Blockbuster films and those oriented to children are the most common examples of these trends, although films appealing to a more narrowly targeted audiences are not exempt. Many movies are obvious and blatant commercials for other products, in addition to their role as cultural commodities themselves.

It also seems obvious that there is far more coordination of these activities, thus the potential for more profits but from fewer ideas. In other words, there is even more deliberate commercialization surrounding the production and distribution of Hollywood films than in the past and with creative, economic, and cultural implications.[6]

Product placement is often justified in terms of contributing to film realism. Indeed, one of the product placement agencies' motto is: "Helping to create a real world" (PropStar Placements). However, it is also possible that narratives may be altered to accommodate products. It also is important to note that the products placed are those of the largest and most powerful producers and thus may not be a true indication of the variety or use of products in the marketplace.

One result of this general acceptance of movies as a viable advertising medium (product placements, in theaters and on video) is that advertisers are likely to get involved in the whole process at a much earlier stage. Beginning with script searches to place products, to advertising and product promotion in theaters, to ads appearing on cassettes, advertisers will attempt to promote specific themes and deliver consistent messages. Throw in promotional tie-ins and merchandising efforts, and it may not be too far-fetched to predict the day when advertisers approve scripts and stars and modify all elements of the motion picture process to suit particular advertising goals.

There also should be concern about the influence of marketing decisions on the creative process, for instance, the push to create toyetic characters or to write in scenes which have merchandisable characteristics. It has been suggested that merchandise is formulaic, relying on established genre and characters. Thus, creativity may be compromised when film scripts and characters must fit into these formulas in order to land valuable merchandising contracts.

It is difficult to generalize about how product placement within films and merchandising possibilities can affect creative decision-making. However, manufacturers and those involved with joint promotions are often aware of script details during pre-production, and may indeed even try to influence the productions in order to maximize the benefits accrued to them. Further, although the marketplace may control the types of films made, an increasing reliance on the revenues from these sources may actually limit the types of films considered for production, as possible spin-offs, tie-ins, and product deals come to play a more important factor in pre-production planning.

Independent producers also may benefit from these sources of production funds. While most product placement and tie-in activity seems to be associated with the big budget, mass appeal films, independent productions that cater to minority or select audiences also are very attractive to manufacturers and advertisers. Nevertheless, product placement ultimately must be seen to strengthen distributors' positions and (again) disadvantage independents.

In addition, there is the inevitable influence on consumption, as films (and society) become further commercialized. The evolution of product as narrative is especially telling in terms of the extent that commercialization pervades society.

Product placements in some films can actually be detrimental, as exemplified by the case of cigarette placements. Despite a 1998 multi-state tobacco settlement banning tobacco companies from marketing directed toward children and banning payments to place tobacco products in films, a 2002 report revealed that tobacco use in the most popular youth-oriented movies had increased by 50 percent. "Tobacco at the Movies" highlighted the health risks to children, who are susceptible to the subtle message sent by famous actors and actresses using tobacco on the big screen.[7]

The most obvious economic consequence is the further commodification of motion pictures. Similar to other forms of mass media, film now represents not only a commodity in itself, but also serves as an advertising medium for other commodities and increasingly generates additional commodities. These developments provide additional profits for film companies, advertising agencies, and product manufacturers, but there seems to be little or no concern about the effects on the society and culture as a whole. Nevertheless, it is possible to argue that the repetition of themes, images, and characters, across media, as well as into other areas of daily life, may limit the expression of ideas and values, forming a *cultural synergy*. This concept will be discussed further in the next section.

## Diversification/Synergy

The major media/entertainment companies have long been diversified with business divisions spread across film, broadcasting, print, etc. However, these companies increasingly are realizing the benefits of promoting their activities across a growing number of outlets, creating a synergy between individual units and producing immediately recognizable brands. Synergy can be defined as the cooperative action of different parts for a greater effect. An *Economist* article on entertainment brands in 1998 described this process as follows:

> The brand is a lump of content – such as News Corp's *The X-Files*, Time Warner's *Batman* or Viacom's *Rugrats* – which can be exploited through film, broadcast and cable television, publishing, theme parks, music, the Internet and merchandising.
>   Such a strategy is not so much vertical or horizontal integration, but a wheel, with the brand at the hub and each of the spokes a means of exploiting it. Exploitation produces both a stream of revenue and further strengthens the brand. Thus when Viacom licenses *Rugrats* toothpaste and *Rugrats* macaroni cheese, it both makes money and promotes the direct-to-video movie launched last year and the full-blown animation feature due out later this year.[8]

This certainly is not a new development, especially for the Walt Disney Company. In fact, "Disney synergy" is the phrase typically used to describe the ultimate in cross-promotional activities and is sometimes seen as the goal for other diversified film companies. It may be instructive, therefore, to look at an example of Disney's use of synergy to further understand how diversification actually works.

## The case of Disney's *Hercules*

From its inception, Disney created strong brands or characters that were marketed in various forms (mostly through films and merchandise) throughout the world. However, the company's synergistic strategies accelerated dramatically in the 1950s when the company opened Disneyland, the theme park that used previously created stories, characters, and images as the basis for its attractions. In addition, the television program *Disneyland* was introduced on ABC, providing further opportunities to promote the theme park as well as Disney's other products. Over the past few decades, the possibilities for synergy have expanded even further with the addition of cable, home video, and other new media outlets.

While there are endless examples of Disney synergy, a closer look at the release of one film may provide some insight into how a motion picture can serve as the base for synergistic activities. Disney's 35th animated film, *Hercules*, was released in US theaters, on June 27, 1997. However, promotional activities and merchandise sales began well before that date.[9] Promotion of Disney's animated films begins with the initial announcement of the film, usually years before its actual release. The pre-production and production process is covered in entertainment and trade magazines, as well as in Disney-owned media. In addition, advance trailers advertise the release of the film. For *Hercules*, 4-minute trailers were shown before the theatrical screening of *101 Dalmations* during the 1996 Christmas season. *Hercules* trailers also were included on videocassette copies of other Disney productions, *Toy Story* and *The Hunchback of Notre Dame*.

In February 1997, Disney organized a 5-month, 20-city MegaMall Tour featuring 11 different Hercules-related attractions. McDonald's and GM participated in the tour, providing giveaways and promotion. Meanwhile, *Hercules on Ice* opened in February – the first time an ice show had opened before the release of a film. Accompanying the tour and the ice shows were concession stands selling Hercules dolls, caps, flags, T-shirts, plastic cups, and other gifts.

Ironically, the film itself presents a tongue-in-cheek portrayal of merchandising and tie-ins, featuring "Air Herc" sandals, "Herculade" thirst quencher and even a "Hercules Store" crammed with figurines. But the "real" licensing process for Hercules merchandise had started much earlier, and was reported to include nearly 100 manufacturers and 6,000 to 7,000 products, which began appearing in stores at least three to four weeks before the film's opening. The Disney Company manufactures its own products as well as licensing specific characters and images to other manufacturers. The company requires a sizable upfront guarantee and a 16 percent royalty fee on wholesale orders, although most other movie tie-ins are around 12 percent.

The marketing/merchandising effort was carefully coordinated by Disney with consistent themes, colors, and gimmicks across a wide range of merchandise, toys, clothing, and publications. For instance, a Greek Decoder Sweepstakes promotion was featured on much of the *Hercules* merchandise, and was promoted across many of the Disney divisions. Other products included the film's soundtrack (released by Columbia Records in May), as well as interactive merchandise such as Disney's Print Studio, Hercules and Disney's Hercules Action Game.

As merchandise started appearing, especially in the Disney Stores, *Hercules* products and promos also were featured by tie-in partners, including McDonald's, Nestlé, Choice Hotels International Inc., Quaker Oats, and General Motors Corp.

Meanwhile, *Hercules* was promoted on the Disney website. The *Hercules* site (http://www.disney.com/Hercules) featured details of the 20-city mall tour, summaries of the Hercules story, information about the characters and "stars" of the animated film, plus other activities and information. "Guests" to the site could download the film's trailer, as well as find out information about purchasing tickets to the film. Yet another example of tongue-in-cheek synergy was represented in the ESPN-inspired page, "OSPN: Olympus Sports Panhellenic Network."

Closer to the release date, segments of the film were highlighted in the media, especially those channels owned by Disney. However, the hype accelerated dramatically during the weekend of June 13–15 with "The Hercules World Premiere Weekend in New York." The event included a wide range of events scattered around the city, which were promoted widely and covered extensively by the media. Ceremonies featuring Disney stars and celebrities were held outside the New Amsterdam Theater (owned by Disney), where the film premiered. The world premiere of the film was followed by "The Hercules Electrical Parade," featuring the new Hercules-edition of Disneyland's "Main Street Electrical Parade."

The Manhattan premiere party and parade were covered live on E! (partially owned by Disney), as well as receiving extensive coverage by other media outlets. Disney promoted its sneak preview weekend and the film's opening through the Disney Stores, Disney On-Line and the Disney Catalog. The on-line site allowed "guests" to purchase special preview tickets and to locate local theaters. When ordering tickets, consumers received character collector pins and special offer coupons. Tickets were also available at the Disney Stores, through the Disney Catalog or through a special hotline.

In addition, Disney aired a special prime time television program introducing the *Hercules* characters and cast on their own television network, ABC. The film's opening was also featured in two specials on The Disney Channel. *Movie Surfers Go Inside Disney's Hercules* explored the movie set and provided facts about the film, while *Disney's Hercules Strikes Manhattan* again featured the "Hercules Electrical Parade" in New York. Meanwhile, the only movie theater in Celebration, Florida – Disney's planned community, south of Walt Disney World – was showing Disney's *Hercules*, and the Hercules Victory Parade opened at the Florida theme park.

Even though the film may not have been the predicted box-office or merchandising success expected by the Disney company, the characters from the film were added to Disney's stable of "classic" characters and continue to be promoted across the company's different media.

*Hercules* represents only one example of how synergy works for at least one of the major studios. Of course, sometimes it works and sometimes it doesn't. Individual films may not perform as expected or may face heavy competition from competing film releases and merchandise. In addition, some film companies have not been as successful at synergy as the Disney Company. For instance, even though AOL Time Warner was created with high expectations of promotion across its wide array of businesses, the synergy has been much less than predicted.

Nevertheless, the highly diversified nature of the entertainment conglomerates which own the major Hollywood studios provides at least the potential to promote the film commodity while marketing derivative commodities and promoting other parts of the corporation at the same time.

## International Markets/Globalization

Hollywood also looks beyond the USA to literally expand the markets for its products. In addition, global markets have become increasingly important to the transnational, entertainment conglomerates that dominate the US film industry.

Several changes have enticed Hollywood into foreign markets over the last few decades. First, some forms of deregulation or privatization of media operations have been developing since the 1980s. The result has been new commercial channels sprouting up all over the globe. The political and economic upheavals in the Soviet Union and Eastern Europe can be included with these changes, as these countries are increasingly looking towards privatized media activities. The expansion of Asian markets, including China, has also attracted increased attention from film companies with wares to sell.

In addition, the development and proliferation of new technologies, such as satellite and cable television, plus home video technologies such as VCRs and DVDs, continue to enlarge the international market, which translates into further sales of entertainment products. Diversified Hollywood companies are particularly well placed to take advantage of such market expansion. Thus, the development and proliferation of new technologies, plus privatization and deregulation actions worldwide have combined to further enhance an already lucrative global market for Hollywood.

Globalization is a widely debated phenomenon in this new century, with the transnational flow of cultural products as the focus of various discussions. However, the international distribution of US films is not a new phenomenon. From the early part of the twentieth century, American motion pictures have been distributed globally and have come to dominate cinema (and video) screens in many parts of the world.

Many reasons for Hollywood's domination of the global film business have been offered by different types of analysts, from academics to industry analysts, and the explanations differ widely. However, Hollywood's domination is actually a complex mixture of historical, economic, political and cultural factors. The next section of this chapter will discuss these factors as well as new developments affecting the international marketing of Hollywood films.

### International revenues

Entertainment is still the second largest net export industry for the USA, after aerospace, and thus plays an important role in trade relations. It is indisputable that Hollywood dominates the global market for motion pictures, even though there may be differentiated situations in specific markets. Hollywood films these days are released internationally anywhere from within a couple of days to as long as six

TABLE 4.3 *Estimated global distributor revenues for US films, 2000 (in billions)*

|                      | North America | International | Total  |
|----------------------|---------------|--------------|--------|
| Theatrical           | $3.8          | $3.0         | $6.8   |
| Home Video           | $9.2          | $5.8         | $15.0  |
| Television and Other | $4.2          | $3.8         | $8.0   |
| Totals               | $17.2         | $12.6        | $29.8  |

*Source*: Grummitt, *Hollywood: America's Film Industry*, 2001

months following domestic release. Distribution in home video formats and to television and cable markets follows shortly thereafter.

One report claims that the major US studios currently control three-quarters of the distribution market outside the USA.[10] Another report states that the US film industry overall earns more than 40 percent of its revenues exporting films to foreign markets.[11] Another claim is that the global box office accounts for 26 percent of the total wholesale revenues for a film released today and worldwide video rentals and sales account for 46 percent.[12]

Foreign box office revenues for the major Hollywood studios – or those belonging to the MPAA – were over $6.5 billion in 2000 (see Table 4.3). The MPAA reports that US films are shown in more than 150 countries worldwide and American television programs are broadcast in over 125 international markets. Further, the US film industry provides the majority of pre-recorded video cassettes seen throughout the world. Meanwhile, according to the American Film Marketing Association (AFMA), foreign box office receipts for US independent films were over three-quarters of a billion dollars in 1999.

The dominant position of US films is clear when examining the top ten films in various countries around the world. A survey of 38 countries during 2000 found US films representing no fewer than 50 percent of the top ten films for each country. Furthermore, for most countries, 80 percent of the top ten films were from the US.

## Why Hollywood dominates

While many sources have discussed Hollywood's international dominance, often the factors contributing to this global strength are either simplified or unstated. The explanations actually are quite complex and involve a range of historical, economic, political and cultural factors. As Miller et al. (2001) have recently argued, Hollywood's power needs to be rethought as a "set of processes and practices" (Miller, et al., 2000). It is important to have a full understanding of the factors that have influenced these processes and practices.

*Cultural factors.*   One explanation for Hollywood's international success is that American films are superior to other countries' productions and/or Hollywood films have universal appeal. Other attempts to explain Hollywood's dominance point more specifically to the strength of the Hollywood movie style, or state quite simply: "a good story, well-executed" (Segrave, 1997). An American producer offers the following answer: "Because of increasingly sophisticated US production standards, and the globalization of American television – by CNN, MTV and others – American films have become the most desired product throughout the world marketplace."[13]

Meanwhile, more elaborate discussions are offered by scholars from a cultural studies perspective, arguing that American films represent a kind of "narrative transparency." Most recently, Olson has developed this argument in his book, *Hollywood Planet*, stating that "the United States' competitive advantage in the creation and global distribution of popular taste is due to a unique mix of cultural conditions that are conducive to the creation of 'transparent' texts – narratives whose inherent polysemy encourage diverse populations to read them as though they are indigenous" (Olson, 1999).

This kind of argument is even offered by economists who use the concept of "cultural discount" – the notion that because of language and cultural specificity, a film (or other product) may not be popular outside of its own country. Thus, because of their "universal appeal" and the widespread use of English around the world, US films have a small cultural discount in foreign markets. Stated another way, "the format and type of drama originated by the American entertainment industry have in the most recent era created a new universal art form which is claiming something close to a worldwide audience" (Meisel, 1986).

*Economic factors.*   The content and style of American films cannot be the only explanation for Hollywood's global success. It is essential to look to economic factors at least for part of the reason for Hollywood's international dominance.

*Home market advantage.*   The USA has a tremendous advantage in that its home market for motion pictures has developed as the largest in the world. Currently, there are around 37,000 screens in the USA, with

American moviegoers accounting for around 44 percent of the global box office. Indeed, the foreign market for Hollywood films is driven by domestic release schedules. Until recently, foreign distribution has been within six months of domestic release in order to build on the domestic "buzz" and advertising of the movie. Jim Zak, former director of theatrical distribution for Orion Pictures once explained, "domestic theatrical is the engine that drives the train."[14] The wide domestic release of studio movies and the advertising power behind them build a strong market for films in foreign territories.

However, "foreign" films seem to be oddly missing from US cinemas. The argument sometimes made is that Americans aren't interested in films from other countries. But there also is evidence that foreign films have some difficulty getting into the American cinema market to begin with, thanks to deliberate efforts by the domestic industry.

While some in the film industry argue that US films depend on international markets to make a profit, it also could be argued that foreign markets are attractive because of the possibilities for additional profits beyond the home market. The concept of "infinite exportability" has been applied here, indicating that the highest costs are incurred in production and thus exporting, which requires only minimal additional costs, becomes quite profitable. Others have discussed films as joint consumption products – a public good that is not used up when consumed. In fact, Hoskins et al. conclude that "(t)he interaction of the cultural discount and market size for a joint-consumption product is at the core of a microeconomic explanation of the competitive advantage bestowed on the country possessing the largest domestic market" (1997, p. 40).[15]

*Economies of scale.* In addition, as in other industries, large corporations in the film industry have advantages not enjoyed by smaller companies. Examples include access to talent for high-concept or blockbuster films backed up with hefty promotion that is geared to specific countries and regions.

Hollywood films are more than ever these days deliberately created for international markets. In other words, the supposed "universal" appeal of Hollywood products, if it actually exists, is not unplanned or adventitious, as creative personnel in Hollywood continue to be urged to "think globally." For instance, the following advice has been offered to aspiring Hollywood screenwriters: "As the world's hunger for film and television grows, producers everywhere are desperate for products that will transcend international borders. Screenwriters can create a successful career specializing in developing stories to feed the global entertainment machine."[16]

The ability to launch huge blockbuster films with mega-stars is possible for the Hollywood majors, who aim for a global audience with action-adventure films that have little "cultural discount." The same source above who advised potential writers explains the success of American action-adventure films: "There are two broad international markets at work here: the mega-budget, massive publicity, vertically integrated revenue stream Arnold-Stallone shoot-'em-ups – and everybody else. The Sly-Arnold films will blow everything else off the screen by sheer magnitude of production budget and distribution clout."

International distribution system.    Hollywood has a well-developed international system for distributing its own films and those of other countries. Indeed, US film distributors have been globally savvy for many years. An example is this advice offered by an entertainment lawyer to producers looking to distribute their product abroad:

> There should also be some room for creative contracting to mold an agreement in light of the local market trends and viewer preferences. For example, producers should be knowledgeable about whether the territory's audience favors big action films or independent films, video or theatrical release, and should tailor the contract to benefit from these sources of income. Moreover, general cultural, political, and economic factors must also be considered in contracting.[17]

To get a motion picture into cinemas around the globe, the most advantageous strategy is to arrange distribution with a major US distributor. Even though the cost may be higher than an independent distributor, Hollywood's global experience is extensive.

Some claim that the Americans are able to flood the market with a surplus of low-priced programming (films and television series) that benefit from the home market advantage mentioned previously. In other words, American products – often already amortized in the US market – are sold at prices much lower than the cost of producing national products. But it is still difficult to assess these claims without direct access to actual production costs and prices – information that is often difficult to obtain.

Hollywood has operated historically in foreign markets through distribution cartels, which market US films as well as other countries' products. The primary example is United International Pictures (UIP), representing Paramount, Universal, MGM/UA, and successor to

Cinema International Corporation (CIC), but other distribution arrangements between the Hollywood majors exists, as well.

Alliances between Hollywood studios to distribute films abroad also help maintain the studios' dominance of foreign markets. These studio partnerships allow for the spreading of risk while participating in a greater number of costly "event" pictures. For example, if a studio thinks a movie is too expensive, it sells off the foreign rights and cuts its expenses in half. Rights splitting increases the number of films a studio can participate in by easing budget constraints.

Besides agreements between studios domestically, foreign entertainment or distribution groups have made alliances with Hollywood studios. For example, Polygram, a Dutch-based entertainment group, signed a joint finance and distribution agreement with Warner Brothers to distribute five films made by Castle Rock, a Warner production subsidiary. Moreover, Polygram and Warner formed a partnership with the Spanish film and television conglomerate Sogecable for a theatrical film alliance in Spain. In Australia, Warner Brothers entered into a five-year feature film production and distribution agreement with Village Roadshow to produce at least 20 Village films.

Indeed, the strength of Hollywood's distribution system cannot be understated. Recently, Miller et al. (2001) have pointed this out, arguing that "historical patterns of ownership and control over distribution have largely determined the scales of production." They further argue that "(t)he key to the high volume of audiovisual trade is not cheap reproduction costs, but the vast infrastructures of distribution that secure financing for production." The authors point especially to Hollywood's exploitation of national cultural labor markets, international co-productions, intellectual property rights and marketing as keys to Hollywood's dominance.

*Historical factors.* While these economic factors are significant and fundamental, many explanations of Hollywood's dominance still lack a historical perspective.

*Hollywood's initial commercial orientation.* While most histories of Hollywood reveal the strong commercial orientation in the evolution of film in the USA, this point is sometimes overlooked when discussing the nature of Hollywood's international marketing strength. David Puttnam (1998) outlines this historical background quite well in his book, *Movies and Money* when he notes that American film pioneers took advantage of early technological advances from Europe and realized that distribution and exhibition were central to making profits in the film business. Puttnam also points to the importance of developing mass marketing and star power. Thus, while film may have developed differently in other countries, motion pictures activities in the USA developed strongly as a profit-oriented, commodity-based industry from early in its history.

World Wars.   A few historical studies help us to understand the significance of the war periods in reinforcing American strength in foreign film markets. Miller et al. (2001) at least mention the two world wars, observing that "The 1914–18 and 1939–45 conflicts left national production across Europe either shut down or slowed. A plentitude of unseen US inventory waited to be unleashed."

Meanwhile, Thompson's (1985) research documents the US film industry's rise in global markets during WWI and the maintenance of that dominant position through the mid-1930s. She points out that it was not only that US films were able to export films during and after the war, but also "because they instituted new distribution procedures abroad, establishing offices in various countries. . . . By eroding the European film industry's base of support abroad, American competition permanently weakened the strong pre-war European producing countries". (See also Ulff-Møller, 2001.)

The US dominance was again strongly reinforced during and after WWII, as European industries were decimated, and again, US products were plentiful. In addition, the US government assured continued dominance through their activities in Europe, especially after the war, as documented by Guback (1969).

Thus, the US film industry benefited immeasurably from the historical circumstances that allowed it to continue producing and distributing films during these global conflicts, as well as being tied to a conquering nation that became a world economic and political power.

Political factors.   Additionally, important political factors are often neglected in explaining the international success of the US film industry. Most significant are Hollywood's own lobbying activities, as well as the support it receives from the US government. While more attention will be given to this area in the next chapter, the international activities will be considered here.

The MPAA: A Little State Dept.   The MPAA describes itself as follows:

> Founded in 1922 as the trade association of the American film industry, the MPAA has broadened its mandate over the years to reflect the diversity of an expanding industry. The initial task

assigned to the association was to stem the waves of criticism of American movies, then silent, while sometimes rambunctious and rowdy, and to restore a more favorable public image for the motion picture business.

As we shall see in the next chapter, the MPAA more recently serves as a lobbying force for its members, which include: Walt Disney Company; Sony Pictures Entertainment, Inc.; Metro-Goldwyn-Mayer Inc.; Paramount Pictures Corporation; Twentieth Century Fox Film Corp.; Universal Studios, Inc.; and Warner Bros.

Support for the film industry (and other American export industries) was especially boosted when the Webb-Pomerene Act was passed in 1918, allowing companies that must compete in the USA to collaborate in foreign markets. The Hollywood majors organized an export cartel that operated as the sole export agent for its members. Formerly the Motion Picture Export Association (MPEA), since 1994 the Motion Picture Association (MPA) represents US film internationally, in other words, sets price levels, terms of trade, etc., for each country. The MPA and MPAA work with the State Dept. and the Office of the US Trade Representative to monitor trade barriers, etc.

As the organization's literature explains, the MPA was organized "to respond to the rising tide of protectionism resulting in barriers aimed at restricting the importation of American films. Since its early days, the MPA, often referred to now as 'a little State Department,' has expanded to cover a wide range of foreign activities falling in the diplomatic, economic, and political arenas."

The US government has supported the film industry in various ways, but especially in overcoming resistance to Hollywood exports in global markets. In addition, the government does its best to protect the US film industry in international treaty negotiations, such as NAFTA, GATT, WTO, etc. The government also provides the clout to back up threats by the industry when countries don't cooperate by opening their markets.

As MPAA head, Jack Valenti explains: "Our movies and TV programs are hospitably received by citizens around the world" (quoted in Miller et al., 2001). Perhaps. But it doesn't hurt to have a little help from friends in high places.

### New developments in the global film business

While the international dominance of Hollywood is nothing new, as explained above, there are some new developments that have reinforced Hollywood's strength, but also may ultimately challenge US dominance.

**Diversification of the film business.**   As discussed previously, the major studios are part of highly diversified, media conglomerates. Not only are Hollywood films distributed internationally, but products associated with those films (i.e. merchandise) are marketed globally, as well. Cross-ownership of other media outlets means that Hollywood products are promoted and linked to products across the media landscape, that is, on television shows, in magazines, newspapers, etc.

In addition, these diverse transnational corporations do not have to rely only on the success of motion pictures, but have various outlets to rely on for overall profits. Independent film companies may have much more difficulty surviving only on the (hopeful) success of their films.

There also are new means of promoting Hollywood's products, for instance, via the Internet, which is being used for previews and other advanced publicity for Hollywood films internationally.

**International ownership of Hollywood companies.**   An interesting development that complicates the issue of American dominance is the recent ownership of many Hollywood studios by companies outside the USA, as outlined in Chapter 2. Remember that Sony (a Japanese company) has owned Columbia Pictures/Tristar for many years now, while the French-based Vivendi company owns Universal Pictures and Australian-based News Corp. controls Twentieth-Century Fox. While films produced by these companies are still typically identified as American, it is doubtful that the ultimate loyalty of the owners is connected to the US.

**Growth of co-productions/runaway production.**   As noted previously, co-productions involving Hollywood companies have been increasing with the studios' attempts to spread the risk of costly productions. While there are different types of co-production deals, some of these arrangements can help to build indigenous film infrastructures and talent pools, although Hollywood has been notorious for raiding such pools over the years. Thus, co-productions and runaway production are highly controversial, especially with Hollywood labor organizations, but also in many foreign countries.

**Resistance to US dominance.**   More often, countries have attempted to resist Hollywood's dominance in various ways. Forms of resistance have been attempted for much of Hollywood's existence, including import quotas, tariffs, licensing, screen quotas, frozen earnings, and local or national subsidies.

For example, import quotas are imposed in China and other countries, where a specific number or quota of films a year can be foreign. In other countries, duties are added to theater tickets. For instance, Indian ticket taxes are 100 percent while Malaysian taxes are 32 percent. In Hungary, a special distribution tax of 20 percent is added for pornographic and violent films. Other nations impose various forms of taxes against foreign films. Turkey maintains a 25 percent municipality tax on receipts from foreign films. Also, Australia charges a 10 percent tax on American distributors who do not market Australian films.

Foreign distributors also encounter local ownership requirements, such as Canada's requirement that non-Canadian distributors must own worldwide distribution rights to a film before it can be distributed in Canada without a Canadian distributor. Hollywood producers have threatened to boycott, so they have been exempt from this law, however, other independent American distributors and foreign distributors, such as Dutch-owned Polygram, have been affected.

Restrictions also prevent American movies from appearing on television in some countries. China allows for 15 percent foreign programming, while Canada and EU nations require a 50 percent minimum of local programming. Screen restrictions in the United Kingdom mandate that a minimum of 20 percent of the screens show British films, where only 10 percent of box office receipts come from British films.

In addition, subsidies for domestic film industries are funded through taxation of foreign movie revenues. In France, a 12 percent tax is added to cinema admissions to fund a $250 million subsidy of local films. While admission taxes are a common means of subsidizing domestic film production, licensing fees, tax rebates, loans and grants are other ways that nations fund their film subsidies.

These various forms of resistance have been aimed at US films in markets around the world for many, many years. Even though some have been successful over the years, Hollywood's overall domination has still continued. It remains to be seen whether or not this kind of resistance, combined with other recent developments, can more seriously challenge Hollywood's dominance in the future. (Another major issue in global markets is piracy, which also will be covered in the next chapter.)

*International anti-trust enforcement.*    Some of the Hollywood studios have recently encountered foreign anti-trust actions. For instance, the European Commission threatened to block UIP operations because of complaints that the company had used block booking, or selling certain films only with others in a package.

Meanwhile, other anti-trust problems have emerged in Korea, where five major US film distributors were found guilty of collusion by the Korean Fair Trade Commission for withholding ads in two Seoul newspapers. Penalties were assessed and the companies warned that future violations would lead to the closing of the US distributors' offices in Korea.

While these actions may be isolated, at least one source has observed, "The strength of studio distribution alliances abroad may also be a weakness when foreign anti-trust laws view these alliances as anti-competitive. Thus, the power of a studio distribution arm abroad does have some risks."[18]

### New formations/competition

Meanwhile, new forms of competition also may challenge Hollywood's global strength. Only a few examples – the European Union and India – will be included in this discussion, but they represent important cases.

#### The European Union

> I'm tired of the dominance of American movies over every facet
> of film-making and cinemagoing. It's time European directors
> made films with reach, punch and intellectual ambition. (Neil
> Jordan, writer/director, in Cowie, 2000)

Though American movies continue to pack in audiences overseas and dominate European markets, a few European films have recently achieved domestic and international success. For instance, *Bean, The Full Monty* and others have attracted revenue that might have gone to US films.

On the one hand, reliance on state support has resulted in many European productions playing to a narrow market. Nevertheless, EU funding of co-productions and distribution, plus box-office-driven policies for awarding subsidies, have encouraged filmmakers to seek a wider audience. However, at least some are concerned about the future of European film if purely commercial motivations are pursued. For instance, Puttnam (1998) "urges Europe to marshal its abundant talents and resources to take the lead in what he expects will be the next audio-visual wave – the convergence of multimedia entertainment and education."

*Bollywood.* Increasingly, some film industries that have previously been relatively provincial are beginning to pay attention to global film marketing. India has not one film industry but several. The largest, and the only one making more films today than a decade ago, is the Hindi-language "Bollywood" industry based in Mumbai. Although the Bollywood industry's output of over 240 films in 2000 made it the largest of India's film industries, the Tamil, Telegu, Malayalam, Kannada and Bengali language industries are also significant, between them producing over 500 films in 2000.

There are various indications that Bollywood is aiming to increase its market share of global film revenues. India's government is encouraging the industry, improving access to bank finance and reforming taxation laws to encourage exports. A BBC report explains: "Behind these measures lies a perception that the film industry, like telecommunications and information technology, is one that can leverage the country's highly skilled workforce and low costs to create an internationally competitive economy." There are just 12 cinemas per million people in India compared to 116 per million in America. However, revenues in India's entertainment industry rose 30 percent in 2001, seven times faster than the economy as a whole. Indian films are already being distributed to markets in the United Kingdom, North America, the Gulf states, and parts of Africa.[19]

## Issue: The new global Hollywood?

It could be argued that Hollywood has always been a global industry, selling its products worldwide since its inception. It also has been noted that Hollywood has dominated world cinemas at least since the 1920s, and possibly much earlier.

What is certain is that the current American film industry's products are sold globally and receive substantial revenues from these global markets. In addition, the American product often displaces indigenous film products, as Hollywood films have become the worldwide standard of commercial filmmaking.

Reactions to this development have been both economic and cultural, as countries around the world have struggled to maintain national cinemas in the face of Hollywood competition. It remains to be seen if these recent efforts to resist such domination will succeed, or if the Hollywood products will continue to rule cinema screens around the world.

## Notes

1  J. Goldsmith, "Vivendi U, Toyota Pact for Promos," *Variety*, 31 July 2001, p. 5.
2  This section relies especially on Turcotte, 1995; Litvak, 1986.
3  Marc Graser, "H'wood Looking to Land Brands," *Variety*, 14 Nov. 2002, p. 1.
4  The case of *Spider-Man* was prepared by Randy Nichols, University of Oregon, and based on material from the trade press (especially *Variety*, *Billboard*, *Advertising Age* and *Brandweek*), business periodicals (especially *The Economist* and *Business Week*), various online sites (especially movieheadlines.com, Boxofficecemojo.com), trade organizations (especially the Video Software Dealers Association), in addition to Kent, 2001, and Sheff, 1993.
5  Randy Nichols, University of Oregon, contributed to this section.
6  Wasko, Phillips and Purdie (1993) pointed to some of these trends in the early 1990s.
7  For more details, see http://www.pirg.org/alerts/route.asp?id2=8330%20.
8  "Size Does Matter," *The Economist*, 23 May 1998, p. 57.
9  The discussion of the promotion of *Hercules* is from Wasko (2001), and draws primarily on information in trade publications, especially *Variety*, *The Hollywood Reporter*, *Business Wire*, *PR Newswire*, and *Amusement Business*, as well as *The Los Angeles Times*.
10 ABN Amro (international investment bank), research report, Sept. 2000.
11 http://www.cameraguild.com/news/genindustry/runaway.htm
12 Vogel, 2001, p. 62, for estimates of worldwide home video revenues.
13 http://hollywoodnetwork.com/Gadney/1movies.html
14 B.A. Blake, "Hollywood Sales Abroad: Market Analysis of Studio Films in Foreign Territories," http://www.optimalegal.com/sys-tmpl/hollywoodsalesabroad/.
15 They further argue that Hollywood's dominance is based on: "possession of the largest domestic market, production in English, characteristics of the US industry, and the Hollywood system" (Hoskins et al., p. 37).
16 "Writing Action-Adventure for the Global Market Interview with Neill D. Hicks," www.hollywoodnet.com/pov/pov2.html.
17 B.A. Blake, "International Film Distribution: Striking a Deal in the Global

Market," http://www.optimalegal.com/sys-tmpl/internationalfilmdistribu-tion/.

18 L.Y. Wang, "Foreign Anti-trust Laws: Restrictions on Studio Distribution Abroad," http://www.optimalegal.com/sys-tmpl/foreignantitrustlaws/.

19 "Bollywood Aims for Global Success," http://news.bbc.co.uk/hi/english/entertainment/film/newsid_1400000/1400367.stm, 21 June 2001; "India's Entertainment Industry Blockbuster," http://news.bbc.co.uk/hi/english/business/newsid_1874000/1874901.stm, 15 March 2002.

# Promoting and Protecting the Industry 5

## Promoting the Industry

Hollywood companies succeed year after year in dominating film markets around the world for a variety of reasons, but it must be stressed that these companies do not simply rely on the strength of their products competing in these markets. As Samuel Arkoff once claimed, "No picture has ever been made that is good enough to sell itself" (Donahue, 1987, p. 82).

Film companies spend massive amounts of money on advertising and promotion to ensure that consumers are aware of their products. In addition, Hollywood encourages press coverage of their activities, not only through film reviews, but various kinds of publicity associated with films and film celebrities. Films also receive attention at festivals and markets, as well as through yearly awards given out by industry and non-industry groups.

Promotion draws attention to the industry's products but Hollywood also employs various strategies to protect its interests, both within the US and internationally. These efforts are carried out by industry organizations that often call upon the US government for assistance and support. This chapter will present an overview of the ways that Hollywood both promotes and protects its business.

### Movie Marketing

The film that is often credited with changing how movies are distributed and marketed was *Jaws* – the first movie to open at a thousand theaters and to use network television to support it. Before that, what are now called marketing departments were publicity departments. In addition, much less money was spent on advertising, with more attention given to publicity and trailers.

After the *Jaws* experience in the 1970s, publicity departments gradually evolved into "multi-disciplined" marketing departments, which include specific divisions for publicity, creating advertising, media buying, and promotion (including product placement and tie-in activities). More recently, a specific area has been developed for Internet promotion. Film companies attempt to keep these activities coordinated and moving together to put out a single message. As one marketing executive explains:

> [I]t's sort of like planning a military invasion. You can't plan to have your air force do something, your artillery do something, and your infantry do something, without any knowledge of their power. So you have to assess the power of each one of your organizations to implement a program before you can design a battle plan. (PBS, 2001)

Not surprisingly, each company arranges marketing activities some-what differently. The same marketing executive cited above explains:

> It's very different from company to company. There are companies that will not put a movie into production without the endorsement of the marketing department. They are as involved in reading scripts, making the decisions on whether or not that movie is going to get made or not as is the production element. [But] some companies really could care less what the marketing department says. (ibid.)

If the average movie costs around $28 million to market, about $3 to $5 million dollars of that is for the production of materials and running the marketing campaign; the balance is the cost of media (ibid.). Although the studios use in-house marketing personnel, outside companies or individuals can also be employed to create specific parts of the campaign, such as the trailers, television commercials, or print material. This process of using outside vendors may be contributing to increasing marketing expenditures, an issue that is considered in the next section.

## Issue: Marketing madness

It might be useful to ask why the marketing costs for films continue to grow. Some industry observers argue that a fear of box office failure and a never-ending cycle of "hyper-competition" have developed as the studios try to outspend each other in promoting their big films. Based on reports on marketing research and competition, more and more money is poured into advertising campaigns and other efforts to boost box-office numbers.

Of special importance is the amount of television advertising that is assumed to be needed to support big, blockbuster films. Certainly, this process has contributed to the further commercialization of the industry, not to mention the waste involved in the massive amounts of money poured into such efforts. But it also has apparently shifted power within marketing departments, and even within the studios themselves. Levin (2000) observes that "people who are more involved in how you put together television commercials – the creative folks who do that kind of work – have risen in importance in these marketing departments. The publicity people have been diminished a little bit against the creative people, and the budgets have soared."

There is so much emphasis on marketing in general that a commonplace assumption in the industry is that if a movie is successful, it was a great movie, but if it was a failure, it was because of weak marketing. In addition, the emphasis on the initial opening, or first weekend, has become intense. The marketing department becomes responsible for a big opening, which, it is argued, "becomes critical for the entire life of the movie" (ibid.). Films that do not manage to attract big bucks during their opening weekend are considered losers, and are relegated to the home video market rather quickly. Thus, marketing campaigns become crucial to the success of major Hollywood films. More details about this process follow in the next few sections.

**Marketing strategies.**    A wide range of considerations is involved in designing marketing plans. In addition to the usual marketing factors, when the film will be released and the competition influence these decisions. The design of the marketing also will take into account the genre, the plot, and the cast. For instance, how much publicity is possible from the film's stars may influence how dependent the marketing campaign needs to be on advertising versus publicity. Promotional partners also may be possible, thus "other people's money" can be used to promote the film.

**Marketing research.**    For many, many years, Hollywood has attempted to use research to foretell a film's success in the marketplace. But it is still a tricky business, as evidenced by the stories that industry people tell about the films that were rejected based on supposedly solid research. For instance, Universal passed on *Star Wars*, Columbia gave up on *E.T.: The Extra Terrestrial* after extensive development, and all of the major studios passed on *Raiders of the Lost Ark* except for Paramount.

As one industry insider explains, "Motion picture research attempts to predict what audiences want to see, when they want to see it, and the best means of motivating them to go to the film" (Donahue, 1989, p. 98). Sometimes it works, but more often it doesn't. Hollywood seems to have mixed feelings about marketing research, especially when it attempts to assess moviegoers' awareness of future movies and their likelihood of seeing them, especially in international markets. As a *Variety* reporter concludes, "Companies are eager for the information, but occasionally skeptical about its reliability."[1]

Nevertheless, filmmakers and distributors still employ outside companies to provide research on which to make decisions. While numerous companies offer such services, the dominant firms are interestingly connected to the industry's trade publications. National Research Group (NRG) dominates the domestic market for film research and has a virtual international monopoly on such services. NRG is owned by VNU, the same company that owns the *Hollywood Reporter* and was discussed in Chapter 3.

In 1997 VNU acquired NRG, which was recently integrated into its Nielsen Entertainment unit. Nielsen offers a range of movie-marketing services, including box office tracking, focus-group testing and surveys, and includes a number of companies that provide information, marketing solutions, and analytical tools to the entertainment industry. Nielsen Entertainment is especially important in measuring box office results, but also tracks music, video/DVD, and book sales. In addition to NRG, the companies involved are Nielsen EDI, Nielsen ReelResearch, Nielsen VideoScan, Nielsen Entertainment Marketing Solutions (EMS) and others.

Domestically, NRG's chief competitor is MarketCast, which is owned by *Variety*'s parent company, Reed Business Information. MarketCast provides market research for motion picture studios, production companies, film exhibitors, television networks, and Internet content providers, supporting them in the development of marketing strategies for movies, television and Internet programming. (More background will be presented on Reed below in the section on the trade press.)

Various methods are used to pre-test concepts, titles, etc., as well as to guide marketing campaigns before and after a film is produced. Market surveys may be used to identify features of a film that have the widest consumer appeal, or that reveal a target audience. Research methods may include "intercept" techniques (pedestrians asked to respond to questions about concepts, stars, or advertising copy). Interviews also are used to elicit responses to advertising.

Test screenings may involve the screening of either a rough cut, the final cut, the trailer or television commercials, followed by questionnaires that attempt to identify what segment of the audience is attracted to the film and why. A test screening can lead to changes in the film, reediting or even reshooting. But information gleaned from test screenings also is used to develop a marketing strategy, often focussing on a target audience. Focus group sessions also are utilized, especially after a target audiences is identified.

Film companies also attempt to use marketing segmentation techniques to target consumers in their advertising and promotional campaigns. For instance, the following scheme is presented on a film company website as a way to categorize American movie audiences:

> *Gen Y Audiences.* Approximately 28 percent of American society aged 14 to 26, and of primary interest to traditional movie marketers. Gen Y actually ranges from 7 to 26 in three distinct waves.
>
> *Gen X Audiences.* Baby Busters – now tagged Generation X approximately 18 percent of American society, aged 26 to 42. Strong audience for independent films, goes their own way, seeks out the unknown and undiscovered.
>
> *Boomer Audiences.* The strong new audience segment, approximately 32 percent of American society, 43 to 56 years old, empty-nesters with time and money and strong appetites for interesting films. (filmprofit.com)

Marketing research also continues after a film opens, sometimes utilizing exit interviews to find out how audience members responded to the film. Subsequent advertising, as well as changes in the release pattern, may be altered based on the findings of such research.

### Issue: Marketing to children

Early in 2002, the Federal Trade Commission reported that the entertainment industry deliberately targeted children and teenagers with advertising for R-rated films, as well as using them in focus groups to test such movies.[2] An example from the documents used in the study showed that MGM/United Artists had tested commercials for the horror film *Disturbing Behavior* on children as young as 12, while using children 9 to 11 to research ideas for another horror movie.

During a later Senate hearing, film executives admitted to being guilty of "competitive zeal" in marketing violent movies to children and offered varying acts of contrition. However, they were divided over whether to end the practice. Some of the companies pledged to alter their policies of advertising adult-rated movies to schools and youth groups, as well as on television shows, websites, and in magazines with primary audiences under age 17. They also agreed to expand their rating systems to help parents better evaluate films, with Warner Bros. planning to add the designations L for profane language, S for sex and V for violence. And all the executives said that their studios had stopped using children in focus groups for R-rated films, unless accompanied by adults. How serious these efforts will be remains to be seen, but represents an attempt by government representatives to place pressure on the industry.

The next sections will present overviews of specific marketing activities, such as publicity, advertising, trailers, and the Internet, followed by some attention to film festivals and markets, critics and reviewers, film awards, and the trade press. Promotional activities such as product placements, merchandising and tie-ins also contribute to the marketing of a film, but were discussed in the last chapter.

## Publicity

Publicity can be defined as unpaid media attention, as opposed to paid promotion or advertising, and includes a wide range of activities, including critics' reviews and film festivals, which will be discussed separately below. Media coverage of a film is not fortuitous, nor is it typically initiated by media outlets. Publicity for Hollywood films is the result of deliberate and calculated planning by publicists and public relations specialists.

Publicity begins even before production, usually after a film receives a green light, but accelerates during the principal photography. A unit publicist or public relations firm is assigned at this time and stays with the film through its release.

Again, publicity on the set is not accidental, but carefully planned by publicists who prepare press releases, invite the press on the set and arrange interviews with talent. Publicists may arrange for video to be shot during production for electronic press kits, music videos, and featurettes or the making-of-the-movie programs, as well as coordinating photos and talent interviews. Publicists also get involved in script and editing changes as well as market research.

As the film nears completion, publicists try to create a buzz for a film in whatever way possible. One way is to get other media to cover the film, including cover stories in national magazines, television programs (news, talk shows, entertainment programs, etc.), as well as other media outlets. The aim is to stimulate coverage of a film outside of the entertainment section of the news media by staging events, drawing attention to stars, etc.

One recent example was the media blitz that accompanied the James Bond release, *Die Another Day*, in November 2002. The film's stars appeared across the media, accompanied by a myriad of cross-promotional advertisements of the branded products in the film. *Time* magazine's coverage was a seven-page color spread, while *Newsweek* devoted four pages to the new release. Numerous other magazine covers featured the images of the film's stars, who also traveled the talk show circuit.

Traditional means of film publicity include press kits or books which supply advertising material for exhibitors (and later, home video companies, etc.) and the press (magazines, newspapers and television) from 6–8 weeks before a film opens. The kit may include story description, photos, star bios, sample stories, etc. Other theater material includes posters, standees or stand-ups, window cards, etc. Electronic press kits include video interviews, behind-the scenes footage, the trailer, perhaps a music video and other material that can be used to publicize the film. Promotional items such as t-shirts, buttons, key chains, and music are also included with press kits, as well as being used as giveaways to the public.

A few months before a film's release, it is shown to the trade (mostly exhibitors) and to the press, as well as to audiences in a few theaters (usually in Los Angeles). In addition to audience information, sneak previews are intended to enhance word of mouth about the film as well as to elicit responses to the film from preview cards. However, previews also can become profitable for blockbuster films when shown at numerous theaters. For instance, during one weekend in November 2002, *Harry Potter and the Chamber of Secrets* was shown at sneak previews in 522 theaters in Britain and gathered $12.5 million, while in Japan the film was sneaked at 777 screens for one day and yielded $3.7 million.

Stars also participate in media junkets and other publicity events. Appearances on talk shows, features on entertainment programs, and most recently, special cyberspace events and chat sessions, can be invaluable in terms of "free" advertising. As films also need to be sold to exhibitors, stars are often requested to attend exhibitors' conventions or other events. Star appearances are especially important in foreign countries, where marketing campaigns are designed separately and revenues can surpass those from the US market. For instance, Vin Diesel, the star of *XXX*, did a 12-country, two-month tour to promote the film, thus upping the gross receipts to over $150 million by the end of 2002.

Distributors also use "fieldmen" to promote a film in major cities around the USA. These employees (or independent agencies) make sure that the film receives local attention in the press, as well as arranging promotional events, contests and giveaways at department stores, radio stations, and other sites.

## Advertising

Advertising costs for a film can be more than the cost of production and, as noted above, have grown dramatically over the last few decades. The MPAA reported that the average for new feature films by member companies was $27.3 million in 2002. Again, advertising campaigns and budgets vary for each Hollywood film (see Table 5.1), but a few common practices still prevail. Advertising is aimed at the film industry itself (especially exhibitors, but also other sectors), as well as consumers in the various markets where a film will be sold.

Trade advertising involves ads in trade papers (*Variety* and *The Hollywood Reporter*) before, during and after production, for various purposes. Distributors typically arrange such advertising, in addition to national campaigns (how these expenses are actually charged or accounted for is another matter, as explained in the section on creative accounting in Chapter 2).

Other advertising efforts are aimed at the national and local level. The amount of money and where it is spent are often related to a film's release pattern. However, national advertising has become increasingly important, as big films open in wide releases across the country. Network television has become common and has driven up the costs of advertising campaigns (see Table 5.2). *Variety* reported that movie studios increased their spending on television ads in 2001 over the previous year by 55 percent on network television and 74 percent on cable. Films also are advertised in other outlets, including newspapers, radio, magazines, and billboards. The major distributors and exhibitors often work with advertising agencies when purchasing

TABLE 5.1   *Advertising costs of individual films, 2000* (in millions of dollars)

| Film | Distributor | Box Office | Advertising | Ratio |
|------|-------------|------------|-------------|-------|
| *Cast Away* | Fox | 233.4 | 23.5 | 9.9 |
| *X-Men* | Fox | 157.2 | 22.7 | 6.9 |
| *Dr. Seuss' How the Grinch Stole Christmas* | Universal | 260.0 | 40.3 | 6.5 |
| *What Women Want* | Paramount | 182.8 | 30.8 | 5.9 |
| *Scary Movie* | Miramax | 157.0 | 26.5 | 5.9 |
| *Mission Impossible 2* | Paramount | 215.4 | 37.2 | 5.8 |
| *What Lies Beneath* | DreamWorks | 155.4 | 28.8 | 5.4 |
| *Meet the Parents* | Universal | 166.2 | 33.9 | 4.9 |
| *Dinosaur* | Buena Vista | 137.7 | 28.3 | 4.9 |
| *Erin Brockovich* | Universal | 125.6 | 27.2 | 4.6 |
| *Miss Congeniality* | Warner Bros. | 106.8 | 23.4 | 4.6 |
| *The Perfect Storm* | Warner Bros. | 182.6 | 40.5 | 4.5 |
| *Gladiator* | DreamWorks | 187.7 | 42.7 | 4.4 |
| *Remember the Titans* | Buena Vista | 115.6 | 26.2 | 4.4 |
| *Charlie's Angels* | Sony Pictures | 125.3 | 28.9 | 4.3 |

*Source*: Grummitt, *Hollywood: America's Film Industry*, 2001.

*Note*: Box office and advertising cost relate to North America; box office is to July 2001.

TABLE 5.2   *MPAA member companies' advertising costs, 2002*

| % of Advertising costs | MPAA Members | MPAA Affiliates |
|------------------------|--------------|-----------------|
| Newspaper | 13.5 | 22.0 |
| Network TV | 23.0 | 25.7 |
| Spot TV | 17.6 | 5.6 |
| Internet/Online | 0.9 | 0.9 |
| Trailers | 4.5 | 6.1 |
| Other Media | 21.4 | 21.1 |
| Other non-media | 19.1 | 18.6 |

*Source*: MPAA.

*Note*: Other media include cable TV, radio, magazines, billboards. Other non-media include production and creative services, exhibition prices, promotion and publicity, market research.

such media time and space. The studios' media buyers, together with their advertising agencies, claim to know the appropriate level and extent of advertising for each film. As one marketing executive explains: "With their budget they plan the strategy as to whom to buy, when to buy and how to buy, so that the result reaches the target audience for each movie with the greatest economy" (Squire, 1992, p. 299). One may wonder, then, why some films are not successful at the box office and why advertising costs keep rising.

Cooperative advertising has come to mean mostly local advertising. Although this expense may be shared by the exhibitor and distributor, there is a good deal of variation depending on the location, the companies involved and the specific film. For instance, New York represents a significant market that can contribute as much as 10 percent of a film's domestic theatrical revenues. However, it also represents high advertising costs and the potential for negative reviews (see especially Donahue, 1987).

## Trailers

Trailers (or movie previews shown in theaters) can be traced back to the 1920s, if not earlier, when they were outtakes or uncut footage. Trailers originally ran at the end of a film showing, but because people were leaving before the trailers were finished, they were moved to before the featured film.

Prior to the 1970s, trailers were produced and distributed to theaters by a company called the National Screen Service (NSS), along with other items such as posters, photos, and material for local advertising. In fact, the National Screen Service has an interesting history that indicates the extent that Hollywood has changed its promotional habits.

NSS was created in 1920 to produce and distribute trailers, which were an important part of the studios' marketing campaigns. NSS prepared trailers for several major studios, and eventually also became involved in distributing "movie paper" (also called standard accessories), which included 8"×10" press stills, lobby cards, half sheets, inserts, one sheets, three sheets, six sheets and twenty-four sheets.

Most of the majors arranged for NSS to handle these materials, together with its affiliate, Advertising Accessories Inc. By the mid-1940s most of the majors used NSS, which continued to be the center for movie paper advertising until the mid-1980s. After this point, the business became more dispersed, although NSS continued to handle approximately 15–20 percent of the advertising paper. In September, 2000, the NSS offices were bought by Technicolor, Inc., which now provides these services, with particular emphasis on the one-sheet.[3]

Today, trailers can range in length from 30 seconds to 4.5 minutes, but average 2.5 to 3 minutes. Shorter teasers can appear as much as a year in advance of a film's opening, serving as an announcement and rarely featuring much actual film footage as the movie is often in production. For instance, during summer 2002, teasers for *The Hulk* were shown, although the film was not scheduled to open until summer 2003.

More than ever, trailers are crucial to a successful film these days. In fact, trailers are probably the most important, effective, and cost-efficient way of marketing a new film. A 2002 survey by *Variety* and Moviefone found that ticket buyers cited trailers as the biggest influence on their movie choices, followed by television, newspapers and Internet.

In addition, trailers have become important with the proliferation of wide releases of films that rely on opening weekends to set their value. "We'll spend five months to a year obsessing about them, every single cut and every single moment that we use," says David Sameth, DreamWorks' head of creative advertising. "That's indicative, I think, of how intense the pressure is on creating the right piece."

Trailers can be produced within the studios, although companies specializing in this type of production also are employed and have proliferated recently. For instance, The Ant Farm is a Los Angeles-based motion picture advertising company that worked on *Lord of the Rings: The Fellowship of the Ring* and *The Sixth Sense*, among others. One of its representatives explained that, "You have to find what is unique in each movie and figure out a way to highlight that and get the audience excited about it."

In light of the significance of trailers, their placement has become particularly important. For instance, because of an agreement between George Lucas' Lucasfilm and Pixar Animation Studios, trailers for *Star Wars: Episode II – Attack of the Clones* were included before *Monsters, Inc.* However, the studios distributing the films (Twentieth Century Fox and Disney, respectively) apparently were not involved or consulted about the decision. The deal prompted some concern at the studios, where (as *Variety* reported), there is "fear of losing control of a valuable element of the Hollywood marketing machine." The issue put into question who has control of the space before the movie – the theater, the studio, the producer or even a star?

## Internet promotion

As noted in Chapter 3, Hollywood companies now utilize the Internet to promote their products. Most films have Internet sites which open long before the movie appears in theaters, primarily to promote the film, but also to gather information about fans.

The technology offers new possibilities for "one-to-one marketing," using databases of moviegoers with preferences and profiles, and targeted email promotions. The sites also can be used to "build communities." An early example: Sony Tristar's *Starship Troopers* site featured "Mobile Infantry" that users could employ to join the battle against the giant alien bugs, while Trooper ID screens provided links to other users' sites. The *Starship* site had attracted over 30,000 users by summer 2000, thus providing free promotion for the film. By 1997, 40 percent of the movie sites online had interactive attributes, such as games or quizzes, and 30 percent had community features (Chowdhury et al., 1997).

Movie sites also may feature product placements or companies that have promotional tie-ins. For instance, the 2002 site for *Die Another Day* featured links to 24 "007 partners," including Finlandia Vodka, Bollinger Champagne, Talisker Scotch Whiskey, and Heineken Beer, as well as Ford, Jaguar, and Aston Martin. The site also offered numerous versions of the film's trailer, music, and videos, in addition to production notes, downloadable screen savers, information about the film's production and release, and photos and material on past Bond films.

## Press coverage and film critics

*Hollywood and the press.* Hollywood has always had an interesting relationship with the press, as the film industry is a source for popular newspaper content as well as a customer for its advertising services. Press coverage of Hollywood involves everything from film reviews to features on film stars' personal lives. During the last decade, it may seem that more press attention has been given to the business of Hollywood, with box office returns regularly reported in local newspapers and a plethora of "entertainment news" programs.

Interestingly, the same companies that own film companies own some of the more popular entertainment news sources. Examples would include periodicals such as *Entertainment Weekly* (AOL Time Warner), as well as television shows such as *Entertainment Tonight* (Paramount). While this type of "entertainment news" sometimes includes stories about the film business, it is mostly fan-oriented with an emphasis on Hollywood celebrities and movie reviews.

One estimate is that there are over 2,000 journalists in the USA who write about Hollywood films. At least, that is the number of press kits that studios often send out for new films (Squire, 1992, p. 300). Another indication of the extent of press coverage is represented by the Hollywood Foreign Press Association (HFPA), a non-profit organization with members representing magazines and newspapers in some 55 countries with a claimed combined readership exceeding 250 million.

The HFPA's background can be traced to the formation of the Hollywood Association of Foreign Correspondents in 1928. A competing group of foreign journalists was organized in 1943 as the Hollywood Foreign Press Association. In 1955, the HFPA united members from the two groups and established definite requirements for membership. Currently, members must submit recent by-lined articles for active status and participation in the association's activities. These include interview opportunities with motion picture talent, plus visits to sets, press days, and film festival events.

But the press does not always need to arrange these events on their own, as noted earlier in the discussion of Hollywood publicity. Studios and other film companies actively court press coverage of upcoming and new films, especially, but also Hollywood activities, in general.

**Film critics.** The term "critics" (or *Variety*'s term, "crix") refers to "persons usually employed by newspapers, television stations or other media who screen newly released movies and provide their subjective views and comments on the movie for the public's information" (Cones, 1992, p. 120).

Over the years, some newspaper columnists and reviewers have developed extremely close relationships with Hollywood. While well-known columnists such as Hedda Hopper and Louella Parsons became Hollywood celebrities themselves, some feel that they were much more manipulated by the studio system than movie critics are by today's media system.

Critics and film reviewers still play a special role in the Hollywood system. Studios regularly schedule critics' screenings in advance of a film's release, hoping to receive favorable reviews. However, if negative reviews are expected, the studio may decide not to screen a picture, hoping to delay the bad publicity as long as possible (although this strategy may backfire as critics may be harsher in their reviews because of the delay).

However, the studios have been known to woo key critics in various ways. In addition to supplying information and material about upcoming films, they may wine and dine critics at previews, arrange special interviews with stars or other key talent, or provide a variety of other special considerations or favors. Marketing and advertising campaigns also sometimes feature quotes from well-known critics, thus improving their reputation and (possibly) encouraging them to make more favorable comments to get their name in film advertisements.

It is assumed, therefore, that movie critics are able to influence the box office success of a film. A "powerful critic theory" is also prevalent in other industries where reviews are often thought to make or break commercial properties such as Broadway plays, books, etc., but the relationship between film critics and Hollywood seems to have become particularly entangled. As one movie marketing executive explains: "Critics . . . I think we've made them important to us. We quote them all the time. We use excerpts from their reviews in our advertising. But we're probably doing that because we don't have enough confidence in our own good work to not use them" (Brouwer and Wright, 1990, p. 520).

Another commonplace assumption by many in the industry is expressed as follows: "if it's not a good movie, gets poor reviews and opens poorly, it might be saved. If it's not a review-driven movie, such as an action or teenage movie, and opens poorly, it probably can't be saved" (Squire, 1992, p. 302).

A number of academic studies have attempted to assess the influence of critics' reviews on motion picture selection, however, with mixed results. Eliashberg and Shugan (1997, p. 77) reviewed these studies and observe that:

> In sum, research evidence on critics' reviews and their effect seems inconclusive. It suggests that the role critics (or movie experts) play may be interpreted as influential, in shaping movie-goers' interest in attending movies. It also suggests a moderate, and possibly different, impact for positive and negative reviews . . . Finally, it suggests that the reviews may only indicate movie-goer tastes.

In their own study, Eliashberg and Shugan found that critical reviews may influence late and cumulative box office receipts but do not have a significant impact on early box office revenues. In other words, critics serve more as leading indicators than as opinion leaders.

Meanwhile, in a recent study, MarketCast reported on a national random sample of moviegoers that found friends' opinions and quotes in ads more important than critics' opinions. Furthermore, over 50 percent of participants in the study reported that they ignore what critics say about a film, feeling that critics can't relate to normal audiences or misled them about movies.

In a more recent study, *Variety* polled four dozen filmmakers in Hollywood and New York in 2000 and found that industry insiders have mostly negative views about critics. A typical opinion was the following: "I can't name one critic that I trust. If there was ever an art to it, it's been lost." The report concluded that "There's a hunger for quality criticism that once played a key role in American filmmaking; moviemakers are angry that it's been replaced by blurbmeisters, report cards, one-to-four-star rankings and thumbs (aloft and below)."[4]

Some filmmakers felt that reviewers in the past had more passion and that, "Now it's about soundbite criticism." However, they also felt that's not always the fault of critics. Now, there are few films that lend themselves to impressive reviews, plus "They're being hit on by the studios to a much greater extent, and they're being hyped." In addition, there was some sympathy for reviewers who are faced with a huge number of films for review these days.

Filmmakers were especially contemptuous of the "most heavily blurbed" TV critics. One filmmaker observed, "If there ever was an art to film criticism, it was lost. It all started with the televising of *Siskel & Ebert*. People stopped reading." One of the key reviewers in the USA, Roger Ebert, illicited a love–hate response from filmmakers. Ebert, with his late partner, Gene Siskel, seems to have created the most familiar image of today's film critic. (Perhaps, ironically, the duo established their name in television through a program produced by one of the majors.)

Jowett and Linton have offered another assessment of the critic-industry relationship:

> While the producer-distributors would prefer to have good critical reviews than bad ones, even the latter will be accepted if the audience has good things to tell its peers about the movie. Such a discrepancy simply adds support to movie-makers' contention that critics are cultural eunuchs who know nothing about the business – let alone the art of making movies. (1989, p. 70)

Some industy people realize that critics are necessary for the business and try to use them to their benefit. As one of the filmmakers interviewed in the *Variety* poll mentioned above explained: "the key to following a critic is knowing how to interpret his tastes for your own needs." Others in Hollywood still wage bitter battles with reviewers, and sometimes those conflicts are quite public. One recent example was director James Cameron's infamous response to Kenneth Turan's negative comments in the *Los Angeles Times* about Cameron and his film *Titanic*. More recently, Castle Rock decided not to screen *The Adventures of Pluto Nash* to critics prior to its release because negative comments on the Internet revealed a "predisposition by reviewers to pan it." Release of the film, which stars Eddie Murphy, had already been delayed for nearly two years for various reasons.

And then there was the group of French filmmakers who were tired of attacks by French film critics and issued a public directive against their attackers. The French directors proposed that negative reviews be suppressed until after opening weekend, an idea that attracted a good deal of attention, but little hope of success.

It is probably not surprising that there are associations for film critics, similar to other professional groups associated with the film industry. Critics have organized groups in many major US cities, including Los Angeles, New York, Chicago, Dallas, Fort Worth and San Francisco. The National Society of Film Critics was formed in 1966 by a group of magazine writers who had been refused admittance to the New York Film Critics, which was comprised exclusively of newspaper writers.

Meanwhile, critics groups are organized in foreign cities (London, for instance) and countries (Australia, for instance) and the International Federation of Film Critics claims to "defend the rights and interests of professional film critics and the improvement of conditions in which they carry out their work." More recently, an Online Film Critics Society has also been formed.

## The trade press

The film industry attracts a good deal of attention and coverage from the popular press, as discussed previously. But the industry also has its own trade press, as does many other industries, where news and information about the business are published.

The industry trade press includes a number of publications, but the most prevalent and influential are *Variety* and *The Hollywood Reporter*. These outlets are primary sources for a wide range of information on the film industry, as well as other media such as television, music, and legitimate theater (in the case of *Variety*). The reliability of that information is another matter, as some of the "news" is influenced by the publicity-seeking nature of Hollywood. Nevertheless, the trade press is an important component of the industry and serves as a focal point for industry players and company activities.

*Variety.* Since 1905, *Daily Variety* has served as one of the main industry trade papers. The weekly version was started in 1933. A more recent addition is *Daily Variety Gotham*, which highlights New York news. The publication claims that it is "Recognized throughout the world as the entertainment industry's business-to-business newspaper of record." This may be true, as the publication covers the global media and entertainment marketplace in 84 countries.

In addition to trade news coverage, the publication features box office reports and film and TV production charts that most industry people read. *Variety*'s film reviews also are valued by many in the industry. In fact, in the poll of filmmakers mentioned previously, Hollywood business papers were viewed as "the most reliable, because in addition to box office prospects and production values, they pinpoint a picture's weaknesses and they don't go off on a tangent." However, it is also acknowledged that the reviews are part of a trade paper mentality. "Every review was about the chances of the film turning a profit in the domestic marketplace, as opposed to being about directing or acting. They were profit-margin reviews."

*Variety* is owned by Cahners Business Information, which is owned by Reed Business International, the business division of Reed Elsevier Group PLC, which claims to be "the world's leading publisher and information provider." The larger Reed Elsevier Group includes legal publishing (under the LexisNexis banner), scientific and medical information and educational materials (Harcourt Education).

Reed Business Information includes more than 135 business-to-business publications, over 125 web sites, and a range of services including web development, custom publishing, research, business lists, and industry events. The company also produces specialized directories, databases, market research, newsletters, conferences, and seminars. The company claims that more than 7 million subscribers read their publications. Reed Business reported revenues of over $2 billion in 2001.

In addition to *Variety* and MarketCast (the research company mentioned earlier in this chapter), the division includes *Video Business, Publishers Weekly, Wireless Week, Multichannel News, Broadcasting & Cable* and *LA411/NY411* (production services directories). The company also owns eLogic, a leading software company and provider of content management and web solutions to media companies.

Almost from its launch in 1905, *Variety* has used its own, distinctive "slanguage." Some of these terms, such as "scribes," "tenpercentery," and "crix," have already been used in this text. Others include words like "ankle," which refers to someone leaving or walking away from a job, or "whammo," "boffo," or "socko," referring to something terrific, especially box office performance. New York is "Gotham" and Australia is "Oz." A "chop-socky slug fest" is a martial arts film, while a "weeper" is a melodrama.

The publication explains that the language was a device to fit long words into small headlines. For instance, one of the best-known *Variety* headlines was used in the 1940s: "Sticks Nix Hick Pix," meant that audiences in rural areas were not interested in attending films about rural life. But the publications also explains that the slang terms also were developed "to create a clubby feel among the paper's entertainment industry readers" (see Appendix C for more examples of *Variety*-speak).

**The Hollywood Reporter.**    A close competitor of *Variety* is *The Hollywood Reporter*, as mentioned previously, owned by VNU Business Publications. VNU is a huge company that manages web sites, electronic products and services, as well as owning over 70 magazines including *Adweek, Billboard, Architecture*, and *Progressive Grocer*. VNU also operates The Entertainment News Wire, an electronic entertainment resource with a news and digital photo service and newspaper, magazine, broadcast and database clients in 32 countries. The News Wire provides general, consumer-oriented coverage of film, music, TV, theater and video. Material is drawn from VNU business publications such as *Billboard* and *The Hollywood Reporter*, as well as other sources.

### Film festivals and markets

Marketing and promotional possibilities for films also are presented by film festivals and markets, which have multiplied at a rather fast rate over the past few decades. Over 600 festivals of one kind or another were reported worldwide by *Variety* in 2002, however, the exact number of festivals is difficult to estimate. For instance, in 2000, the European Coordination of Film Festivals reported over 150 festivals in Europe alone (Turan, 2002).

The attention given to some festivals and the awards they give to individual films can be alluring and advantageous for some filmmakers and companies. Some of the key festivals have also added markets to their events, offering further opportunities for buying and selling products and making industry contacts. These events have become especially important for smaller or independent films as press and audience attention can generate invaluable word-of-mouth promotion. Again, festivals may be particularly lucrative for smaller or independent films, as positive attention may attract distributor attention and ultimately affect a film's success, especially in international markets.

Yet, some filmmakers and distributors are wary of festivals, fearing the potential damage of a negative response. There also can be relatively high expenses associated with participation, including the cost of travel. Some of the major Hollywood blockbusters may not need to be screened at festivals and thus avoid these additional expenses.

*Los Angeles Times* reviewer, Kenneth Turan, has categorized film festivals as those with aesthetic, business or geopolitical agendas. He identifies and discusses Havana, Sarajevo and Midnight Sun as having geopolitical goals, while Pordenone, Lone Pine and Telluride are examined for their primarily aesthetic goals. Meanwhile, Cannes, Sundance and ShoWest represent festivals with distinct business agendas (Turan, 2002). Only a few of the more prominent festivals and markets are discussed briefly here.

The *Cannes Film Festival* is actually the Festival International du Film and has been organized on a regular annual basis since 1951. The event is probably the best-known film festival, and, in fact, has been called the world's largest yearly media event: "a round-the clock cinematic billboard that in 1990 attracted 3,893 journalists, 221 TV crews, and 118 radio stations representing 81 countries" (Turan, 2002, p. 14). But Cannes also includes a film market where as many as 600 films are screened in hopes of attracting buyers. Cannes is said to have a love–hate relationship with Hollywood, yet has been known to give major Hollywood films important awards that are then used in marketing pitches.

Meanwhile, the *Sundance Film Festival* was started 1978 in Salt Lake City, growing to become "the flagship of the burgeoning American independent film movement" after being adopted by Robert Redford's Sundance Institute in 1985 and relocated to Park City, Utah. However, the event has become increasingly useful for the major studios, as well. Redford's explanation is an example of how the mainstream film industry catches up with and eventually encompasses the independent, the marginal or the peripheral:

> When the first studio people showed up, I dragged them off the street and into the screening rooms. . . . Eventually – and this caught me by

surprise – people began flocking here because they were interested in the wonderful, diverse menu of films we were screening that started with *El Norte* and gained steam with *Sex, Lies, and Videotape*. Sundance was suddenly so cool that Hollywood simply couldn't ignore it. In fact, Hollywood wanted to be "in" with it. When Hollywood came, the merchants came. And when the merchants came, fashion came. And when fashion came, the media came and voted, Sundance was a part of the mainstream.[5]

At the same time, *ShoWest* is basically a convention organized mostly for exhibitors every March in Las Vegas, but it is also a focal point for "mainstream filmmaking and filmgoing" (Turan, 2002, p. 51). In addition to numerous film screenings, the huge gathering (up to 12,000 people often attend) features information and panels on industry issues as well as a trade show. For instance, at the 2002 event, a panel was organized on engineering standards for digital cinema. A wide range of vendors (sometimes over 500) participate in the trade show, but also sponsor events, such as receptions, etc. Awards also are given for various reasons, everything from achievements in international exhibition and distribution to achievements in popcorn processing.

The first ShoWest took place in 1974, but moved to its Las Vegas site in 1979. It is organized by Sunshine Group Worldwide, which also stages a smaller event called ShowEast for smaller market exhibitors, and CineAsia for Pacific Rim exhibitors.

Although the event can be expensive for the studios, it also is acknowledged as a key promotional device (the trade press, as well as the popular press, cover the event extensively), and serves to cultivate valuable relations within the industry, especially "camaraderie" between exhibitors and distributors (ibid., p. 55).

Another important event for independent film is the *American Film Market*, sponsored by the American Film Marketing Association. The AFMA is the trade association for independent film and television distributors and producers. AFMA's global membership distributes (and often produces) non-studio films and claims that its members generate more than $4 billion annually in worldwide distribution revenues. The organization includes over 130 independent film and television companies.

The American Film Market is held annually in Los Angeles and claims to be the world's largest film market, attracting more than 7,000 film and television industry professionals, including acquisition and development executives, producers, distributors, agents, attorneys, buyers, and film financiers. The organization reports that "hundreds of films are financed, packaged, licensed, and greenlit, sealing over half a billion dollars in business for both completed films and those in preproduction."

**Festival choices.** The selection process at film festivals often relies on personal trust, long-time friendships, and subjective opinion. While there are usually festival selection committees, gatekeepers or political lobbyists have emerged on the festival circuit. These characters operate between filmmakers and festival heads, influencing the films that are offered and chosen. While big titles by well-known directors or films from the US majors rarely are affected by these maneuvers, international exposure can be crucial for smaller or independent films.

Festivals have distinct images and getting a film into the right festival is also crucial for smaller films, especially. The biggest industry exposure is said to come from around ten of the top festivals: Rotterdam, Berlin, Cannes, Locarno, Montreal, Venice, Toronto and San Sebastian, plus Annecy for animation and Amsterdam for documentaries. As a *Variety* reporter explains:

> Getting the wrong fest – or even the wrong section of a fest – can be counterproductive to a movie's launch. Is it too small for the giant screen of Locarno's Piazza Grande or too populist for its competition? Is it edgy enough for Berlin or too cutting edge for Cannes? Will a nice but unflashy Euro pic be lost in a U.S.-dominated fest like Sundance; would it be better appreciated at Venice?[6]

Sometimes production companies or distributors hire a full-time person just to coordinate festival entries. In fact, some companies have asked festivals to pay service fees to cover these additional costs.

**Festival sponsorship.** Even film festivals are becoming more commercialized, as more businesses are offering sponsorship for the events. Because the presumed impact of traditional advertising is weakening, festivals offer companies with expensive products access to an ideal audience. In other words, festivals attract educated middle-aged consumers with above-average incomes. For example, a recent printed program from the Sundance Film Festival included advertisements from over 125 corporate sponsors.

Corporate funding has been typical for many festivals, but primarily in the form of charitable donations. Recently, however, a more intense partnership has developed between sponsoring companies and festivals, involving marketing departments and advertising agencies. Companies have become interested in a more active and visible role, while these corporate alliances provide festivals with additional funds for promotion.

## Film awards

Hollywood companies attempt to draw attention to their products through press coverage and critical reviews. But attention and acclaim also can be generated through various awards that originate both from inside and outside the film industry.

*Academy Awards.* The best-known film awards are presented by the Academy of Motion Picture Arts and Sciences, or in other words, by the industry itself. The Academy Awards were first organized in 1929 and have grown to become benchmarks for filmmaking, as well as playing an important economic role for the industry.

Regular awards are presented for outstanding individual or collective efforts in 24 categories. Up to five nominations are made in most categories, with balloting for these nominations restricted to members of the Academy branch concerned; directors, for instance, are the only nominators for Achievement in Directing. Nominations for awards in the foreign language and documentary categories are made by large committees of members drawn from all branches. Best Picture nominations and final winners in most categories are determined by the entire membership.

Nomination ballots are mailed by the Academy in January to its members (there were over 5,600 voting members in 2002). The secret ballots are sent to PricewaterhouseCoopers, the professional services firm formerly known as Price Waterhouse. The results of nomination balloting are announced in early February. Then, final ballots are mailed in early March and members have two weeks to return them. After ballots are tabulated, only two partners of PricewaterhouseCoopers are claimed to know the results until the envelopes are opened on stage during the Awards Presentation in March. The Academy Awards Presentation program is itself a media event, attracting worldwide audiences and extensive media coverage.

The nominations and awards are considered some of the best ways to promote a film and can potentially lead to a substantial increase in revenues. Dodds and Holbrook (1988) evaluated the impact of Academy Awards on film revenues, and found significant effects of

Best Picture, Best Actor, and Best Actress awards on post-award revenues. Another study found that theatrical revenue can increase 5–10 percent if a film is nominated, while actually receiving an award can enhance a film's value for cable and network television by 50– 100 percent (Donahue, 1987, p. 81).

Thus, receiving a nomination and ultimately an award are seen as adding value to a film commodity. Serious efforts are made to attract these honors and expensive campaigns to influence voting begin in November each year. In the past, elaborate strategies have been used involving targeted advertising and promotional gimmicks. Studios, independent distributors, and publicists use various strategies to make sure that the Academy members view their film. Special screenings are held, free admissions are offered to commercial runs of a film or video cassettes are shipped to the voters. For several years, the Academy has aggressively monitored campaigning and has issued guidelines that limit company mailings to those items that "actually assist the members in their efforts to assess the artistic and technical merits of a film."

However, at least one author and film critic believes that the campaigns around the Academy Awards have become "nastier, more aggressive, more expensive and more sophisticated." Emanuel Levy, chief film critic for *Screen International* and the author of *Oscar Fever: The History and Politics of the Academy Awards*, notes that "aggressive campaigns have been run for Oscars as far back as the 1940s."[7]

The campaigning may indeed affect the outcome, as over the years there have been some classic examples of films that won (or didn't win) because of political and/or economic reasons. For instance, in 1941 *Citizen Kane*, directed by Orson Welles and based on newspaper mogul William Randolph Hearst, lost to *How Green Was My Valley*. It was widely suggested Hearst's influence in Hollywood had much to do with ensuring that Welles did not triumph. In 1959 screenwriter Ned Young failed to win an Oscar for *The Defiant Ones* because he was blacklisted. His pseudonym, Nathan E. Douglas, won it instead. More recently, in 1998, intense and heavy spending by Miramax was believed to have helped *Shakespeare In Love* defeat *Saving Private Ryan*, widely regarded as the favorite.

**Other awards.** There are a huge number of awards made yearly that involve Hollywood films.[8] While many of these are relatively insignificant, a few important awards are given by organizations or associations connected to the industry. The Hollywood Foreign Press Association presents the Golden Globe Awards at the end of January every year, while the Los Angeles, New York and London Film Critics Associations also present yearly accolades.

Awards also are given by the Hollywood guilds. What has been called Hollywood's pre-Oscar Final Four – the quartet of guild award shows the first two weekends of March – includes trophies from the Producers Guild, the Writers Guild, the Screen Actors Guild, and the Directors Guild.

Meanwhile, the National Board of Review hands out awards that often serve as "signposts" to the winning Oscars. The organization was created as a censorship group in 1909, but its current board is composed of around 150 members from varying professions, including educators, doctors, lawyers, historians, and few former industry insiders. The membership is said to be a mystery to most people in the film business. Although the group's selections tend to favor the specialty market, with an emphasis on breakthrough performances and emerging talent, the board's choice has agreed with 41 percent of the Academy's best picture choices since 1980.

While the artistic and creative merit of these various awards can be disputed endlessly, the promotional and potential financial benefit is less debatable. Any kind of nomination or award is typically used extensively in advertising and promotional activities, and often boosts a film's overall revenues.

## Protecting the Industry

Similar to other industries, Hollywood employs strategies to protect its products and business interests both in domestic and global markets. These efforts include a strong trade association and ongoing efforts to enlist the state in supporting the industry.

### MPAA

The Motion Picture Association of America (MPAA) and its international counterpart, the Motion Picture Association (MPA) are the associations that officially promote and protect the industry's interests. The MPAA was founded in 1922 mostly to defend the industry against critics that were pushing strongly for national censorship of motion pictures. But the organization has expanded its role over the years to reflect an expanding industry. The organization defines itself as "the voice and advocate of the American motion picture, home video and television industries." However, the MPAA works principally for its members, the Hollywood majors.

In addition to administering the Ratings and Classification System discussed in Chapter 3, the MPAA is especially active in fighting various threats to the industry, everything from government intervention and trade policies to copyright infringement and First Amendment issues. The tactics used include promotional and educational campaigns, as well as legal actions on behalf of its members. A good deal of the work that the MPAA does, however, involves influencing and working with local, state, and national governments, as will be discussed below.

The MPAA's activities are carried out through its staff, as well as outside PR firms. However, much of the public attention often focuses on its zealous leader, Jack Valenti. As Chairman and CEO of the MPAA since 1966, Valenti speaks out on any subject that relates to the film industry, but has been especially active in releasing policy statements to the press on issues such as trade relations, ratings, copyright and piracy issues, and future technologies. The silver-haired orator is often called upon to testify on these issues at Congressional hearings, where he is not shy about reminding everyone about the value of the film industry's products. An example from a House Appropriations Committee hearing in April 2002:

> The facts are these: The Copyright Industries are responsible for some five percent of the GDP of the nation. They gather in more international revenues than automobiles and auto parts, more than aircraft, more than agriculture. They are creating NEW jobs at three times the rate of the rest of the economy. The movie industry alone has a *Surplus* balance of trade *with every single country in the world*. No other American enterprise can make that statement. And all this at a time when the U.S. is bleeding from some $400 Billion in *Deficit* balance of trade. [emphasis in original] (Valenti, 2002)

Valenti is well suited for the Hollywood spokesperson position with notable past political experience (he worked in the Lyndon Johnson White House).[9] Of course, he is handsomely rewarded for his efforts on behalf of the industry and was the first lobbyist to cross the $1 million mark. In 2000, he was paid $1.15 million, in addition to $18,851 in perks, and ranked fifth among the top ten highest-paid trade-organization heads.

Although the MPAA is well organized and (mostly) an effective advocate for its members, the organization relies heavily on the state for support and to protect the industry from various threats.

## Hollywood and the State

From coverage in the popular press, it might be assumed that Hollywood is a target of a government that monitors, criticizes, and attempts to regulate the film industry. Indeed, some local and national government officials seem to devote considerable attention to criticizing film content, especially its influence on young people.

Yet it is absolutely clear that the industry looks for and receives a good deal of support from the state, not only in the global arena but in the domestic marketplace, as well. In other words, the film industry does not just rely on its own resources to protect its business, but receives considerable support and assistance from the US government.

State support does not come automatically, however, and the industry works hard to lobby for such assistance. The MPAA and other industry representatives are involved in lobbying that is carried on at the highest level of the government, with special attention given to the presidency as well as cabinet officials. It certainly hasn't hurt matters that some presidents have already had close ties to Hollywood. Ronald Reagan, the Hollywood actor, was the most obvious example but Bill Clinton also had Hollywood connections through close friends in the industry and extensive political support from entertainment notables.

Hollywood's lobbying efforts are not just aimed at the political party in office. For instance, one might think there would be some concern during Republican administrations, as Hollywood tends to support the Democratic Party. Of course, the industry and its power players are huge political contributors. For instance, the entertainment industry contributed $10 million in various political contributions in 1999.[10] But a survey by the Associated Press in 2002 concluded that when Hollywood gives to political causes, the money almost always goes to legislators associated with the Democratic Party. The survey found that 42 heads of studios, directors and producers in the music, television, and film businesses contributed $613,633 to the Democratic National Committee and various Democratic candidates, while only minimal amounts were given to Republicans.

Thus, when Republicans control the presidency and the legislative bodies, one might think that the film industry would suffer. However, Hollywood seems to cover all of its political bases. As Valenti proclaims: "We have friends on both sides of the aisle." Futhermore, as *Variety* concludes, "Despite the fact that Hollywood itself is predominantly Democratic, the current crop of Tinseltown lobbyists is adept at working the political apparatus of both parties."

As noted previously, the industry relies on the government to become involved in a wide range of issues. As we have already seen, the State supports the film industry extensively with trade negotiations and removing barriers to trade. The industry also works closely with the State on copyright protection and piracy problems, while some groups in the Hollywood community have turned to the government for relief from runaway production. A bit more detail on these two issues will further exemplify this deep-rooted industry/State relationship.

## Examples of Hollywood/State cooperation

*The perennial problem of piracy.*    The MPAA and MPA claim that the US motion picture industry loses in excess of $3 billion annually in potential worldwide revenue due to piracy. The organization states that this figure does not include Internet piracy losses because of difficulties in calculating such amounts. However, those damages are claimed to be substantial. For instance, one estimate was that there were 4 million illegal downloads of *Star Wars* and *Spider-Man* during May 2002. (Current forms of piracy or copyright abuses are discussed at the end of this section.)

To combat these supposed losses, the MPAA/MPA organized an international anti-piracy program in the USA in 1976. The organization states that the program attempts to "implement and strengthen existing copyright protection legislation, assist local governments and law enforcement authorities in the investigation and prosecution of piracy cases, initiate civil litigation on behalf of its member companies against copyright infringers, and conduct education outreach programs regarding the harmful effects of piracy."

These efforts have been extended globally through the MPAA's support of what it calls "legitimate markets" and the castigation of illegal activities. In 2000, the MPA launched over 60,000 investigations into suspected pirate activities. Working with local authorities around the world, the association was involved in another 18,000 raids against pirate operations. The MPAA/MPA coordinate these activities from headquarters in Encino, California, but also maintain regional offices in Washington, D.C., Brussels, New Delhi, Rio de Janeiro, Singapore, Mexico City, Toronto, and Jakarta.

The organization points out that when piracy of a film occurs at any point in its release sequence, all subsequent markets are negatively affected. An example was the 1999 release of the film *Star Wars: Episode 1 – The Phantom Menace*. Pirated copies of the film that were created by using camcorders flooded the Asian market, even while the film was still showing in US theaters. When the film opened in Asian theaters, attendance was far below the distributor's expectations. The MPAA/MPA also claimed that home entertainment retailers lost business because of pirated copies.

Again, the industry does not rely on its own efforts to counteract piracy, but looks to the State for support and enforcement. Hollywood lobbied hard for strong anti-piracy legislation as part of the Copyright Act of 1976. The Act was amended in 1982 to increase the penalties for the illegal duplication of copyrighted material and make such offenses felonies on the first offense. Copyright owners can file civil lawsuits against copyright infringers, while the government may file criminal charges. Furthermore, the new US Sentencing Commission guidelines have reinforced these penalties. In addition, the Communications Act of 1984 and later amendments provided comparable penalties and remedies for cable TV and satellite pirates. Clearly, the government has responded to the industry's appeal to protect copyright in the US, at least.

However, the US government also assists in global efforts to combat piracy. The MPA actively works to strengthen the copyright laws that currently exist in more than 80 nations. In some parts of the world where copyright laws are weak or nonexistent, successful charges have been brought against pirates under other statutes, such as receiving stolen goods, trademark violations, smuggling, and failure to pay custom duties. In addition, intellectual property relations between the USA and most foreign countries are governed by an array of multilateral treaties and conventions as well as bilateral agreements, including the Universal Copyright Convention (UCC) and the Berne Convention.

The government does not shy away from threatening countries because of copyright violations. Political pressure has been placed at the highest levels in many countries in an effort to force stronger copyright enforcement. Indeed, the industry/government partnership has been quite successful in countries such as Malaysia, Indonesia, and Singapore, where trade sanctions were threatened unless copyright adherence was improved. Other forms of pressure are also used, for instance, in Korea, where US government pressure forced the Korean film industry to open up to American distribution companies.

The industry/government alliance also has been at work in Eastern Europe, which represents a lucrative market where pirating is seen as a special problem. Not only video copying is rampant, but copying film prints is also common. For example, 80 percent of video activity in Bulgaria is reported by the industry to be illegal. The US film industry has applauded the efforts in countries such as Poland and Hungary to crack down on piracy.

While governments are essentially responsible for copyright legislation and enforcement, the trade organizations have been actively assisting in the process. Both the MPA and AFMA boast of working with governments to get old copyright laws updated and "appropriate penalties" formulated. Once the laws are on the books, the MPA often offers to send high-level teams to some countries to help develop anti-piracy programs.

Finally, various trade agreements also encourage the free flow and protection of intellectual property among nations. The MPA encourages foreign governments to abide by, and fully implement, important agreements such as the Trade Related Aspects of Intellectual Property Rights (TRIPS) agreement and the World Intellectual Property Organization (WIPO) treaties.

**Forms of piracy.**   Despite all these enforcement activities, the different types of piracy continue to grow with the ongoing development of new forms of media technology. Indeed, Hollywood's embrace of new technologies often leads to inevitable breaches of copyright laws, a contradictory dilemma that is perhaps unavoidable. As the industry employs new technologies to expand its markets, products distributed via those same technologies often are susceptible to unauthorized or unpaid use. The MPAA's list of different kinds of piracy is included on their web site, as well as the organization's efforts to combat these activities. A few of these are discussed briefly here.

*Theatrical print theft* involves 35 or 16 mm film prints stolen from a theater, film depot, courier service or other industry-related facility to make illegal copies. Relatively high quality copies are possible from these prints, although the practice is not as common as other forms of content theft. For instance, *signal theft* – or the act of illegally tapping into cable TV or satellite signals – is far more prevalent. Meanwhile, *broadcast piracy* involves the on-air broadcasting of a bootleg videocassette of a film or the on-air showing of legitimate films or television programs without permission from the copyright holder.

*Videocassette piracy* includes the use of video cameras to record motion picture films off theater screens and then copy them on blank videocassettes or optical discs for illegal distribution. In addition, illegal copies of videocassettes are sometimes made from legitimate advance copies used for screening and marketing purposes. Duplicating facilities or "laboratories" are set up to create and distribute pirated videocassettes, often producing hundreds of thousands of illegal videocassette copies each year. Copies (sometimes in counterfeit videocassette boxes) are distributed to a variety of outlets including swap meets, co-operating video dealers, and street vendors. As noted previously, the MPAA works with governments to raid such operations, seizing thousands of illegal tapes each year. In 2000, approximately 350,000 illegal videocassettes and 4,000 VCRs were seized in North America alone. In addition, the MPAA claims to initiate over 600 investigations into suspected piracy in the USA each year and at any one time has approximately 400 active cases.

Several forms of illegal activity may be involved in *internet piracy*. *Downloadable media* pertains to digital files that allow for motion pictures to be compressed and uploaded for direct download onto a computer. Pirates use downloadable media formats to illegally offer and distribute motion pictures to other Internet users. *Hard goods piracy* is the illegal online sale, distribution and/or trading of copies of motion pictures in any format, including videocassettes and all optical media product. *Streaming media* refers to the transmission or transfer of data that is delivered to the online user or viewer in a steady stream in near real time. *Circumvention devices* are any physical media or digital files that permit the circumvention of content protection devices on films, videos, discs, etc. An example is the software utility DeCSS that breaks the copy protection on DVDs making it possible for motion pictures in DVD format to be decrypted and illegally copied onto a computer's hard drive for further distribution over the Internet or other means.

The MPAA again relies on the government to police and prosecute Internet copyright violations through amended federal copyright statutes such as the No Electronic Theft Act (NET Act) and the Digital Millennium Copyright Act (DMCA). In international settings, the industry works with national governments to combat Internet piracy. An example is the case of movie88.com in Taiwan. Early in 2002, the MPAA announced that the Taiwan authorities ("with assistance provided by the Motion Picture Association") ordered the closure of the web site which offered to stream movies without the permission of copyright owners. The site was charging one dollar for mostly major Hollywood movies. As Jack Valenti explained: "We are grateful to the Taiwanese authorities for their swift action in shutting down movie88.com."[11]

*Optical disc piracy* may involve laser discs, video compact discs and digital versatile discs or DVDs. In 2000, the MPA claimed that 4.5 million videos were seized worldwide, but over 20 million pirate optical discs were confiscated during the same period. An average illegal videocassette duplication facility with 100 VCRs can, in a 10-hour period, produce about 400 pirated cassettes, while pirates with the right CD pressing equipment can produce thousands of perfect DVDs daily.

Although it does not involve the government, the major US distributors have been implementing near simultaneous foreign release dates mostly because of international film piracy problems. While all of these efforts may help solve some of the piracy puzzle, it is likely that the problem will continue to be a thorn in the side of the Hollywood majors for years to come.

**Runaway production.**   The concerns over runaway production were discussed in Chapter 1, but this issue also represents an example of how the industry looks to the government for solutions to its problems, as well as the political nature of that process. As discussed previously, the runaway production problem has been persuasively documented in industry and government reports. However, the solutions to the problem have proven to be more controversial. While a number of industry coalitions have called for government intervention, there has been disagreement as to the best remedy.

The Film U.S. alliance, which includes the DGA, the American Film Marketing Association, the Producers Guild and a number of film commissions, has supported a *federal wage-based tax credit*, a rarely granted incentive allowing production companies to write off part of employee wages.

Meanwhile, the Film & Television Action Coalition (FTAC) (backed by SAG and the protectionist Made in the USA Foundation) initiated a Countervailing Tariff Petition with the US Dept. of Commerce to determine the legality of subsidies granted by the Canadian Government. The *countervailing tariff remedy* would combat runaway production by forcing US producers to give up Canadian government subsidies. In other words, if a studio gets a $1 million subsidy to shoot in Canada, the studio would then be required to give that money to the US government. Furthermore, the countervailing tariff would be a condition for clearing a film for US distribution. The coalition argued that industry-specific subsidies are illegal under the General Agreement on Tariffs and Trade (or GATT).

Countervailing tariffs have not been supported by Film U.S., the MPAA, IATSE, or a number of other Hollywood groups. The opposition to the tariff petition has been because of the dependence on the industry on foreign markets; the potential for retaliation (Canada and other governments could, for instance, impose a tax on box office tickets or on American TV equipment); and, the negative impact on legislative efforts. As one Congressman explained: "The quickest way to kill runaway production legislation is this tariff proposal. Congress will not support protectionism." The MPAA and others lobbied heavily with the Bush administration and other Washington politicians on this issue, and the petition was withdrawn in January 2002. The FTAC then asked the World Trade Organization to rule that Canadian production subsidies are illegal. The FTAC also filed a NAFTA Section 301(a) petition asking the US Trade Representative to initiate negotiations with Canada to remove its subsidies, backed by the threat of intervention by the WTO if it does not comply.

Meanwhile, important runaway production legislation in California failed in 2002 due to budget problems. The bill would have provided as much as $650 million in tax credits to producers between 2004 and 2010, and thus might have lured producers back to California.

Although the runaway production problem continues, it represents another example of how the industry looks to the State for support and assistance in solving its problems. Ironically, however, this particular problem seems to be related to contradictions within the industry itself. One might ask who is responsible for runaway production, anyway. And the answer would be producers – Hollywood producers – who are attracted to advantageous exchange rates, as well as other economic advantages such as cheaper labor costs. Thus producers are taking their business to locations outside of southern California and even outside the USA, to the detriment of the Hollywood labor force. While no solution seems near at hand, as they say in the movies, stand by . . .

## Issue: State/industry partnerships

While the interaction between the film industry and the US government is not unusual, it is important to acknowledge and understand the relationship. Industries often rely on the State in various ways to assure their survival as well as their prosperity in domestic and global markets. Hollywood is not necessarily unique in this sense, however, the major companies have been relatively successful in calling on State support, especially in global markets where resistance is often present. These practices call into question the idealistic notions of "free" markets, as well as the autonomy of the private sphere. However, these arguments are not the only questionable claims that are often made about the motion picture business, as we shall see in the concluding chapter.

## Notes

1 For instance, in September 2002, United International Pictures announced it would drop National Research Group's tracking service, though the international distributor will have a continuing relationship with the firm for other sorts of overseas research.

2 F. Fiore, "Hollywood Admits Marketing Violent Movies to Young Kids," *Los Angeles Times*, 29 September 2000, p. C-1.

3 http://www.learnaboutmovieposters.com/NewSite/INDEX/ARTICLES/ nss_history.asp

4 J. Bing, "PIX NIX CRIX SHTICKS: Reviewers Get Thumbs-Down from Filmmakers," *Variety*, 13 March 2000, p. 1.

5 "Turning an Industry Inside Out: A Conversation with Robert Redford," *Harvard Business Review*, May 2002, Vol. 80, Issue 5.

6 D. Elley, "Underground Network Plays Politics with Pix," *Variety*, 26 Aug 2002, p. 1.

7 D. Campbell "Hollywood Knives are Out as Oscars get Nasty," *The Guardian*, 16 March 2002.

8 For an extensive list of awards and festivals, see http://www.imdb.com/ Sections/Awards/Events.

9 Valenti's advertising and political consulting agency, Weekley & Valenti, was in charge of the press during the visit of President Kennedy and Vice President Johnson to Texas. As the MPAA web site explains: "Valenti was in the motorcade in Dallas on November 22, 1963. Within hours of the murder of John F. Kennedy, Valenti was on Air Force One flying back to Washington, the first newly hired special assistant to the new President." http://www.mpaa.org/jack/jack/index.htm

10 See http://www.opensecrets.org/alerts for more information on political contributions.

11 http://www.mpaa.org/jack/index.htm

# Why it Matters How Hollywood Works 6

This book is an attempt to explain how Hollywood works as an industry that manufactures and markets commodities. While these commodities are often engaging and exciting entertainment products, it is still important to understand the process by which they are produced and distributed.

The previous chapters have described how a film concept becomes a film commodity, passing through the production, distribution, and exhibition/retail stages. During this process, Hollywood films are becoming more commercial through product placement, as well as spawning new commodities such as merchandise and other media products. The corporations that control the industry – the Hollywood majors – are part of diversified entertainment conglomerates that operate at a global level, constantly searching for new markets. Though the majors dominate domestic and global markets, their products do not simply compete with other commodities in these marketplaces, but are heavily promoted and publicized, as well as protected and defended through various strategies that rely on the State.

## Film Industry Illusions

Along with the details of this industrial process, this book has challenged a few of the assumptions that are often made about the film business. While sensational stories, legends and myths about movie stars, directors, screenplays, and writers seem to flourish in the film industry, much of the prevailing wisdom about the business of film also appears slightly deceptive. A few of these illusions are summarized briefly here, as they have been detailed in the previous chapters.

### Illusion #1: "There's no business like show business."

Economists and other industry observers insist that film production and distribution is a unique and risky business. However, both of these assumptions need to be more carefully qualified.

While the US film industry may have some unique characteristics, it is nevertheless an industry organized around profit and thus not unique in that sense. From a film's inception as an idea or concept to its distribution to a wide range of outlets and locations, film industry insiders explain that the motivating force is the bottom-line. Furthermore, even though each product may be singular and unique, the techniques and strategies that are used to produce and promote Hollywood films are comparable. In other words, an industrial process is in place that does not always appear to be peculiar or unusual.

While film production and distribution is consistently claimed to be a risky business, much of the "risk" has been introduced and sustained by the industry itself. Expensive blockbuster, star-studded features promoted by massive marketing campaigns are characteristic of Hollywood's attempt to attract massive box office revenues, as well as to build further profits from subsequent distribution outlets. These skyrocketing costs are one of the main reasons why Hollywood filmmaking is said to be risky.

But is the film business actually a risky business at all? A common assumption is that Hollywood films rarely return their investments at the box office and companies survive from the successes of a few blockbuster films. This assumption, however, belies the fact that box office receipts are not the only source of income for film commodities. As we have seen, theaters are only the beginning of a chain of windows or markets where little additional investment is needed, but more income and, not infrequently, extensive profits are produced.

For the film industry, more distribution outlets have translated into less risk. Videocassette, DVD, and cable release have provided especially lucrative rewards for films that do well in theaters, as well as giving "legs" to films that have not performed well in theatrical release. Moreover, globalization and privatization have opened international markets that further reduce the risk of distributing these infinitely exportable products. Obviously, these factors must be taken into account when considering the claim that Hollywood's "unique" business is inherently "risky."

## Illusion #2: "It's a dog-eat-dog business."

Some claim that the industry is extremely competitive. However, it is obvious by looking at the breakdown of market shares for the retail outlets where feature films are bought and sold that Hollywood represents a concentrated industry. From the theatrical box office, to VHS and DVD sales, to the sale of films to television and cable outlets, the Hollywood majors rule the film business as a reigning oligopoly. While there may be some competition (for instance, between major releases), the studios also cooperate in typical oligopolistic fashion to determine industry policies and to protect and promote the industry.

This dominance is echoed in the clout that is demonstrated in the various deals that characterize the industry – power deals that involve the major studios and Hollywood's power players, with little room for independents or smaller companies to compete for talent or other resources. The majors' strength can be contrasted to an independent company that only produces films, and thus is unable to capitalize or draw strength from diversified revenues or from a conglomerate owner.

While the film industry accommodates independent production, the majors ultimately set the agenda and reap the bulk of the rewards. Through their control over film distribution, as well as by pursuing various strategies to reduce risk, and protect and promote their products, the Hollywood majors have maintained their dominance of the US film industry, as well as much of the world's film business.

## Illusion #3: ". . . a supremely democratic form of entertainment."

A film executive once described the industry as democratic because "customers vote for one movie over another by simply putting down hard cash" (Squire, 1992, p. 24). Another assumption about Hollywood is that the industry offers audiences a wide range of entertainment choices.

While hundreds of films are produced and distributed each year, it may be possible to argue that audience choice is still somewhat constrained by the many formulaic and recycled films that Hollywood consistently distributes to theaters and other outlets that crave these kind of products. Even though audiences are said to influence the films that are produced and distributed, such influence is mainly a matter of choosing between the films that are actually made available.

Certainly, much of American popular culture (including Hollywood films) is mass-produced, thus it is not created by public preference but by industrial intentions. In this sense, the claim of consumer choice is somewhat overstated. Again, Hollywood films are produced and distributed within specific industrial parameters that privilege profit over other goals such as artistic merit or public enlightenment.

## Illusion #4: "That's entertainment!"

Serious discussions of the film industry are often met with a typical response: "Well, it's only entertainment." Despite this commonly held assumption, it must be insisted that Hollywood is not just about entertainment. As we have seen, it's a business that produces and distributes products that have significant economic, political, and cultural implications. Hollywood films may offer engaging fantasies and convenient escape from the drudgeries of daily life, but they also offer explicit visions of the world and lessons for living in that world. In addition to their obvious economic importance, motion pictures are ideological products and thus are socially and politically significant as well. Consequently, understanding how Hollywood works is a necessary component to discerning film's overall social significance.

## Hollywood in the twenty-first century

Hollywood seems to thrive on myths and illusions, even those that pertain to the business of film. These illusions become more problematic upon closer inspection of how the industry actually works. Indeed, several general economic trends are alive and well in Hollywood. As with many other capitalist industries, the processes of concentration, commodification, and commercialization currently govern the US film industry. Furthermore, the industry contributes to the growing trend of consumerism that dominates Western societies through the ceaseless manufacture of redundant merchandise, as well as the heightened commercialization involved in the manufacture and marketing of film commodities.

Of course, the megacorporations that dominate the entertainment world are not invincible. Challenges abound, from the potential competition posed by new technologies to ongoing threats from intellectual property infringement. Furthermore, there are no guarantees that Hollywood companies or players will always make the correct decisions to ensure their survival. After all, Hollywood must still depend on the ability to attract audiences, as well as sometimes confronting hostile politicians and other political and economic vagaries. Ultimately, their own grand plans may prove fatal, as sometimes predicted when considering the constantly increasing costs of talent and the continually expanding budgets for major Hollywood films.

Meanwhile, the major Hollywood players move on. With the enhanced need for product to feed new technologies and expanding entertainment markets, the Hollywood majors remain poised and ready to supply it. While the majors already receive income from diverse resources, new distribution outlets mean even further diversification and profits. They continue to build alliances with other companies as well as developing interdependencies between old and new technologies. In addition, they have worked to ensure relaxed government regulation and a supportive State, thus merging into large synergistic corporations that control huge chunks of popular cultural production, not only in the USA, but also around the world.

In other words, the majors – bolstered by their ownership by global entertainment conglomerates – are well positioned to maintain their prominence, not only in the traditional film industry, but also in new forms of entertainment, as well as in the culture industry as a whole. Currently, that means selling film commodities in new outlets such as DVD, the Internet and video-on-demand, commercializing films through product placements, creating new commodities through merchandising, and expanding into global markets. Though the technologies and the players may change, and the strategies used to promote and protect the film business may shift in subtle ways, the motives are likely to remain the same.

Thus it also seems likely that understanding how Hollywood works as an industry that produces and distributes commodities will remain an important requirement for understanding motion pictures in the twenty-first century.

*General Audiences – All ages admitted.* Signifies that the film rated contains nothing most parents will consider offensive for even their youngest children to see or hear. Nudity, sex scenes, and scenes of drug use are absent; violence is minimal; snippets of dialogue may go beyond polite conversation but do not go beyond common everyday expressions.

*PG Parental Guidance Suggested.* Some material may not be suitable for children. Signifies that the film rated may contain some material parents might not like to expose to their young children – material that will clearly need to be examined or inquired about before children are allowed to attend the film. Explicit sex scenes and scenes of drug use are absent; nudity, if present, is seen only briefly, horror and violence do not exceed moderate levels.

*PG-13 Parents Strongly Cautioned.* Some material may be inappropriate for children under 13. Signifies that the film rated may be inappropriate for pre-teens. Parents should be especially careful about letting their younger children attend. Rough or persistent violence is absent; sexually-oriented nudity is generally absent; some scenes of drug use may be seen; some use of one of the harsher sexually-derived words may be heard.

*R Restricted.* Under 17 requires accompanying parent or adult guardian (age varies in some jurisdictions). Signifies that the rating board has concluded that the film rated may contain some adult material. Parents are urged to learn more about the film before taking their children to see it. An R may be assigned due to, among other things, a film's use of language, theme, violence, sex or its portrayal of drug use.

*NC-17 No One 17 and Under Admitted.* Signifies that the rating board believes that most American parents would feel that the film is patently adult and that children age 17 and under should not be admitted to it. The film may contain explicit sex scenes, an accumulation of sexually-oriented language, and/or scenes of excessive violence. The NC-17 designation does not, however, signify that the rated film is obscene or pornographic in terms of sex, language or violence.

*Source*: MPAA.

| 1 | *Titanic* | Paramount | 1997 | $600,788,188 |
| 2 | *Star Wars* | Fox | 1977 | $460,998,007 |
| 3 | *E.T. – The Extra-Terrestrial* | Universal | 1982 | $434,974,579 |
| 4 | *Star Wars: Episode – The Phantom Menace* | Fox | 1999 | $431,088,295 |
| 5 | *Spider-Man* | Sony | 2002 | $403,706,375 |
| 6 | *Jurassic Park* | Universal | 1993 | $357,067,947 |
| 7 | *Lord of the Rings: Two Towers* | New Line | 2002 | $337,526,600 |
| 8 | *Forrest Gump* | Paramount | 1994 | $329,694,499 |
| 9 | *Harry Potter Sorcerer's Stone* | Warner | 2001 | $317,575,550 |
| 10 | *Lord of the Rings: Fellowship* | New Line | 2001 | $313,364,114 |
| 11 | *The Lion King* | Buena Vista | 1994 | $312,855,561 |
| 12 | *Star Wars: Episode II – Attack of the Clones* | Fox | 2002 | $310,672,361 |
| 13 | *Return of the Jedi* | Fox | 1983 | $309,205,079 |
| 14 | *Independence Day* | Fox | 1996 | $306,169,255 |
| 15 | *The Sixth Sense* | Buena Vista | 1999 | $293,506,292 |
| 16 | *The Empire Strikes Back* | Fox | 1980 | $290,271,960 |
| 17 | *Home Alone* | Fox | 1990 | $285,761,243 |
| 18 | *Shrek* | DreamWorks | 2001 | $267,665,011 |
| 19 | *Harry Potter Chamber of Secrets* | Warner | 2002 | $261,970,615 |
| 20 | *Dr. Seuss' How the Grinch . . .* | Universal | 2000 | $260,044,825 |
| 21 | *Jaws* | Universal | 1975 | $260,000,000 |
| 22 | *Monsters, Inc.* | Buena Vista | 2001 | $255,873,250 |
| 23 | *Batman* | Warner | 1989 | $251,188,924 |
| 24 | *Men in Black* | Sony | 1997 | $250,690,539 |
| 25 | *Toy Story 2* | Buena Vista | 1999 | $245,852,179 |
| 26 | *Raiders of the Lost Ark* | Paramount | 1981 | $242,374,454 |
| 27 | *Twister* | Warner | 1996 | $241,708,928 |
| 28 | *My Big Fat Greek Wedding* | IFC | 2002 | $241,438,181 |
| 29 | *Ghostbusters* | Columbia | 1984 | $238,600,000 |
| 30 | *Beverly Hills Cop* | Paramount | 1984 | $234,760,478 |

| 31 | Cast Away | Fox | 2000 | $233,632,142 |
|----|-----------|-----|------|--------------|
| 32 | The Exorcist | Warner | 1973 | $232,671,011 |
| 33 | The Lost World: Jurassic Park | Universal | 1997 | $229,086,679 |
| 34 | Signs | Buena Vista | 2002 | $227,966,634 |
| 35 | Rush Hour 2 | New Line | 2001 | $226,164,286 |
| 36 | Mrs. Doubtfire | Fox | 1993 | $219,195,051 |
| 37 | Ghost | Paramount | 1990 | $217,631,306 |
| 38 | Aladdin | Buena Vista | 1992 | $217,350,219 |
| 39 | Saving Private Ryan | DreamWorks | 1998 | $216,173,322 |
| 40 | Mission: Impossible 2 | Paramount | 2000 | $215,409,889 |
| 41 | Austin Powers in Goldmember | New Line | 2002 | $213,117,789 |
| 42 | Back to the Future | Universal | 1985 | $208,242,016 |
| 43 | Austin Powers 2 | New Line | 1999 | $205,444,716 |
| 44 | Terminator 2: Judgment Day | Tristar | 1991 | $204,843,345 |
| 45 | The Mummy Returns | Universal | 2001 | $202,019,785 |
| 46 | Armageddon | Buena Vista | 1998 | $201,578,182 |
| 47 | Pearl Harbor | Buena Vista | 2001 | $198,542,554 |
| 48 | Indiana Jones – The Last Crusade | Paramount | 1989 | $197,171,806 |
| 49 | Toy Story | Buena Vista | 1995 | $191,780,865 |
| 50 | Men in Black 2 | Sony | 2002 | $190,418,803 |

Source: Variety and EDI FilmSource data, 20 April 2003.

Note: "Box Office Data Sources: The data for the box office charts on Variety.com is gathered by Variety and Nielsen EDI. Box office receipts are calculated via reports from the studios and from the exhibitors, and are subject to early estimates and later corrections." Variety.com

## Excerpts from *Variety*'s Slanguage Dictionary

**ad-pub**   relating to the advertising and publicity department of a motion picture studio.

**Alphabet web**   the ABC television network.

**ankle**   a classic (and enduring) *Variety* term meaning to quit or be dismissed from a job, without necessarily specifying which; instead, it suggests walking.

**anni**   anniversary.

**arthouse**   motion picture theater that shows foreign or non-mainstream independent films, often considered high-brow or "art" films.

**aud**   audience.

**Aussie**   Australian. (See also Oz)

**ayem**   a *Variety* coinage meaning morning (a.m.).

**Beantown**   *Variety* slanguage for Boston, Mass.

**Beertown**   *Variety* slanguage for Milwaukee, Wisconsin.

**BevHills**   Beverly Hills.

**b.f.**   an abbreviation for boyfriend, usually used in reviews (also g.f. – girlfriend).

**biopic**   a *Variety* coinage meaning biographical film.

**bird**   a *Variety* term for satellite.

**biz**   shorthand for business or "the business" – show business.

**Blighty**   Britain.

**blurb**   TV commercial.

**B.O.**   box office or box office receipts.

**boff** (also **boffo, boffola**)   outstanding (usually refers to box office performance). (See also, socko, whammo)

**bow**   (n.) opening or premiere; (v.) to debut a production.

**chantoosie**   female singer (chanteuse).

**Chi** (also **Chitown**)   Chicago.

**chopsocky**   a martial arts film.

**cleffer** a songwriter.

**click** a hit.

**cliffhanger** a melodramatic adventure or suspense film or TV show; usually a serial with a to-be-continued ending.

**(the) Coast** Hollywood, Los Angeles.

**coin** money, financing.

**Col** (also **Colpix**) Columbia Pictures.

**commish** commissioner, commission.

**competish** competition.

**confab** convention or professional gathering.

**conglom** conglomerate.

**corny** a term in common usage originally coined by *Variety*, meaning sentimental, obvious or old-fashioned, out of it.

**crix** critics.

**deejay** (also **d.j.**) commonly used term originally coined by *Variety* meaning disc jockey.

**distribbery** distribution company.

**ducats** tickets.

**exec, exex** executive, executives.

**exhib** exhibitor (movie theater owner).

**Eye web** the CBS television network.

**fave** favorite.

**feevee** pay TV.

**fest** film or TV festival.

**flop** (also **floppola**) failure at the box office.

**f/x** special visual effects.

**Gotham** New York City.

**hardtop** indoor movie theater.

**helm** direct a film or TV program.

**helmer(n.)** a director.

**hoofer** dancer.

**horse opera** Western film.

**hotsy** strong performance at the box office.

**huddle** (v.) to have a meeting; (n.) a meeting.

**indie** independent film, filmmaker, producer or TV station.

**infopike** information superhighway (Internet).

**ink** to sign a contract.

**kidvid** children's television.

**Kiwi** New Zealander.

**Kudocast** *Variety* term for an awards show.

**legs** stamina at the box office.

**lense** to film a motion picture.

**(the) Lion** (also **Leo**)   *Variety*-ese for Metro-Goldwyn Mayer (MGM) Studios, so referred to because of the company's legendary "Leo the Lion" logo.

**meller**   melodrama.

**mitting**   applause.

**moppet**   child, especially child actor.

**Mouse** (also **Mouse House**)   the Walt Disney Co. or any division thereof.

**nabe**   a neighborhood theater.

**netlet**   fledgling networks UPN and the WB; any network with less than a full weekly schedule of programming.

**nix**   reject, say no to; as in the famous *Variety* headline "Sticks Nix Hick Pix," meaning that audiences in rural areas were not interested in attending films about rural life.

**oater**   Western film, referring to the preferred meal of horses.

**Oz**   Australia.

**ozoner**   drive-in movie theater.

**pact**   (n.) a contract; (v.) to sign a contract.

**passion pit**   drive-in theater, so called owing to their privacy factor and romantic allure for teenagers.

**Peacock web**   the NBC television network, named for its colorful mascot.

**pen**   (v.) to write.

**percenter** (also **tenpercenter**)   agent.

**pic(s)** (also **pix**)   motion picture(s).

**pinkslip**   to lay off or fire from a job.

**pour**   cocktail party.

**powwow**   a meeting or gathering.

**PPV**   pay-per-view; "The fight will be presented as a PPV event in the spring."

**PR** (also **p.r.**)   public relations

**praiser**   publicist.

**praisery**   public relations firm.

**preem**   (n.) an opening-night or premiere performance; (v.) to show a completed film for the first time.

**prexy** (also **prez**)   president.

**scribbler**   writer.

**sesh**   session or meeting; also a time frame, such as a weekend.

**sex appeal**   a term coined by *Variety* now in common usage, meaning to be attractive to audiences owing to sexual aura.

**sleeper**  a film or TV show that lacks pre-release buzz or critical praise, but turns into a success after it is released, usually due to good word-of-mouth.

**sock** (also **socko**)  very good (usually refers to box office performance).

**sprocket opera**  film festival.

**sudser**  soap opera.

**tabmag**  tabloid-style TV magazine show.

**tix**  tickets.

**toon**  cartoon.

**topper**  the head of a company or organization.

**tubthump**  to promote or draw attention to, from the ancient show business custom of actors wandering the streets banging on tubs to drum up business.

**veep** (also **veepee**, **VP**)  vice president.

**web**  network.

**weblet**  fledgling networks UPN and the WB; any network with less than a full weekly schedule of programming.

**whammo**  a sensation (bigger than boffo).

**whodunit**  a mystery film (or show).

**wrap**  to finish production.

**yawner**  a boring show.

**zitcom**  a television comedy aimed at teenagers.

# Select Bibliography

Acland, C.R. (2003) *Screen Traffic: Movies, Multiplexes and Global Culture*. Durham, NC: Duke University Press.

Aksoy, A. and Robins, K. (1992) "Hollywood for the 21st Century: Global Competition for Critical Mass in Image Markets," *Cambridge Journal of Economics* 16 (1): 1–22.

Albarron, A.B. (1996) *Media Economics: Understanding Markets, Industries, and Concepts*. Ames, IA: Iowa State University Press.

Alexander, A., Owers, J., and Carveth, R. (eds) (1993) *Media Economics: Theory and Practice*. Hillsdale, NJ: Lawrence Erlbaum Associates.

Allen, R. and Gomery, D. (1985) *Film History: Theory and Practice*. New York: Alfred A. Knopf.

Anonymous (1998) *The Hollywood Rules: What You Must Know to Make it in the Film Industry*. Beverly Hills, CA: Fade In Books.

Auletta, K. (1997) *The Highwaymen: Warriors of the Information Superhighway*. New York: Random House.

Bagdikian, B. (1997) *The Media Monopoly*. Boston, MA: Beacon Press.

Balio, T. (ed) (1976) *The American Film Industry*. Madison, WI: University of Wisconsin Press.

Bart, P. (1999a) *The Gross: The Hits, The Flops – The Summer that Ate Hollywood*. New York: St. Martin's Press.

Bart, P. (1999b) *Who Killed Hollywood? . . . and Put the Tarnish on Tinseltown*. Los Angeles, CA: Renaissance Books.

Baumgarten, P.A., Farber, D.C., and Fleischer, M. (1992) *Producing, Financing, and Distributing Motion Pictures*, 2nd edn. New York: Limelight Editions.

Benedetti, R. (2002) *From Concept to Screen*. Boston: Allyn and Bacon.

Bettig, R. (1996) *Copyrighting Culture: The Political Economy of Intellectual Property*. Boulder, CO: Westview Press.

Bordwell, D., Staiger, J. and Thompson, K. (1985) *The Classical Hollywood Cinema: Film Style and Mode of Production to 1960*. New York: Columbia University Press.

Brouwer, A. and Wright, T.L. (1990) *Working in Hollywood*. New York: Crown Publishers.

Chowdhury, S., Bluestein, W.M., and Davis, K.S. (1997) "Promoting Films Online," *The Forrester Report: Entertainment and Technology*, 1 (5), August.

Clark, D. (1995) *Negotiating Hollywood: The Cultural Politics of Actors' Labor*. Minneapolis: University of Minnesota Press.

Compaine, B. (ed) (1982) *Who Owns the Media? Concentration of Ownership in the Mass Communications Industry*. White Plains, NY: Knowledge Industry Publications.

Conant, M. (1978) *Antitrust in the Film Industry*. Los Angeles: University of Calfornia Press.

Cones, J.W. (1992) *Film Finance and Distribution: A Dictionary of Terms*. Los Angeles: Silman-James Press.

Cones, J.W. (1997) *The Feature Film Distribution Deal: A Critical Analysis of the Single Most Important Film Industry Agreement*. Carbondale, IL: Southern Illinois Press.

Cowie, P. (ed) (2000) *Variety International: Film Guide 2000*. Los Angeles: Silman-James Press.

Daniels, B., Leedy, D., and Sills, S.D. (1998) *Movie Money: Understanding Hollywood's (Creative) Accounting Practices*. Los Angeles: Silman-James Press.

Davis, P. (2002) "Fine young cannibals in the US motion picture industry exhibition market." online at econ.ise.ac.uk/staff/pjdavis/papers/EntryMovies.pdf

De Vany, A. (2002) "Contracting in the Movies When Nobody Knows Anything: The Careers, Pay and Contracts of Motion Picture Directors," paper presented at Rotterdam Conference on the Economics of Culture.

De Vany, A.S. and Eckert, R. (1991) "Motion Picture Antitrust: The Paramount Cases Revisited," *Research in Law and Economics*, 14: 51–112.

DeVany, A.S. and Walls, D. (2001) "How Can Motion Picture Profits Be So Large and Yet So Elusive? The Alpha-Stable Distribution," paper presented at the Third Business and Economics Scholars Workshop in Motion Picture Industry Studies.

Dodds, J.C. and Holbrook, M.B. (1988) "What's an Oscar Worth? An Empirical Estimation of the Effect of Nominations and Awards on Movie Distribution and Revenues," in B.A. Austin (ed), *Current Research in Film: Audiences, Economics and the Law*, Vol. 4. Norwood, NJ: Ablex Publishing.

Donahue, S.M. (1987) *American Film Distribution: The Changing Marketplace*. Ann Arbor, MI: UMI Research Press.

Eliashberg, J. and Shugan, S.M. (1997) "Film Critics: Influencers or Predictors?" *Journal of Marketing*, 61, 2: 68–78.

*Encyclopedia of American Associations* (2003) 39th edn. Vol. 1, Part 2. New York: Thompson Gale Publishers.

Fink, G.M. (ed) (1977) *Labor Unions*. Westport, CT: Greenwood Press.

Garnham, N. (1979) "Contribution to a Political Economy of Mass Communication," *Media, Culture and Society*, 1: 123–46.

Garnham, N. (1990) *Capitalism and Communication: Global Culture and the Economics of Information*. London: Sage Publications.

Golding, P. and Murdock, G. (1991) "Culture, Communication, and Political Economy," in J. Curran and M. Gurevitch (eds), *Mass Media and Society*. London: Edward Arnold, pp. 11–30.

Goldman, W. (1983) *Adventures in the Screen Trade: A Personal View of Hollywood and Screenwriting*. New York: Warner Books.

Gomery, D. (1989) "Media Economics: Terms of Analysis," *Critical Studies in Mass Communication*, 6 (1): 43–60.

Grummitt, K.-P. (2001) "Hollywood: America's Film Industry," Leicester: Dodona Research.

Guback, T. (1969) *The International Film Industry: Western Europe and America Since 1945*. Bloomington, IN: Indiana University Press.

Guback, T. (1978) "Are We Looking at the Right Things in Film?" paper presented at the Society for Cinema Studies conference, Philadelphia, PA.

Guback, T. (1989) "Should a Nation Have Its Own Film Industry?" *Directions*, 3 (1): 489–92.

Guiles, F.L. (1975) *Hanging on in Paradise*. New York: Conestoga Press.

Hamsher, J. (1997) *Killer Instinct: How Two Young Producers Took on Hollywood and Made the Most Controversial Film of the Decade*. New York: Broadway Books.

Hark, I.R. (ed) (2001) *Exhibition: The Film Reader*. New York: Routledge.

Harmetz, A. (1983) *Rolling Breaks and Other Movie Business*. New York: Alfred A. Knopf.

Harmon, R. (1994) *The Beginning Filmmaker's Business Guide: Financial, Legal, Marketing, and Distribution Basics of Making Movies*. New York: Walker and Co.

Harries, D. (ed) (2002) *The New Media Book*. London: BFI Pubishing.

Hartsough, D. (1995) "Crime Pays: The Studios' Labor Deals in the 1930s," in J. Staiger (ed), *The Studio System*. New Brunswick, NJ: Rutgers University Press.

Horne, G. (2001) *Class Struggle in Hollywood, 1930–1950: Moguls, Mobsters, Stars, and Trade Unionists*. Austin, TX: University of Texas Press.

Hoskins, C., McFadyen, S., and Finn, A. (1997) *Global Television and Film: An Introduction to the Economics of the Business*. New York: Oxford University Press.

Huettig, M.D. (1944) *Economic Control of the Motion Picture Industry*. Philadelphia, PA: University of Pennsylvania Press.

Jowett, G. and Linton, J.M. (1980) *Movies as Mass Communication*. Beverly Hills, CA: Sage Publications.

Kawin, B.F. (1992) *How Movies Work*. Berkeley, CA: University of California Press.

Kent, N. (1991) *Naked Hollywood: Money and Power in the Movies Today*. New York: St. Martin's Press.

Kent, S.L. (2001) *The Ultimate History of Video Games*. New York: Prima Publishing.

Kindem, G. (ed) (1982) *The American Movie Industry: The Business of Motion Pictures*. Carbondale, IL: Southern Illinois University Press.

Klingender, F.D. and Legg, S. (1937) *Money Behind the Screen*. London: Lawrence & Wishart.

Koenig, A.E. (ed) (1970) *Broadcasting and Bargaining*. Madison, WI: University of Wisconsin Press.

Lardner, J. (1987) *Fast Forward: Hollywood, the Japanese and the Onslaught of the VCR*. New York: W.W. Norton.

Leedy, D.J. (1980) *Motion Picture Distribution: An Accountant's Perspective*. Self-published booklet.

Levy, E. (1999) *Cinema of Outsiders: The Rise of American Independent Film*. New York: New York University Press.

Levy, F. (2000) *Hollywood 101: The Film Industry*. Los Angeles: Renaissance Books.

Lewis, J. (2000) *Hollywood v. Hard Core: How the Struggle Censorship Saved the Modern Film Industry*. New York: New York University Press.

Litman, B.L. (1998) *The Motion Picture Mega-Industry*. Boston: Allyn and Bacon.

Litwak, M. (1986) *Reel Power: The Struggle for Influence and Success in the New Hollywood*. New York: New American Library.

Litwak, M. (2002) *Dealmaking in the Film and Television Industry from Negotiations through Final Contracts*, 2nd edn. Los Angeles: Silman-James Press.

Lukk, T. (1997) *Movie Marketing: Opening the Picture and Giving it Legs*. Los Angeles: Silman-James Press.

McDonald, P. (2000) *The Star System: Hollywood's Production of Popular Identities*. London: Wallflower Press.

Meisel, J. (1986) "Escaping Extinction: Cultural Defense of an Undefended Border," in D. Flaherty and W. McKercher (eds), *Southern Exposure: Canadian Perspectives on the United States*. Toronto: McGraw-Hill Ryerson.

Miller, T., Govil, N., McMurria, J., and Maxwell, R. (2001) *Global Hollywood*. London: BFI Publishing.

Moore, S.M. (2000) *The Biz: The Basic Business, Legal and Financial Aspects of the Film Industry*. Los Angeles: Silman-James Press.

Moret, D. (1991) "The New Nickelodeons: A Political Economy of the Home Video Industry with Particular Emphasis on Video Software Retailers," MA thesis, University of Oregon.

Mosco, V. (1996) *The Political Economy of Communication: Rethinking and Renewal*. London: Sage Publications.

Murdock, G. and Golding, P. (1974) "For a Political Economy of Mass Communications," *Socialist Register*, pp. 205–234.

Murdock, G. and Golding, P. (1979) "Capitalism, Communication and Class Relations," in J. Curran, M. Gurevitch, and J. Woollacott (eds), *Mass Communication and Society*. Beverly Hills, CA: Sage Publications.

Nielsen, M. (1985) "Motion Picture Craft Workers and Craft Unions in Hollywood: The Studio Era, 1912–1948," PhD dissertation, University of Illinois.

Nielsen, M.C. and Mailes, G. (1995) *Hollywood's Other Blacklist: Union Struggles in the Studio System*. London: British Film Institute.

Obst, L. (1996) *Hello, He Lied – And Other Truths from the Hollywood Trenches*. Boston: Little, Brown and Company.

O'Donnell, P. and McDougal, D. (1992) *Fatal Subtraction: How Hollywood Really Does Business*. New York: Doubleday.

Olson, S.R. (1999) *Hollywood Planet: Global Media and the Competitive Advantage of Narrative Transparency*. Mahwah, NJ: Lawrence Erlbaum Associates.

PBS (2001) "The Monster that Ate Hollywood." Online at http://www.pbs.org/wgbh/pages/frontline/shows/hollywood/.

Pendakur, M. (1990) *Canadian Dreams and American Control: The Political Economy of the Canadian Film Industry*. Detroit: Wayne State University Press.

Pendakur, M. (1998) "Hollywood North: Film and TV Production in Canada," in G. Sussman and J. Lent (eds), *Global Productions: Labor in the Making of the "Information Society"*. Cresskill, NJ: Hampton Press.

Petrikin, C., Hindes, A., and Cox, D. (eds) (1999) *Variety Power Players 2000: Movers and Shakers, Powerbrokers and Career Makers in Hollywood*. New York: Perigee/Berkeley Publishing.

Picard, R. (1989) *Media Economics: Concepts and Issues*. Newbury Park, CA: Sage Publications.

Prindle, D.F. (1988) *The Politics of Glamour: Ideology and Democracy in the Screen Actors Guild*. Madison, WI: University of Wisconsin Press.

Prindle, D.F. (1993) *Risky Business: The Political Economy of Hollywood*. Boulder, CO: Westview Press.

Puttnam, D. (1998) *Movies and Money*. New York: Alfred Knopf.

Resnik, G. and Trost, S. (1996) *All You Need to Know about the Movie and TV Business*. New York: Simon & Schuster.

Rosenbaum, J. (2000) *Movie Wars: How Hollywood and the Media Limit What Movies We Can See*. Chicago, IL: A Capella Books.

SAG/DGA (1999) "US Runaway Film and Television Production Study Report." Online at http://www.sag.org/PDF/runawayALL.pdf.

Schwartz, N.L. (1982) *The Hollywood Writers' Wars*. New York: Alfred A. Knopf.

Segrave, K. (1997) *American Films Abroad: Hollywood's Domination of the World's Movie Screens from the 1890s to the Present*. Jefferson, NC: McFarland & Co., Inc.

Sheff, D. (1993) *Game Over*. New York: Random House.

Sherman, E. (1999) *Selling Your Film: A Guide to the Contemporary Marketplace*, 2nd edn. Los Angeles: Acrobat Books.

Shorris, S. and Bunby, M.A. (1994) *Talking Pictures: With the People Who Made Them*. New York: The New Press.

Smith, A. (2001) *Popped Culture: The Social History of Popcorn in America*. Washington, DC: Smithsonian Press.

Smythe, D.W. (1960) "On the Political Economy of Communication," *Journalism Quarterly*, Autumn, pp. 563–72.

Squire, J.E. (ed) (1992) *The Movie Business Book*, 2nd edn. New York: Simon and Schuster.

Storper, M. and Christopherson, S. (1987) "Flexible Specialization and Regional Industrial Agglomerations: The Case of the U.S. Motion Picture Industry," *Annals of the Association of American Geographers*, 77 (1).

Stumer, M. B. (1992) "Show-Biz Unions, Guilds: A Practitioner's Guide; Cutting-Edge Issues," *Entertainment Law and Finance*, August, p. 1.

Sychowski, P.V. (2000) *Electronic Cinema: The Big Screen Goes Digital*. London: Screen Digest.

Taub, E. (1994) *Gaffers, Grips and Best Boys*. New York: St. Martin's Press.

Taylor, T. (1999) *The Big Deal: Hollywood's Million-Dollar Spec Script Market*. New York: William Morrow and Co.

Thompson, K. (1985) *Exporting Entertainment: America in the World Film Market 1907–34*. London: British Film Institute.

Turan, K. (2002) *Sundance to Sarajevo: Film Festivals and the World They Made*. Berkeley, CA: University of California Press.

Turcotte, S. (1995) "Gimme a Bud! The Feature Film Product Placement

Industry," a Professional Report presented as partial fulfillment of the requirements for the Master of Arts in Advertising at the University of Texas at Austin. Online at http://advertising.utexas.edu/research/papers/Turcotte/Toc.html

Ulff-Møller, J. (2001) *Hollywood's Film Wars with France: Film-Trade Diplomacy and the Emergence of the French Film Quota Policy*. Rochester, NY: University of Rochester Press.

US Dept. of Commerce (2001) *The Migration of U.S. Film and Television Production Impact of "Runaways" on Workers and Small Business in the U.S. Film Industry*. International Trade Administration report.

Valenti, J. (2002) "A Clear Present and Future Danger," prepared for the House Appropriations Committee, Subcommittee on Commerce, Justice, State, the Judiciary, and Related Agencies. Reprinted online at mpaa.com.

Vogel, H.L. (1998) *Entertainment Industry Economics: A Guide for Financial Analysis*, 4th edn. New York: Cambridge University Press.

Wasko, J. (1982) *Movies and Money: Financing the American Film Industry*. Norwood, NJ: Ablex Publishing.

Wasko, J. (1994) *Hollywood in the Information Age: Beyond the Silver Screen*. Cambridge: Polity Press.

Wasko, J. (1998) "Challenges to Hollywood's Labor Force in the 1990s," in G. Sussman and J. Lent (eds), *Global Productions: Labor in the Making of the "Information Society"*. Cresskill, NJ: Hampton Press.

Wasko, J. (2001) *Understanding Disney: The Manufacture of Fantasy*. Cambridge: Polity Press.

Wasko, J., Phillips, M. and Purdie, C. (1993) "Hollywood Meets Madison Avenue: The Commercialization of US Films," *Media, Culture and Society*, 15 (2): 271–93.

Wasser, F. (2001) *Veni, Vidi, Video: The Hollywood Empire and the VCR*. Austin, TX: University of Texas Press.

Weinberger, E. (1995) *Wannabe: A Would-Be Player's Misadventures in Hollywood*. New York: St. Martin's Press.

Wiese, M. (1989) *Film and Video Marketing*. Studio City, CA: Michael Wiese Productions.

Wilson, J.M. (1998) *Inside Hollywood: A Writer's Guide to Researching the World of Movies and TV*. Cincinnati, OH: Writer's Digest Books.

Wyatt, J. (1994) *High Concept: Movies and Marketing in Hollywood*. Austin, TX: University of Texas Press.